AGING WELL

AGING WELL

Surprising Guideposts to a Happier Life

from the Landmark Harvard Study

of Adult Development

GEORGE E. VAILLANT

LITTLE, BROWN AND COMPANY
Boston   New York   London

FIRST EDITION

The author is grateful for permission to reprint the following excerpts: vignettes of
Bill Dimaggio and Eric Carey, from G. E. Vaillant, *The Wisdom of the Ego* (Cambridge,
Mass.: Harvard University Press, copyright © 1993 by the President and Fellows of
Harvard College); H. Zinsser, *As I Remember Him* (Boston, Mass.: Little, Brown, 1940);
vignette of Mary Fasano from *The Harvard Gazette;* the 15 lines from G. Garrett's
translation of Sophocles' *Oedipus at Colonus* by University of Pennsylvania Press; the
excerpt from *The View from Eighty* by Malcolm Cowley, copyright © 1976, 1978, 1980
by Malcolm Cowley. Used by permission of Viking Penguin, a division of Penguin
Putnam, Inc.; the 3 lines from W. B. Yeats, "Sailing to Byzantium," from *The Poems of
W. B. Yeats: A New Edition,* edited by Richard J. Finneran. Copyright © 1928 by
Macmillan Publishing Company, copyright renewed © 1956 by George Yeats. Used
with the permission of Scribner, a division of Simon and Schuster, Inc., and with the
permission of A. P. Watt Ltd., London; the 8 lines from R. Humphries' translation of
Ovid's *Metamorphoses* by Indiana University Press, copyright © 1963.

For information on Time Warner Trade Publishing's online publishing program,
visit www.ipublish.com.

Library of Congress Cataloging-in-Publication Data
Vaillant, George E.
Aging well : surprising guideposts to a happier life from the landmark Harvard study
of adult development / George E. Vaillant. — 1st ed.
p. cm.
Includes bibliographical references and index.
ISBN 0-316-98936-3
1. Aging — Social aspects — United States — Longitudinal studies. 2. Aging —
Psychological aspects — United States — Longitudinal studies.   I. Title.
HQ1064.U5 V35 2002
305.26'0973 — dc21   2001030651

10 9 8 7 6 5 4 3 2 1

Q-FF

Book design by Fearn Cutler
Printed in the United States of America

For Caroline
With love and gratitude

CONTENTS

CHAPTER ONE

THE STUDY OF ADULT DEVELOPMENT

> I enjoy talking with very old people. They have gone be-
> fore us on a road by which we, too, may have to travel, and I
> think we do well to learn from them what it is like.
>
> Socrates, in Plato's *The Republic*

Having entered the new millennium we are bom-
barded with contradictory information about what it means to
grow old. News reports of people living longer than ever are jux-
taposed to horror stories of life in nursing homes and elders
wishing for death. Inspiring anecdotes of energetic 85-year-old
marathon runners or CEOs or composers who seem as young as
ever are followed on the nightly news by stories on the barrenness of life in gated retirement communities filled with decrepit
old people who feel superfluous. Will the longevity granted to us
by modern medicine be a curse or a blessing? How can we control our last years? These are the questions for which we need answers.

"To know how to grow old is the master-work of wisdom,
and one of the most difficult chapters in the great art of living";
so wrote Henri Amiel in 1874.[1] More than a century later, as
more and more of us are destined to live into our eighties, his
challenge becomes more pressing than ever; and we need to decide from whom to gain that knowledge. As we go through life,
we meet octogenarians who offer us rare role models for growing
old. We meet vigorous, generative great-grandparents, and we

wonder how they became that way. We wonder about their origins — about how their pasts might illuminate our own futures. Foolproof answers, of course, are not possible. But if we are to understand successful aging, we need to ask very old people about the road they travel. The demographers have told us, have they not, that today's young adults can expect to live past 80. If so, we all need models for how to live from retirement to past 80 — with joy.

Based on what is arguably the longest study of aging in the world — the Study of Adult Development at Harvard University — this book attempts to offer such models. The Study of Adult Development consists of three separate cohorts of 824 individuals — all selected as teenagers for different facets of mental and physical health more than half a century ago and studied for their entire lives. Therefore, this book will allow the reader to watch the adult life cycle, in its entirety, unfold. It will provide a theoretical framework, as well as data, for understanding how older people end up fulfilled or not.

The Study includes a Harvard Law School graduate who died a derelict's death in a seedy residential hotel but also men who became ambassadors and cabinet members, bestselling novelists, and captains of industry. The Study includes brilliant women, from Lewis Terman's study of gifted children, derailed from career paths by the sexism of their era, but also women whose creativity flowered brilliantly after age 65. The Study includes a number of men who began their lives as Inner City high school dropouts but have gone on to achieve not mere occupational distinction, but great success in living. What is special about the Study of Adult Development is that it consists of grandparents and great-grandparents who have been followed since adolescence. Old age is like a minefield; if you see footprints leading to the other side, step in them.

The Study of Adult Development offers significant, reliable data that tell us what successful aging is and how it can be achieved. Some may argue that the term *successful aging* is an oxymoron. For is not *aging* inextricably associated with loss, decline, and approaching death? Is not *success* inextricably associated with gain, winning, and a zestful life? Perhaps, but the fact is that the majority of older people, without brain disease, maintain a sense of modest well-being until the final months before they die.[2,3] Not only are the old less depressed than the general population, but also a majority of the elderly suffer little incapacitating illness until the final one that kills them. No, successful aging is not an oxymoron.

Too often, however, the successful great-grandparents whom you or I admire seem a freak of nature — like the doughty Frenchwoman Jeanne Louise Calment, who went on smoking French cigarettes until she was 122 years old. We imagine that there must be something in their lives — something beyond our grasp — that explains their remarkable vigor. We may fear that at 75 or 80 we will ask, "Is this all there is?" But from everything I have learned from the Study of Adult Development, those among the old-old who love life are not exceptions — they are just healthy. As they surmount the inevitable crises of aging, the Study members seem constantly to be reinventing their lives. They surprise us even as they surprise themselves. In moments of sorrow, loss, and defeat many still convince us that they find their lives eminently worthwhile. They do not flinch from acknowledging how hard life is, but they also never lose sight of why one might want to keep on living it.

For example, over the years on the biennial questionnaires sent to the Study members, there were certain questions that produced unusually revealing answers. One such question was: What is the most important thing that makes you want to get out of bed in the morning? An 84-year-old Study member answered, "To live, to work, to learn something that I didn't know yesterday — to enjoy the precious moments with my wife."

To the same question a 78-year-old Study member replied, "All the many plans for the day. I love life and all I do. I love the out of doors. . . . It is a joy to be alive and living with my best friend." He was referring to his wife of fifty years with whom his sex life was still "very satisfying."

Over the past thirty-five years I have enjoyed the privilege of studying and interviewing these generous people who agreed to participate in an experiment lasting for their entire adult lives. Their outcomes often provided surprises that no one would have guessed at the beginning.

* * *

Consider 70-year-old Anthony Pirelli. Initially, he experienced most of the early perils that resiliency experts tell us stand in the way of a successful life, including low socioeconomic status, parental marital discord, a depressed mother, an uneducated father, and seven siblings all crowded into a small tenement apartment. These risk factors do, indeed, predict poor life adjustment in young adulthood.[4-6] Until the Study of Adult Development, no one had investigated whether these same factors also doomed youth to a miserable old age. This sixty-year follow-up revealed that Anthony Pirelli, predicted to fail in young adulthood, has become a stunning success as an old man.

Both of Anthony Pirelli's Italian-born parents could barely read English. As a semiskilled factory worker, his father had worked steadily for Depression wages and then spent both his spare income and his spare time drinking in disreputable neighborhood bars. He was "mean" and would give "terrible beatings" to Anthony's older brothers with "whatever was at hand." They would come out of the cellar "screaming and bloody . . . bodily injury meant nothing to him." Pirelli explained that during his early childhood, such beatings were a nearly weekly occurrence for his brothers, but that he and his sister had been spared.

When Pirelli was 3 years old, his mother became stricken with manic-depressive illness. She was unable to exert control over her children, and as a result they lost respect for her as a disciplinarian. When together, Pirelli's parents fought continuously and marital separations were frequent. When he was 13, his parents separated permanently. Pirelli went to live with his father, who appeared to the Study staff at the time to be unconcerned by his son's truancy.

In 1941 the first of five Study interviewers to visit Anthony Pirelli's home was struck by the sparse furnishing of his dilapidated fifth-story tenement flat without central heating in "one of the poorest sections" of Boston's West End. The Study investigator noted that it was "quite lacking in comfort and is very unattractive. It shows the lack . . . of anyone who cares about its appearance." As a boy Anthony Pirelli had seemed very different from the extroverted, tanned tycoon who in 1998 was to show the fifth Study interviewer his stunning high-rise apartment. The Study psychiatrist described the 13-year-old Pirelli as:

> Unaggressive, sensitive and fearful of parental disapproval. . . . This is a very mild appearing boy. Wants to make a good impression. Does what he thinks is expected of him, never is quite at ease. Plainly quite insecure in a social way. On the whole, he is so conventional that it is very hard to get any true opinion that is his own. He is quite inhibited in action, never joined in any vigorous athletics but has numerous quiet hobbies of his own such as stamp collecting and ship model building. We do get the impression that he is quite sensitive and has aesthetic tastes.

In addition, the psychiatrist observed that Pirelli was "emotionally stable . . . considerate of family feelings . . . presents a perfect example of how children, reared under miserable circumstances, survive through intelligence and character."

At the end of each school year, in order to celebrate advancing to a new grade, the students were supposed to wear a special outfit. Pirelli's parents could not afford these clothes so they were supplied by the school. Sometimes his parents were challenged even to put food on the table. Later, Pirelli wondered why his father hadn't done anything to better himself. "I almost think he didn't want to. Why didn't he?" Nor could Pirelli understand why his mother had not learned English given that she had come to the United States as a young girl. Years later his much older sister, Anna, explained to Pirelli that she had raised him from infancy to 7 or 8. For unlike children in many dysfunctional families, the eight Pirelli children banded together as a unit and looked after one another. That made all the difference. At school Pirelli was on the honor roll. He graduated from a trade high school, and at 17 he enlisted in the air force. Just before he was released from the service, Pirelli met his future wife at a USO dance; when he was 19, they were married. He loved his in-laws. He explained that, unlike his own home, "it was always fun at their house . . . they never had any real problems."

After discharge from the air force, Pirelli found work as a skilled laborer. His brother Vince became the most important person in Pirelli's early adulthood. Vince would take him out to lunch once a week to talk over Pirelli's plans for the future. It was Vince who insisted that he go back to school.

The second interviewer was struck by the bungalow that Pirelli at age 25 had bought under the GI bill and by "its charming living room." The interviewer also noted that Pirelli "has considerable drive, a very hard worker, mature." At night Pirelli pursued a degree in accounting at Bentley School of Accounting and Finance. He was a grateful student and reported that his teachers had had a profound impact on him. In particular, he admired the school's founder, Harry C. Bentley, who he believed had practically invented modern accounting. He wanted to get good grades for Mr. Bentley, who explained to him, "If you learn accounting, you can do anything." Pirelli never forgot.

Five years later, the third interviewer was struck by his "beautifully landscaped" split-level ranch house. He also noted that Pirelli "has worked hard during this period . . . very serious about providing for his sons a better environment than what he had." Pirelli was "obviously devoted" to his two children. In the early years of their marriage Pirelli's wife had worked to help out financially. Later, she helped in his restaurant with interior decorating and personnel problems. What Pirelli found most special about his wife was her "ability to cope with difficult situations." When he and his wife had problems, they would sit and "talk them out. . . . She attacks the problem right away." He was grateful for this since it helped circumvent "my stubbornness." In their spare time both Pirelli and his wife loved dancing together.

But then gratitude was one of Pirelli's strong suits. By the age of 30 Pirelli was a certified public accountant and had long since left his job as a skilled laborer. His clients trusted him, and Pirelli's "love for business" and, more important, his friendliness and sense of joy opened one door after another and helped establish him in the business world.

When Pirelli was 47 his large suburban house, swimming pool, tennis court — and the strength of his marriage — impressed the fourth Study interviewer. "They are both sympathetic toward the other." Pirelli seemed to "give thought to each question before he answered it, and he was intelligently curious about the Study." The interviewer wrote that Pirelli "was appreciative when I said that we could send him some articles about the outcome. He felt honored to be part of [the Study] and hoped that the information he had given would prove to be of help to someone else."

Consistent with Reinhold Niebuhr's famous Serenity Prayer, Pirelli had developed throughout his life the courage and perseverance to change the things he could and the serenity to accept the things that he could not. On the one hand, at 47, after discussing the unexpected deaths of both his brother Vince and his closest friend, Pirelli had remarked to the interviewer that life was "like a book filled with many different chapters." He said that when one chapter was finished, you must then go on to the next chapter — not a bad prescription for growing old. On the other hand, continued Study follow-up revealed that this once "unaggressive, sensitive, fearful" boy with a trade school education had triumphed over a large international conglomerate in a patent dispute. Pirelli could fight when he needed to.

At age 63 Pirelli suffered a serious heart attack and retired. He realized that he was "getting old." He turned his accounting business over to his children. By age 65 he had turned almost all his many business interests over to trusted colleagues. He wanted to enjoy his life and do things that he and his wife had always hoped to do while their health was still good. Unlike many high achievers, Pirelli always retained a clear sense of when to let go. He auctioned off his beloved and very valuable stamp collection in order that others could glean the same pleasure that he had enjoyed in adding rare stamps to his collection.

At age 70 Anthony Pirelli met still a fifth Study interviewer at the door of his high-rise Boston condominium. Pirelli was dressed casually but neatly in a brightly colored tennis shirt and fashionable navy tennis warm-up pants. He sported a full head of white hair, and his face was still tan from a trip to his winter beachfront house on the Gulf Coast of Florida. Despite recent coronary bypass surgery, he glowed with energy and good health. Pirelli loved being retired.

Anthony Pirelli escorted the interviewer to a picture window. The interviewer was impressed by spectacular views of the Boston Public Garden and its swan boats, the gold-domed State House and, in the distance, the Charles River. On the left stately trees divided the grand town houses that march along Commonwealth Avenue. Pirelli, however, drew the interviewer's attention to the right-hand side of the view, to where the blighted tenement of his blighted childhood once stood — the tenement whose barren interior had so depressed the first interviewer.

Pirelli's narrative of his family had now softened. His memory had transformed a painful childhood into a glass half-full. Forgiveness, as well as gratitude, had become a strong suit. Pirelli expressed compassion toward his mother. He explained that she was "the kindest woman in the world. . . . It drove her up the wall not being able to communicate because she couldn't find out about how her kids were doing in school. She felt embarrassed to come to school activities; and she was bothered that she couldn't help with schoolwork. There was nothing that she would not do for her children." He remembered his parents as being committed to taking care of the children and not of themselves. He marveled at how his mother was able to hold the family together for so long and on so little money.

Pirelli seemed unconscious of his increasing capacity for forgiveness over time. He believed that it was his father, not himself, who had mellowed with age. He now recalled his father as a "good family man" who made sure that his sons went to school. His father took care of the garden, and "it was the best garden in the neighborhood." He abused his older sons only because "he was such a failure that he took it out on his kids." He reiterated his father was not abusive to Pirelli or to his younger sister; "We were never touched." He wondered why. Perhaps, he mused, "Times were a little better when my sister and I came along." After all, his older siblings were able to help out, and his father had received a small promotion. He also wondered if "age itself was a healing factor." As we shall see, forgiveness leads to successful aging more often than does nursing old resentments.

Nevertheless, asked what effect he thought his early experiences with his parents had upon his adult personality, Anthony Pirelli replied that they had "a direct impact. I wanted to be the opposite of my father. I didn't want to be an ordinary nothing. My goal in life was to be ambitious." Only during his fifth interview did Pirelli reveal that as a child not only his sister, Anna, but also a financially successful uncle and aunt, invisible to the original investigators, had also been important to him. They were "very warm" and had treated Pirelli and his siblings "wonderfully." At every age we tell our life story in a different way. Clues to the future are present in any life history, but the difficulty arises in distinguishing real clues from red herrings.

In contrast to many self-made men, Pirelli, in retirement, was grateful for how well his successors continued to run his businesses. Pirelli still spent one to two hours a week at his car dealership (another of his many ventures), but he could rely on the good management that he had there. When he went into the office, he explained, he would "just get in the way." In other words, in old age he knew enough not to take himself too seriously.

At age 70 when asked who has been his closest friend over the last forty years, Pirelli shot back, "My wife, without a doubt." Asked how they depended on each other, he replied, "One would be lost without the other." They had just celebrated their fiftieth anniversary. One of his children had earned a Ph.D. in mathematics from Columbia University; the other had attended two years of college.

Pirelli may have been *ill,* considering his heart attack and open-heart surgery, but he did not feel *sick.* He was as physically active as ever, and he continued to play tennis. Asked what he missed about his work, Pirelli exulted, "I'm so busy doing other things that I don't have time to miss work. . . . Life is not boring for me." Thus, at age 70 Pirelli enjoyed life as much as anyone in the entire Study. The point of this story is not that yet another poor son of immigrants became a rich man. The real lessons of Pirelli's life are: he was not a prisoner of childhood; he gave to his children what he could not have himself; he loved his wife for fifty years; and he never felt sick, even when he was ill. Ultimately, he could turn what he had built over to others with gratitude, not resentment. The past often predicts but never determines our old age.

·   ·   ·

In the general population only a third of adults alive at 60 will live past 80; but in the three Study of Adult Development cohorts, 70 percent of college-educated members alive at 60 will be alive at 80 — twice as many as expected. In other words, many Study members are now enjoying the exceptional longevity and the prolonged retirement that will become the rule for American children born in year 2000. Throughout this book, biographies of men and women — older than Pirelli — will reveal ingredients essential to successful aging. For as Study members, ten to twenty years older than I, trudge through the minefields of life, I have for three decades now been studying and trying to step in the footsteps they leave behind. In this book I invite readers to join me. Pirelli's story tells us that if we look hard enough, we can find hidden clues that help explain how a person ends up differently from what we might expect.

Among the many significant findings to emerge from the Study of Adult Development thus far are the following:

- It is not the bad things that happen to us that doom us; it is the good people who happen to us at any age that facilitate enjoyable old age.
- Healing relationships are facilitated by a capacity for gratitude, for forgiveness, and for taking people inside. (By this metaphor I mean becoming eternally enriched by loving a particular person.)
- A good marriage at age 50 predicted positive aging at 80. But surprisingly, low cholesterol levels at age 50 did not.
- Alcohol abuse — unrelated to unhappy childhood — consistently predicted unsuccessful aging, in part because alcoholism damaged future social supports.
- Learning to play and create after retirement and learning to gain younger friends as we lose older ones add more to life's enjoyment than retirement income.
- Objective good physical health was less important to successful aging than subjective good health. By this I mean that it is all right to be ill as long as you do not feel sick.

In a world that seems ruled by genetic predestination, we need hope that we still can change. The lives of the Study members offer us guides. They allow us to anticipate and to shape our own lives according to developmental rules. Benjamin Spock and the researchers from whom he borrowed taught mothers to anticipate child development and to understand what could be changed and what had to be accepted. Similarly, this book tries to do the same for late adulthood. Remember the words of Scrooge in

Charles Dickens's *A Christmas Carol:* "Men's courses will fore-shadow certain ends, to which, if persevered in, they must lead. But if the course be departed from, the ends will change." The prospective nature of this book allows us to understand facets of our lives which if departed from will allow our lives to change.

Positive Aging Defined: A First Pass

I shall return to these and other important findings of the Study in the pages ahead. Along the way, I shall develop and expand my definition of positive aging, but it's important to first explain a few key assumptions; for commentators from social scientists to poets can't seem to agree on whether aging is a good thing or not. Do we believe Robert Browning, who invites us to "Grow old along with me! / The best is yet to be"? If so, should not King Lear and Cordelia end their play by riding off into some Walt Disney sunset? Indeed, that is how the play did end before William Shakespeare adapted it to conform to his own pessimistic vision of old age.

In support of Browning's view a distinguished Study novelist wrote to us:

> Contrary to all expectations, I seem to grow happier as I grow older. I think that America has been sold on the theory that youth is marvelous but old age is a terror. On the contrary, it's taken me sixty years to learn how to live reasonably well, to do my work and cope with my inadequacies.
>
> For me youth was a woeful time — sick parents, war, relative poverty, the miseries of learning a profession, a mistake of a marriage, self-doubts, booze and blundering around. Old age is knowing what I'm doing, the respect of others, a relatively sane financial base, a loving wife and the realization that what I can't beat I can endure.

All well and good, but in *As You Like It* another distinguished author, William Shakespeare, asserts that old age "Is second child-ishness and mere oblivion, / Sans teeth, sans eyes, sans taste, sans everything." Shakespeare makes King Lear's senile narcissism seem unbearable; and even when the bard was feeling kindly about old age, he defined it in a sonnet as:

> *That time of year thou mayst in me behold*
> *When yellow leaves, or none, or few, do hang*
> *Upon those boughs which shake against the cold,*
> *Bare ruin'd choirs, where late the sweet birds sang.*

There can be no definitive answer to this debate. Both sides are right. Old age can be both miserable and joyous. It all depends on the facets we choose to examine. But one thing we do know is that positive aging must reflect vital reaction to change, to disease, and to conflict. Thus, perhaps there is a third way for us to view old age — one that does not try to paint old age as either black or white. A 55-year-old Study poet underscored the dignity even in dying. He rhetorically asked, "What's the difference between a guy who at his final conscious moments before death has a nostalgic grin on his face, as if to say, 'Boy, I sure squeezed that lemon' and another man who fights for every last breath in an effort to turn time back to some nagging unfinished business? Damned if I know, but I sure think it's worth thinking about." He also addressed the difference between successful and unsuccessful aging: "What is the difference? One, I guess you would call 'the celebrant sense' or that wonderful hippie word, 'Wow!' I think it's an important component in the whole adaptive process. Life needs to be enjoyed!" And so whenever in this chapter I write pedantically of *successful aging* — think *joy*. The heart speaks with so much more vitality than the head.

Certainly, there will be many paths to successful aging; and there will never be a right way to grow old. But the goal is straightforward: How can we make the journey past three-score-and-twenty one that we will be glad we made? That question will be the focus of this book.

But we shall need to ask the very old to point the way. Thus far, I have been quoting 50-year-olds. Sixty-year-olds. When they wrote with such authority about old age, Browning, Shakespeare, the Study novelist, and the Study poet were middle-aged. What did they know? Even Anthony Pirelli is only seventy.

When he turned 80, the accomplished American literary critic Malcolm Cowley had the same misgivings about the chroniclers of old age.[7] Ralph Waldo Emerson wrote his essay "Old Age" at 57; Alex Comfort wrote *A Good Age* at 56; Simone de Beauvoir wrote *The Coming of Age* at 60; and arguably the most quoted of all, Cicero, wrote *De Senectute* at 62. In his splendid book *The View from Eighty,* Cowley points out, "Those self-appointed experts on old age knew the literature but not the life." I agree.

Ideally, we would want to consult individuals like the 122-year-old Madame Calment. What does life hold when with the passage of time the elder becomes too frail to attend his land conservation meeting or too hard of hearing to attend the lectures at her genealogy society? Since Madame Calment is neither alive nor studied, we may do well to listen to the 84-year-old Study member whose voice we heard earlier in this chapter. Positive aging means to love, to work, to learn something we did not know yesterday, and to enjoy the remaining precious moments with loved ones.

The Study of Adult Development

At this point let me describe the Study in greater detail. The Study of Adult Development is a rarity in medicine, for quite deliberately it set out to study the lives of the well, not the sick. In so doing it has integrated three cohorts of elderly men and women — all of whom have been studied continuously for six to eight decades. First, there is a sample of 268 socially advantaged Harvard graduates born about 1920 — *the longest prospective study of physical and mental health in the world.* Second, there is a sample of 456 socially disadvantaged Inner City men born about 1930 — *the longest prospective study of "blue collar" adult development in the world*. Third, there is a sample of 90 middle-class, intellectually gifted women born about 1910 — *the longest prospective study of women's development in the world*. (To call a study *prospective* means that it studies events as they occur, and not in retrospect.)

The Harvard (Grant) Cohort

The "Grant Study" of adult development was begun at Harvard University by Arlie Bock and Clark Heath.[8] These two student health service physicians had received a gift from a philanthropist, William T. Grant, to study healthy development. Never dreaming that in the year 2000 the Study members would still remain active participants, Arlie Bock, in a press release dated September 30, 1938, described the Study's aims:

> Doctors traditionally have dealt with their patients after troubles of many sorts have arisen. The Department of Hygiene . . . proposes to revise this procedure and will attempt to analyze the forces that have produced normal young men. . . . A body of facts is needed to replace current supposition. All of us need more do's and fewer don'ts.

In the original selection process, about 40 percent of each Harvard class were arbitrarily excluded because there was some question as to whether they would meet the academic requirements for graduation. Usually this meant a freshman grade average of C or lower. The health service records of the remaining 60 percent of each freshman class were then screened, and half the remaining men were excluded because of evidence of physical or psychological difficulty. Each year the names of the remaining 300 sophomores were submitted to the Harvard deans, who selected about 100 boys whom they recognized as "sound."

Over a four-year period, 1939–1942, 268 sophomores were selected for study. Twelve of these students withdrew while they were still in college, and 8 more withdrew over the next half-century. For nearly sixty years (or until their deaths), the remaining 248 men have continued to participate with remarkable loyalty. They have received questionnaires about every two years, provided records of physical examinations every five years, and been interviewed about every fifteen years. The men's wives and their children have also been asked to provide details of their own lives, as well as observations about how they viewed their Study husband or father.

In 1940 men who went to Harvard were not always rich or privileged. But they were almost always white and their grandparents had usually been born in the United States. Oldest children were definitely overrepresented and only 2 percent of the men chosen were left-handed as contrasted to 10 percent of the general population. Put differently, the Harvard cohort had been chosen for their capacity to equal or to exceed their natural ability, and most did so. Four of the 268 ran for the United States Senate. Another net would have had to be cast to include happy-go-lucky dependent, but equally stable, college men.

After being accepted into the Study, each man was seen by a psychiatrist for about eight interviews. These interviews focused on the man's family and on his own career plans and value systems. The Study psychiatrists made an effort to get to know the men as people, not patients.

A family worker, Lewise Gregory Davies, also saw the Harvard men. She took a careful social history from each sophomore subject. She then traveled the length and breadth of the United States to meet their parents. In each boy's home she took a family history that included characterizations of grandparents, aunts, uncles, and made an estimate of social status. She also obtained from the mother a history of each boy's infant-and-child development and any family history of mental illness.

Originally, data were recorded in ink in huge leather ledgers and analyzed by manual counting. Data were not put onto punch cards until 1965, not onto magnetic tape until 1975, and not into the hard drive of an office desktop computer until 1990. Now, as I write in the year 2000, all of the data of sixty years of study resides in a laptop on my desk at home.

Socioeconomically, the Harvard sample men were mainly drawn from a privileged group but not exclusively so. In 1940 a third of their parents had made more than $15,000 a year, but one father in seven made less than $2,500 ($1.25/hr) annually. (In those days a year at Harvard cost $1,500, and a registered nurse made $2,000 a year.) If one-third of the men's fathers had some professional training, one-half of the men's parents never graduated from college. During college almost half of the men were on scholarship and/or had to work during the academic year.

World War II forced the Harvard men into a common experience that permitted them to be compared with their fellow citizens on grounds other than academic excellence. Only 11, instead of a statistically expected 77 out of 268, were rejected for service because of physical defects. Instead of an expected 36 out of 268, only 3 were rejected for psychiatric reasons.

With a few exceptions, like the man whose father made two million dollars a year in the midst of the Depression, the 1940 generation of Harvard men were upwardly mobile and more successful than their fathers. Returning from active military service in World War II, the Harvard men benefited from high employment, a valuable dollar, and the GI bill that virtually guaranteed them an affordable graduate school education. The men themselves were just young enough to be influenced by the health-promoting trends of 1960–1980, like smoking cessation and middle-aged physical fitness.

At age 47 the average earned income of the Harvard sample was about $105,000 in current dollars. Yet the men were Democrats more often than Republicans. In 1954 only 16 percent of the Harvard men had sanctioned the McCarthy hearings; and in 1968, 91 percent had advocated de-escalating our involvement in Vietnam. To generalize, the Harvard sample had the incomes and social status of corporate managers; yet they drove the battered cars and pursued the hobbies, politics, and lifestyle of college professors.

More important to this book, at age 75 the mortality of the Harvard sample is only half that expected of white males in their birth cohort, and their mortality is only three-quarters that of their Harvard College classmates. Sixty percent of the men have survived or will survive past their 80th birthday; only 30 percent of white American males born in 1920 will live that long.

The Inner City Cohort
(The Gluecks' Nondelinquent Controls)

In 1939 Sheldon Glueck, a young law professor at Harvard Law School, obtained funding to conduct a prospective study of 500 youth sent to reform school and of 500 matched schoolboys who at age 14 had not been in any legal trouble.[9] Sheldon Glueck and his wife, Eleanor, a distinguished social worker, restudied both groups of men at ages 17, 25, and 32.[10] Like the Harvard men, the Inner City men originally agreed to be studied by a multidisciplinary team of physicians, psychologists, psychiatrists, social investigators, and physical anthropologists. The Gluecks' research study has produced two classic texts in criminology. One, written by the Gluecks themselves and published in 1950, is *Unraveling Juvenile Delinquency*,[11] and the other, *Crime in the Making*,[12] was written forty-four years later by Robert Sampson and John Laub, two criminologists who were still in grammar school when the Gluecks died.

The nondelinquent youth — the controls to whom the reform school boys were compared — shared the same social risk factors that helped doom the delinquents. They had attended the same inner city schools and had the same tested intelligence (mean IQ = 95) as the delinquents. One nondelinquent in four had repeated two grades or more of school. The controls were also matched with the delinquents for high-crime neighborhoods and ethnicity. The majority of their parents were foreign born; for two-thirds of the boys this meant Italy, Ireland, Great Britain, or Canada. In childhood, half of these Inner City nondelinquents, like Anthony Pirelli, had lived in clearly blighted slum neighborhoods. Half of their homes had lacked a tub or shower. By way of contrast, in 1940 only 16 percent of all Boston dwellings were without tub or shower. Half of the Inner City men came from families known to five or more social agencies, and more than two-thirds of their families had recently been on welfare.

The Gluecks had last interviewed the Inner City sample in 1960–1962.[13] At that time, for financial reasons, they reduced the sample to 456 by excluding the 44 youngest boys. Until I obtained the funds to reinterview them at age 47 (c. 1975),[14] for fifteen years all contact had been lost. Since their 40s, when I inherited the Study from the Gluecks, the men, like the Harvard men, have returned biennial questionnaires; the most recent one was received in the year 2000 when the men were 68 to 74. They, too, have provided physical examinations every five years. When they were 60 the Study still knew whether all but two of the 456 Inner City men were alive or dead.

The Terman Women Sample

For a female comparison group to the Harvard cohort, the Study selected 90 women from the Stanford (Terman) study of gifted children.[15,16] The Terman Study began in 1922 when Lewis Terman, a professor of education at Stanford University, attempted to identify all of the grammar school children in urban California with IQs of 140 or higher. Before this, Professor Terman had established his reputation by adapting the French Binet intelligence test for use in America. From the grammar schools of Oakland, San Francisco, and Los Angeles Professor Terman had first selected the 7 percent of children identified by their teachers as the brightest in each class. He then retested this group individually with the Stanford-Binet Intelligence Test. In this fashion he identified the 1 percent of Californian urban schoolchildren with IQs greater than 135 to 140. Most were born between 1908 and 1914.

Originally the aim of Terman's selection process was to identify most of the brightest children in his three-city area. But when he went back and checked entire schools, he found that he had probably captured only 80 percent. The intelligence of unattractive and shy children tended to be overlooked by their teachers. In addition, all children who attended California private schools (Terman did not approve of private education) or Chinese-speaking schools were arbitrarily excluded. Thus, bright upper-class and Chinese-American children were excluded. Bright children for whom English was a second language were also at risk for inadvertent exclusion, for the teachers of that day revealed enormous ethnic prejudices. For example, the father of one Terman woman was a poet, a chess master, and a former mayor of his town; in addition, he had obtained three years of graduate education in his profession as a horticulturist. His daughter's teacher, however, had disdainfully referred to this cultured man as a "Japanese gardener."

Beginning with Lewis Terman, who studied his "gifted children" from 1922 to 1956[17] and then continuing with his successors — first Melitta Oden, 1956–1970,[18] then Robert Sears (himself a member of the Terman Study), 1970–1989,[19] and, finally, Albert Hastorf, 1990–2000 — the Terman cohort has been studied for almost eighty years. These four generations of investigators have followed the Terman men and women by questionnaire about every five years and by personal interview in 1940 and 1950. After sixty-five years of follow-up, attrition, for reasons other than death or invalidism, is still less than 10 percent. Unfortunately, the Terman women were not asked to provide regular physical exams.

In personality traits, the Terman women showed significantly more humor, common sense, perseverance, leadership, and even popularity than their classmates. They were as likely as their classmates to marry, but their physical health was better. Compared to their classmates, they had better nutrition, better mental stability, fewer headaches, and fewer middle-ear infections. Their siblings suffered only half the childhood mortality experienced by the siblings of their classmates. Finally, by age 80, like the Harvard sample, the Terman women have enjoyed a mortality only half what would be expected for white American women in their birth cohort.

In 1987, through the generosity of Stanford professors Robert Sears and Albert Hastorf, my wife, Caroline Vaillant, and I were permitted to select for reinterview a representative subsample of 90 women from Terman's original sample of 672. We found that 29 of these 90 women had died; and owing to bad health or poor cooperation, 21 surviving women were not seen. We reinterviewed the remaining 40 women. Their average age at interview was 78 — the same age as the men of the Harvard cohort who were last followed up in 1999. Except for the vastly inferior physical health reported in their questionnaires, available data suggested that the 50 uninterviewed women did not differ significantly from the 40 women whom we did interview.

Comparison of the Three Cohorts

At the time of their last study, all the Terman women were old-old (seventy to seventy-nine), and a third of the Harvard men were entering the world of the oldest-old (eighty plus).[20] Only half of the Inner City men had passed from being young-old (sixty to sixty-nine) to old-old. In terms of physical decline the mortality of Inner City men at sixty-eight to seventy was the same as that of the Terman and Harvard cohorts at age seventy-eight to eighty.[21] Most of this difference in health could be explained by less education, more obesity, and greater alcohol/cigarette abuse among the Inner City cohort. When these four variables were controlled, their much lower parental social class, IQ, and current income were not important. Put differently, the health of the 29 Inner City men who graduated from college was identical at age 70 to the health of the Harvard College graduates at age 70.

Although each of the three cohorts in the Study of Adult Development was in itself relatively homogeneous, the samples were very different from each other. A third of the Harvard men's fathers, but none of the Inner City men's fathers, were in social class I (physicians, successful lawyers, and businessmen).[22] A third of the Inner City men's fathers, but none of the Harvard men's fathers, were in Social Class V (unskilled laborers with less than ten grades of education). The parents of the Terman women were largely middle class or skilled laborers (Social classes III and IV); few of their fathers were as privileged as those of the Harvard men or as disadvantaged as those of the Inner City men.

The table illustrates the contrasts between the three cohorts. As noted, the mean (Binet) IQ of the Terman women was 151; the mean (Wechsler-Bellevue) IQ of the Inner City sample was 95; the estimated mean (army alpha) IQ of the Harvard sample was between 130 and 135. The mean education of the Terman women's fathers was twelve years in contrast to eight years for the fathers of the Inner City men and sixteen years for the fathers of the Harvard men. While none of the Inner City mothers had gone to college, a third of the mothers of the Harvard men had graduated from college — twice as many as the mothers of the Terman women. A third of the Inner City men had less than ten grades of education, while a quarter of the Terman women and three-quarters of the Harvard men obtained a graduate school degree.

•   •   •

One final commonality of how these three prospective studies were conducted was that all relied on interviews with the Study members *and* with parents *and* teachers. The Study often made use of recorded sources of public information. Ambiguity about whether a life was successful could often be resolved by the use of multiple sources of information. In this book, I may illustrate a point by quoting what a member said during an interview, but my conclusions are almost always supported by more objective evidence. Behavior, not words, predicts the future and reflects the past.

For example, the stepfather of an Inner City man was described by his wife as a man who until recently had been "quite a heavy drinker who would drink anything," but who now "only bought a small bottle of wine every day." She claimed that he was

Comparison of the Three Cohorts

	Harvard Cohort	Inner City Cohort	Terman Women Cohort
Dates of birth (mean)	1921	1930	1911
Date entered study	1939–42	1940–44	1920–22
Number in study	268	456	682
Last study contact	1999	2000	1988[A]
Dead at last study contact	38%	37%	37%
Frequency of questionnaires	every 2 years	every 2 years	every 4–5 years
Physical exams	every 5 years	every 5 years	not obtained
Caucasian	100%	99%	99%
IQ	c. 130–135	95	151
Social class of most parents[B]	I–III	III–V	II–IV
Graduate school degree	76%	2%	23%
Dead by age 70	23%	37%	c. 20%
Mean income at 50 in current $	$105,000	$35,000	$35,000

A.   1988 refers to the data reported in this book; the Terman men and women are still being studied.

B.   I = upper class; II = upper-middle class; III = middle class; IV = skilled labor; V = unskilled labor/welfare
(Hollingshead and Redlich, *Social Class and Mental Illness*)

a social drinker and that his use of alcohol never interfered with his work. Field investigation revealed a very different story. Five years earlier a social agency had noted the stepfather had been laid off from work "probably from drunkenness," and that he had a long arrest record for *drunkenness*. A child welfare agency noted that the "stepfather is apt to be too drunk to be a companion." Two years after the interview, the stepfather had been arrested three more times for drunkenness and twice was committed to a state hospital for alcohol abuse. Five years after his wife alleged that he "only brought home a small bottle of wine," his death certificate noted the primary cause of his death as "cirrhosis and alcoholism." In similar ways, assessments of vague but important

---

The lives of all three cohorts repeatedly demonstrated that it was social aptitude — sometimes called emotional intelligence[23] — not intellectual brilliance or parental social class that leads to a well-adapted old age.[24]

judgments like the quality of parental affection or marital support could be substantiated from several points of view and at several different points in time.

* * *

On the one hand, none of the three cohorts can be viewed as representative of the general population. On the other hand, the three samples do have the virtue of being demographically vastly different from each other; yet *within* each sample there was considerable homogeneity. Thus, the *similarities between* the groups and the *differences within* the groups may be generalizable to other American Caucasian samples. Like the proverbial half loaf of bread, these studies are not perfect; but for the present they are, arguably, the best lifelong studies of adult development in the world.

At times readers may be irritated that the Harvard examples outnumber stories of women and of the less socially privileged Inner City men. The Study has, for a variety of reasons, more information about the Harvard cohort. But usually the conclusions drawn from each of the three groups were the same.

The Author

As we shall see, this book is filled with both data and judgment calls; and in many ways, the latter are the most emphasized. That being the case, the reader is more than entitled to some acquaintance with the person making most of the judgments, namely me. After all, I have my biases and prejudices that I cannot guarantee haven't affected my observations. So the reader needs to take them into account. I was born in New York City in 1934. My father died when I was ten. When I was thirteen I found myself fascinated to read the report of his Harvard College class of 1922 twenty-five years after graduation. Of course, I did not then anticipate that twenty years later I would be interviewing the men of the class of 1942 at their twenty-fifth reunion. I attended Harvard College, and one way or another I have maintained a Harvard connection for almost fifty years. Like many, I fancy myself a political independent, but longitudinal hindsight reveals that over 44 years I have voted only for Democrats for president.

Unlike my archaeologist father I took no courses in college in the social sciences and, certainly, none in anthropology. Instead, I learned the history of science from a young section man named Tom Kuhn, took premed courses, but majored in the humanities. I attended Harvard Medical School with plans to become a community psychiatrist in the public sector. Instead, I became fascinated by interviewing "remitted" schizophrenics and abstinent heroin addicts whose clinical records from ten to fifty years before I had managed to discover. I was intrigued by the changes in their lives, which to me looked a lot like maturation. Adult development happened, and to understand it further seemed worth my professional lifetime.

Thus, in 1967, in the Harvard cohort's thirtieth year, I was excited to join the Grant Study, as it was then called. I became a research professor instead of a community psychiatrist. Although I had always denied interest in his field of archaeology, I now found myself more than twenty years after my father's death rummaging through dusty files in search of artifacts from the past of Harvard men and muttering to myself, "I've turned into a goddamned archaeologist after all." In 1967 the Study members had begun returning to their twenty-fifth Harvard reunions. As a 33-year-old psychiatrist who had just reviewed their extensive records, I was able to interview them in the flesh. I marveled as before my fascinated eyes the men metamorphosed from adolescents in the Study records — even more callow than I — into mature fathers of adolescents. At age 47 many of these "normal" men were at the top of their game. For years I had been trained to study pathology; now it seemed equally exciting to study health.

By 1972 I had reinterviewed a hundred Harvard men at an average age of forty-seven and had experienced enough troubles of my own to have a fuller sense of the ups and downs of any life trajectory. Yet I was more exhilarated than distressed by the complexity of the lives I was studying. In 1977, when the men were fifty-five, I published a book on adult maturation, *Adaptation to Life*.[25] By that time I assumed that the college men had stopped growing. What did I know? I was only forty-three.

Rich as these lives were, however, the demographic biases implicit in any study of Harvard men meant that the picture I was getting of adult development was necessarily skewed. If I was going to understand "how people keep well and do well" I needed to study a less rarified sample.

In 1970, because of my long-term follow-up of heroin addicts, Sheldon and Eleanor Glueck on their retirement appointed me as one of the three curators of their groundbreaking case files of juvenile delinquents and matched controls. These disadvantaged but resilient controls, of course, made a splendid foil for the "overprivileged" Harvard men. Funded by the National Institute of Alcohol and Alcohol Abuse, my colleagues and I spent the years from 1974 to 1978 reinterviewing the Inner City men. They were the same age as the Harvard men when I had first interviewed them.

Interviews with Study members were consistently exhilarating and exhausting. Indeed, because so much was known about each member, there was an intensity to many of the interviews that was both gratifying and surprising. Talking with Study members was often like resuming an old friendship after a period of separation. Study members who had always found loving easy made me feel warmly toward them, and led me to marvel at their good fortune in belonging to such an enjoyable project. In contrast, Study members who had spent their lives fearful of other people and who had gone unloved in return often made me feel incompetent and clumsy. With them I often felt drained and depressed as if I had done all of the work in the interviews while they took much and gave nothing.

By 1980 the inexorable thrust of adult development had continued. The Harvard men were now 60 and I had just attended my own twenty-fifth Harvard reunion. It had become clear that not only was I committed to following these men for the rest of their lives, but also that I was embarked on a study of aging. Up to that time I had entertained as little interest in gerontology as I had once shown for archaeology. But now, at 46, I was becoming as interested in understanding what life after retirement might be like as I once had been in learning about what it was like to be 45. Besides, since I had already studied the "recovery" process from maladies thought by many to be incurable — schizophrenia, alcoholism, heroin dependence, and personality disorder, to study positive mastery of "old age" seemed a challenging next step. My funding source shifted from the National Institute of Alcohol and Alcohol Abuse to the National Institute of Aging. In 1985 I finally grew up enough to realize that I could not understand human development if I just studied men — a minority group. Thanks to the generous help from the Henry A. Murray Center at Radcliffe (now Harvard) and from Stanford University — especially from Professor Albert Hastorf — my wife, Caroline Vaillant, and I reinterviewed Lewis Terman's gifted women. When we interviewed them in 1987 the Terman women were seventy-six to seventy-nine. I was still fifty-two. Not until I had grown up for another ten years and begun interviewing the Harvard men between seventy-five and eighty did I really begin to appreciate the lessons that the three groups were teaching. Adult development affects us all. Now I, too, get a Social Security check.

The Importance of Prospective Study

I have stressed that the significance of the Study of Adult Development is that it is prospective. But why is that important? The extraordinary value of a prospective study lies in the uniqueness of its perspective. A longitudinal follow-back study must depend on memory; a prospective study records events as they happen. Thus, if we wish to understand how our octogenarian role models became that way, it is critical that the elderly survivors should have been followed since adolescence. There are several reasons why this is so.

First, prospective study allows us to view the happy, successful great-grandparents against a background of peers who died young. Is death at an early age merely one more manifestation of God playing dice with the universe, or could many such premature deaths have been prevented? Are those who die young less well loved and less mentally healthy than those who die old? Or is it just genes? Previous studies of "successful aging" have usually not begun until age sixty or seventy; they have not possessed the prospectively gathered data to address such questions. In them premature deaths are invisible. Chapter 7 of this book will answer the above questions.

Second, prospective study means that we do not have to depend on the subject's memory of what happened yesteryear. It is all too common for caterpillars to become butterflies and then to maintain that in their youth they were little butterflies. In October 1941 a young Harvard member had said of America's increasing hostility toward Germany on the eve of our entry into the war: "I am extremely disheartened. I feel the war in Europe [is] none of our business." By the winter of 1966–1967, however, he fully subscribed to Lyndon Johnson's military policies in Vietnam and condemned his sons for actively protesting American involvement. He had completely forgotten his own public demonstrations against American involvement in World War II.

Third, only prospective study permits one to demonstrate objectively the Freudian concept of repression. As a Harvard sophomore, Fritz Lethe had assured the Study that there was no truth in Freud's sexual theories. He boasted to the Study psychiatrist that he would drop a friend who engaged in premarital sexual intercourse. The psychiatrist observed, however, "While disapproving of sexual relations, Fritz is frankly very much interested in it as a topic of thought." At 19, Lethe was also terribly prejudiced against "sneaky liberals" and tore up "propaganda" from the Harvard Liberal Union. He also told the psychiatrist, "I have a drive — a terrible one. I've always had goals and ambitions that were beyond anything practical."

Later, Lethe rewrote his life story. At age 30 he saw his earlier "terrible drive" as derived from his mother. He saw her as his greatest personal problem. "All my life I have had her dominance to battle against . . . the major change in my philosophy is relevant to my goals in life. My goals are no longer to be a great in science, but to enjoy working with people." By age 49 Mr. Lethe also believed in Freud and premarital sex. The goals of "sneaky liberals" were no longer contemptible. He now believed that "the world's poor [were] the responsibility of the world's rich."

In his interview at age 50, Lethe proclaimed, "God is dead and man is very much alive and has a wonderful future." He now maintained that he had doubted the validity of religion and had stopped going to church as soon as he had arrived at Harvard. Such a memory did not jibe with the fact that as a Harvard sophomore, he reported going to Mass four times a week!

But his memory distortions did not stop there. When Fritz Lethe was 55, I sent him the above vignettes so that he might grant me permission to publish them in my book on the Harvard sample, *Adaptation to Life*. He sent my text back with a terse note: "George, you must have sent these to the wrong person." He was not trying to be funny. He could not believe that his college persona could have ever been him. Maturation makes liars of us all.

Fourth, prospective study also reveals that distortions of memory can be adaptive and creative. Let me offer an example from the life of a Terman woman, Matilda Lyre. At age 78, when asked if she had been interested in becoming a doctor, Lyre replied reprovingly, "You have to remember women have come a long way. I never even thought about being a doctor as a possibility." In point of fact, at 14 she had told the Terman staff that she wanted to be a doctor. In college she had majored in premedical studies, and at age 30 her Strong Vocational Interest Inventory had suggested medicine as the vocation best suited to her interests. Indeed, as a child, Matilda Lyre, besides wanting to be a doctor, had wanted to be an astronomer *and* a poet *and* a scientist.

But her rewriting of history was healing. When Lyre was 20,

one of the Terman staff described her as someone "who seems to adorn anything she attempts." At Berkeley she became editor of the college literary magazine. She was on their all-star swimming team, and as a very young woman, she traveled throughout California giving lectures and writing articles. Then gender bias and limited economic opportunities during the Great Depression combined to squash Matilda Lyre's talents. As a result she began her young adulthood as a part-time physical education teacher in a small town. When her husband found work, she had to give up even that job; for during the 1930s if their husbands obtained jobs, California female teachers had to resign from theirs. School jobs were too scarce for one family to have two.

When she was 78 we also asked Matilda Lyre how she had dealt with the gap between what society had allowed her to achieve and her potential. She responded, "I never knew I had any potential . . . I had to learn to cook and raise a garden." Her life story, then, became in part a reconstruction to make a life frustrated by prejudice, the Great Depression, and poverty in a small town bearable.

However, the saga of Matilda Lyre reveals that developmentally blighted lives can enjoy happy endings, that the futures of the elderly matter, and that they are interesting. When she was 30 Matilda Lyre's Strong Vocational Interest Inventory revealed that besides being suited to being a doctor, she was well suited to becoming a musician. For most of her adult life, Matilda had not allowed herself to develop this side of her persona; finally, at age 60, she took violin lessons. A little later, after she divorced her husband, she inherited a beautiful violin from her best friend, and her musical career took off. For the last six years this one-time-unemployed physical education teacher has been giving solo violin concerts in Los Angeles and loving it. And at age 78 there was no evidence that her new career would not continue.

A fifth reason why prospective study is valuable is that such study allows its members time enough to overcome shame — and deliberate falsification. For example, one man explained to the Study, "My replies have been frank, but with a period of delay. Whenever anything was badly wrong I tried to suppress it, and on the next Grant Study questionnaire I tried to claim that everything was going fine, but that was an effort. The effort convinced me that I had better do something about the situation. If you want to find out what is really happening to me — read the next questionnaire or the one after that. Having to face my situation, having to formulate an attitude and then having to conceal the situation temporarily have been in the long-run healthy for me."

Sixth, perhaps the most important benefit of prospective study is that it permits distinguishing effect from cause — cart from horse, as it were. For example, in interviewing these individuals I often concluded that those who had abused alcohol had done so as a home remedy for their clinical depression. They agreed. However, review of their ongoing case records by two independent psychiatrists, one focusing on alcohol abuse and the other on depression, revealed a quite different conclusion. The symptoms of their alcohol abuse had usually come first; the symptoms of major depression came only later. Like most individuals afflicted with both maladies, the members of the Study could acknowledge their depression but not their alcoholism; and so their retrospective narratives reversed cause and effect.[26] Prospective review of those narratives put them back in order.

Drawbacks to Prospective Studies

If prospective longitudinal studies are so important, why don't we do more of them? The short answer is *expense.* Prospective studies of human lifetimes are extremely expensive in four currencies: money, luck, investigator perseverance, and subject loyalty. First, granting agencies are reluctant to continue funding the "same old study." Therefore, many promising prospective studies of lives have starved to death financially. To keep the Study of Adult Development going for six to eight decades has cost millions of dollars in consecutive grants from roughly twenty different funding sources.

Second, it took not only talent and dogged perseverance, but it also took unusually good luck for Joe DiMaggio to hit safely in fifty-six consecutive games. Similarly, it has taken enormous luck for the Terman Study, the Glueck Study, and the Harvard Study to survive academic and funding vagaries, not only to the maturity of their subjects, but into their old age. Third, many studies have fallen victim to lack of perseverance or the death of the original investigators. Thus, it has been also due to the patience of its several generations of directors that the Study has survived.

But, to be more honest and more humble, it is the fourth expense, the extraordinary loyalty and patience of its members, that is most essential to create a valuable prospective study. Attrition from a prospective study, like the breakage of unique antiques, cannot be repaired. Thus, low attrition frees study conclusions from a bias that usually plagues prolonged prospective studies — selective loss of members. (The Study of Adult Development has been blessed with the lowest attrition rate of any comparable study in the world — except perhaps the Lundby Study in Sweden.[27])

Besides expense, a second problem that besets prospective studies is "halo effects." By halo effect I mean that to know of someone's past biases our judgment of their present. An ordinary wine tastes very different if poured from a bottle with a Château Lafitte label than from a screw-top jug labeled Thunderbird. To avoid this limitation we took many precautions. Raters of the Study members' childhoods were, of course, blind to the future; and raters of the present were kept blind to the men's and women's childhoods. Raters were also blinded to ratings by other judges. Perhaps thirty different research assistants have worked on this Study. Most were asked to make independent ratings before they, too, became biased. As director of the Study for thirty years, my judgments of the present have been profoundly influenced by my knowledge of the members' past. For that reason, I have rarely provided numerical ratings for the Study database. The thoughtful reader may also ask whether a third disadvantage to prolonged study is that it alters the members' lives. What about the so-called

Heisenberg effect? Do we not always change that which we study? As a psychotherapist I must reply, "Alas, if only changing the course of human lives were so easy." If occasionally watching people over the course of a lifetime changed their lives, intensive psychotherapy would be a much more effective force for change than it is. It is true that the Heisenberg effect may apply to electrons studied by physicists, but our own close inspection of a speeding bullet does not usually alter its course. So it is with subjects in a longitudinal study. By studying the members for long periods we may distort what we see, but we don't, necessarily, change them.

A final and very important disadvantage of long-term prospective studies is that they are not representative. They are always limited in size, in historical time, and in composition. Since the Study subjects were all selected for health or nondelinquency or intelligence, they can only illustrate how life unfolds under favorable circumstances. Therefore, the reader may fairly ask how a book about relatively prosperous white Americans chosen for mental health can teach us anything about general humanity. My answer is that in order to understand normal biological development, climate and growing conditions should be optimal.

Had I tried to study successful aging in a random sample of 10,000 of the world's population, my cohort, while being "representative" and "politically correct," would have been so heterogeneous as to boggle both mind and computer. Besides, randomness is neither normal nor healthy. In addition, unlike sociologists and demographers, biologists do not study all of the creatures of Noah's ark simultaneously. Biologists study liver enzymes in purebred rats; they study genetics in the fruit fly; and they study neurophysiology in a single ganglion of the sea snail. Furthermore, control of confounders is essential. For example, the rate of onset of physical disability was dramatically different if Study men had had ten years or sixteen years of education. Thus, in order to study some causes of physical disability other variables must be held constant.

Readers must decide for themselves when the Study members and their behavior reflect people as they know them and when it seems they are reading about unfamiliar tribes. My own belief is that cross-cultural studies will show that mental health from one part of the world to another does not differ as much as we might think. Consider, for example, that the diets of a New York construction worker, of a Japanese aristocrat, and of an Australian aboriginal appear extraordinarily different; but the healthy balance of basic food groups in each diet that makes it nutritious is rather constant. Be that as it may, the three Study cohorts are all unrepresentative. Readers must exercise proper caution about any conclusions that I may draw.

* * *

A few years ago a wise participant and Study member, Ted Merton, wrote to me "testily but cordially":

> Here you have these wonderful files, and you seem little interested in how we cope with increasing age. You ask us what we can no longer do, what our politics are, whether we're spiritual, how bad is our health, etc., but I detect little curiosity about our adaptability, our zest for life, how our old age is, or isn't, predictable from what went before. You seem mostly to want to chronicle progressive deterioration instead of taking advantage of a database with which to examine aging as thoroughly, as imaginatively, and as vigorously as you did our youth and early adulthood. Young people are always more attractive than the elderly, but they're not necessarily more interesting. We may be has-beens, but does the Study have to be? I write to call your attention to the repeated innuendo that our futures no longer matter . . .

The rest of this book will be an effort to respond to his wise advice. I will use true-life narratives to offer a guide for positive, interesting old age. The next five chapters will describe the developmental processes that make old age vital. Then, chapters 7 through 10 will try to unpack critical components of the last two decades of life: first, being ill without feeling sick; second, regaining a capacity for creativity and play in retirement; third, the acquisition of wisdom; and fourth, the cultivation of spirituality. The final two chapters, 11 and 12, will summarize the lessons that I have learned from the Study. I shall attempt to leave readers with greater hope for their final decades than is provided by Simone de Beauvoir in her brilliant monograph *The Coming of Age*[28] or by the equally brilliant but equally dispiriting quip "Old age is not for sissies."

In his fifties, in *The Seasons of a Man's Life,* Daniel Levinson wrote gloomily that men approaching 60 may "feel that all forms of youth . . . are about to disappear, . . . a man fears that the youth within him is dying and that only the old man — an empty dry structure devoid of energy, interest or inner resources — will survive for a brief and foolish old age."[29] In contrast, Betty Friedan in her seventies wrote in *The Fountain of Age:* "We have barely even considered the possibilities in age for new kinds of loving intimacy, purposeful work and activity, learning and knowing, community and care. . . . For to see age as continued human development involves a revolutionary paradigm shift."[30] This book will provide clear evidence to support such a paradigm shift.

•　　•　　•

To convey Study findings, I have selected examples that reflect important issues for more than one member of this Study. I hope they will describe many others outside of it. Any resemblance between individuals in this Study and persons living or dead will be entirely intentional; but I have used pseudonyms and altered identifying detail and specific affiliations. Thus, if the narrative detail fits anyone of the reader's acquaintance too closely, it will almost certainly turn out that he or she has identified the wrong person. Study members who are still living have granted me their permission to print their disguised biographies.

CHAPTER TWO

RIPENESS IS ALL: SOCIAL AND EMOTIONAL MATURATION

> I have that within to show the alchemy of life that has made gold from dross.
>
> Ted Merton, 78-year-old Study member

Not only is aging a very complex concept; it carries very different meanings for different people. For example, consider the following multiple-choice question:

Aging means:
  a. Decay (e.g., after age twenty we lose millions of brain cells a year)
  b. Seasonal change (e.g., the maiden's alluring blonde curls become the grandmother's beloved white bun)
  c. Continued development right up to the moment of death (e.g., an oak tree or a fine Château Margaux wine)
  d. All of the above

The right answer, of course, is "All of the above."

The first answer, (a), is certainly correct; as Woody Allen reminds us, no one gets out of this world alive. The second possible answer, (b), is a theme throughout this book: the more things change, the more they stay the same. This chapter, however, unpacks the third answer, (c). What takes place during adult development? What can septuagenarians do better than twenty-five-year-olds? In reply, I shall discuss the second half of life from two points of view: social maturation and emotional maturation. These two concepts undergird the whole book.

Unfortunately, the theory of adult development is still waiting for the sage who can provide universal principles that transcend cultures and centuries. I am not that sage. For the present the best I can do to explain social development is to stand on the shoulders of that wise artist-anthropologist-psychoanalyst Erik Erikson. To explain emotional development, the best I can do is to stand on the shoulders of Sigmund Freud and chart the maturation of involuntary coping mechanisms (a.k.a. defense mechanisms). Some readers may fuss at my parochialism, but, for the present, those two pairs of shoulders provide a pretty good view.

Social Maturation:
The Sequential Mastery of a Series of Life Tasks

Only in the last century did physicians and parents learn to appreciate predictable development in the personality of children. In the nineteenth century many physicians still considered children as adults in miniature. As a medical specialty pediatrics has emerged only during the last hundred years. In addition, parents' recollections of the milestones of child development are notoriously poor. Only through the invention of the photograph, the baby book, the family doctor's case files, and finally through prospective studies of growth and development are we able to circumvent the distortions of time upon parental memory. Today, thanks to the work of researchers like Jean Piaget and Nancy Bayley, and popularizers like Benjamin Spock, we can predict child development — just as our savage ancestors learned to predict the orderly waxing and waning of the moon. As our children shift from phase to phase, we pray; we cross our fingers; we worry or are grateful; but we are not totally surprised.

However, adult development is still a mystery. Human beings do not stop developing in childhood as Saint Ignatius Loyola declared, "Give me a child until he is 7, and I will show you the man." They do not stop developing at the law's 18 or 21. Men do not even pay mind to William James when he wrote: "Habit is thus the enormous flywheel of society. . . . It dooms us all to fight out the battle of life upon the lines of our nurture or our early choice . . . in most of us, by the age of thirty, the character has set like plaster and will never soften again."[1] Nor do women listen to Sigmund Freud's notion that by age 30 a woman "often frightens us by her psychical rigidity and unchangeability."[2]

In the Middle Ages and the Renaissance, intellectuals found the ages of adult life of considerable interest.[3] They painted these ages and wrote about models of life span development at some length. The difficulty was that their models were represented in principally mystical, spiritual, and astrological terms. Adult development as a subject for scientific study is a very new field.

In 1842 Adolphe Quetelet was the first scientist to suspect that "man is born, grows up and dies according to certain laws that have never been properly investigated."[4] Many decades were to pass before anyone even began to investigate these "certain laws." As late as 1914 the father of geriatrics in America, Ignatz Nascher, had difficulty finding a publisher interested in his landmark book on the subject.[5]

In 1922 Stanley Hall, the creator of Clark University and popularizer of the term *adolescence,* did find a publisher for his book *Senescence,*[6] but its sales were meager. In 1928 the first laboratory to study the psychology of later maturity was founded at Stanford University by the Carnegie Corporation with the munificent endowment of $10,000. Only after World War II, when scientists had already mastered atomic fission, were learned societies devoted to the study of gerontology founded in the United States.

In the 1930s at the University of California at Berkeley, the world's first prospective study of personality development in children was begun under the leadership of Berkeley psychologists Harold Jones, Nancy Bayley, and Jean MacFarlane. The Institute of Human Development, which they founded, directly impacted the research of Erik Erikson, about whom I will have a lot to say. During the same period Berkeley psychologists Charlotte Bühler and her student Else Frenkel-Brunswik collected four hundred biographies and autobiographies of ordinary people.[7] To study the laws of adult development, they tried to learn retrospectively what happened to human beings over time. Frenkel-Brunswik, in turn, influenced a number of Berkeley graduate students and junior faculty who would become future chroniclers of adult development: Jane Loevinger, Betty Friedan, Daniel Levinson, and Erik Erikson.

Bühler and Frenkel-Brunswik conceptualized adult development very much like German folk artists from 1600 to 1900. The folk artists had depicted adult development as steps ascending until age 50 and then descending inexorably downward toward the grave.[8] "Around the forty-fifth year of life," Frenkel-Brunswik wrote, "symptoms of decline can be observed, and with these signs, the third period, called the period of regressive growth is ushered in. . . . One can observe a decline, a form of retirement from life."[9] She would have chosen to answer the question at the start of this chapter by checking answer *a*. So would Shakespeare. After all, he warns us, "And so, from hour to hour we ripe and ripe,/And then from hour to hour we rot and rot.[10]

Yet in Frenkel-Brunswik's own data, unrecognized by her, was a contradiction of her pessimistic view of aging. She had noted that in late midlife "the actor becomes a director, the athlete becomes a trainer" and "although the general sociability lessens, the more philanthropic activities begin first at this time."[11] In her investigation of "duties and wishes" Frenkel-Brunswik noted that at 25, "92% of all wishes are directed towards the individual himself," but by age 60 "only 29% of wishes were directed toward the self, 32% towards the family and 21% toward mankind in general." She was describing the same adult maturational pattern that Erik Erikson was later to term a "widening social radius" and "Generativity."[12]

Erik Erikson, a Danish art student without a college degree, became, through his affiliation with Anna Freud, a psychoanalyst in the early 1930s. In 1934 he emigrated to America, and in 1939 he arrived at Berkeley via Harvard and Yale. During the 1940s Erikson was among those privileged to harvest data from the Institute of Human Development. Years later Erikson recollected, "The study gave me an opportunity to chart a decade of the life histories of about fifty (healthy) children and to remain somewhat informed about the further fortunes of some of them."[13] For the next half-century Erikson continued to be influenced by continuing to observe the evolution of these children and their parents.[14] Together with his cross-cultural studies, Erikson used his prospective view of child development to replace Freudian speculation with anthropologically grounded common sense. Erikson respectively translated Freud's poetic "orality," "anality," "Oedipal," and "latency" into the more down-to-earth "Basic Trust vs. Mistrust," "Autonomy vs. Shame," "Initiative vs. Guilt," and "Industry vs. Inferiority." In *Childhood and Society*[15] Erik Erikson became the first social scientist to conceptualize clearly adult development as progress, not decline.

Through a sequence of stages, he believed adults participated in life within a widening social radius. Life after age 50 was no longer to be a staircase leading downward but a path leading outward. Adult development passed through the four stages of "Identity vs. Identity Diffusion," "Intimacy vs. Isolation," "Generativity vs. Stagnation," and "Integrity vs. Despair."

Perhaps the best empirical evidence for Erikson's generalization of a widening social radius has come from Berkeley psychologist Norma Haan's fifty-year follow-up of adult personality development at the Institute of Human Development.[16] When they were over 70, she studied the same individuals who as children had been studied by Erikson. For both men and women Haan noted that over time three broad components of personality increased very significantly; all three reflected the development of social skills. These three components were *outgoingness* (for a subject described as "gregarious," "arouses liking," "associative," "initiates humor"), *self-confidence* ("turned to for advice," "productive"), and *warmth* ("warm," "sympathetic," "protective," "giving").

•   •   •

The Study of Adult Development at Harvard has allowed me to study Erikson's theory empirically. Similar to time-lapse photography of blooming flowers, the Study of Adult Development permitted me to remain the same and watch Study members evolve from adolescents into great-grandfathers and great-grandmothers. For example, as an adolescent, one Harvard Study man had loved "modern" jazz. At 50, having replaced jazz with classical composers, he had only contempt for his children's passion for "modern" rock and roll. He thought that the musical tastes of the young had deteriorated while his had remained the same. But reading the whole record in a single afternoon made it clear to me that it was he who had changed.

Like Erikson I have concluded that one way to conceptualize the sequential nature of adult social development may lie in appreciating that it reflects each adult's widening radius over time. Imagine a stone dropped into a pond; it produces ever-expanding ripples, each older ripple encompassing, but not obliterating, the circle emanating from the next ripple.[17] Adult development is rather like that.

In describing my revision of Erikson's model, let me begin by noting that for charting adult development a term like Robert Havinghurst's *developmental tasks*[18] is more scientifically correct than Erikson's *stage*. In adult development the term *stage* is only a metaphor. In addition, the process of adult development that I observed in the Study members was not nearly as orderly as intellectual development of children. For Piaget the mastery of the next sequential "stage" always required mastery of all the earlier tasks that he and his students observed in developing children. Adult developmental tasks are more often than not sequential — but not always.

In order to assess adult development I have examined each Study member's first mastery of certain life tasks. In theory the social radius of each task fits inside the next. In my model there are six sequential tasks. First, the adolescent must evolve an *Identity* that allows her to become separate from her parents. Then, the young adult should develop *Intimacy,* which permits him to become reciprocally, and not narcissistically, involved with a partner. Next comes *Career Consolidation,* a task that I added to Erikson's eight. Mastery of this task permits the adult to find a career that is both valuable to society and as valuable to herself as she once found play. After that comes the task of *Generativity,* a broader social circle through which one manifests care for the next generation. The penultimate task is to become a *Keeper of the Meaning,* another task that I have added to Erikson's eight. This task involves passing on the traditions of the past to the next generation. It leads to a social circle wider than that produced by Generativity. Becoming a Keeper of the Meaning allows one to link the past to the future. Finally, there is *Integrity,* the task of achieving some sense of peace and unity with respect both to one's own life and to the whole world.

The six adult life tasks are as follows:

• **Identity:** Prior to entering the adult world it is well that the adolescent achieve a sense of what Erik Erikson titled Identity: a sense of one's own self, a sense that one's values, politics, passions, and taste in music are one's own and not one's parents'. Only then can the young adult move on to the next stage of life, Intimacy, and forge close reciprocal emotional bonds with a mate.

Erikson's *Identity* requires mastering the last task of childhood: sustained separation from social, residential, economic, and ideological dependence upon family of origin. It must be emphasized that such separation derives as much from the identification and internalization of important childhood figures as it does from the ability to master modern life. Nor is Identity just a product of egocentricity, of running away from home or of marrying to get out of the family. There is a world of difference between the instrumental act of running away from home and the developmental task of knowing where one's family values end and one's own values begin. Admittedly, to some degree such separation/individuation is a lifelong process.

Among those Study members who failed to reach *Identity*, even by age 50, were men and women who never achieved independence from their family of origin or from dependence upon institutions. In middle life, such individuals were not able to commit themselves either to gratifying work or to sustained intimate friendship.

• *Intimacy:* The task of living with another person in an interdependent, reciprocal, committed, and contented fashion for a decade or more often seems neither desirable nor possible to the young adult. Initially this task involves expanding one's sense of self to include another person. Once achieved, however, the capacity for intimacy may seem as effortless as riding a bicycle. For several single women in the Terman sample, intimacy was achieved with a close woman friend. Sometimes the relationship was completely asexual. For the participating men in our Study, this person was almost invariably a wife. In part this heterosexual emphasis was because only 2 percent of the College sample viewed themselves as homosexual (although two such College men waited until age 65 to tell us), and because the homosexual Inner City men withdrew from the Study. Superficially, mastery of intimacy may take very different guises in different cultures and epochs, but "mating-for-life" and "marriage-type love" is built into the wiring of many warm-blooded species.

• *Career Consolidation:* Mastery of this task involves expanding one's personal identity to assume a social identity within the world of work. On a desert island one can have a hobby, but not a career; for careers involve other people. Individuals with severe personality disorder often manifest a lifelong inability to work. In his own work Erikson discussed Career Consolidation only obliquely and sometimes did not distinguish self-identity from career identity. But I believe that there are four crucial developmental criteria that transform a "job" or hobby into a "career": contentment, compensation, competence, and commitment. Obviously, such a career can be "wife and mother" — or in more recent times, "husband and father."

To the outsider the process of Career Consolidation often appears "selfish," but without such a "selfishness" one becomes "selfless" and has no "self" to give away. Henrik Ibsen in his play *A Doll's House* depicts Nora's "selfish" escape from her husband. Her husband, who in the pejorative sense really is selfish, demands that Nora care only for him and the children. Since Career Consolidation never justifies the abandonment of children, Nora's leaving her family behind is a metaphor, not a recipe for living to be literally copied. Nevertheless, unless Nora slams the doll house door and develops her own satisfying career, she can never hope to become a generative mentor to her daughter's generation.

• *Generativity:* Mastery of the fourth task, *Generativity,* involves the demonstration of a clear capacity to unselfishly guide the next generation. Generativity reflects the capacity to give the self — finally completed through mastery of the first three tasks of adult development — away. Just as Intimacy reflects a capacity for mutual interdependence; just so Generativity reflects a different sort of capacity — to be in relationships where one "cares" for those younger than oneself and, simultaneously, respects the autonomy of others. Generativity (and leadership) means to be in a relationship in which one gives up much of the control that parents retain over young children and learns to hold loosely.

Generativity means community building. Depending on the opportunities that the society makes available, Generativity can mean serving as a consultant, guide, mentor, or coach to young adults in the larger society. Research reveals that between age 30 and 45 our need for achievement declines and our need for community and affiliation increases.[19] We may view deans, matriarchs, and business magnates as the products of crass ambition and infantile narcissism. But in so doing we ignore the psychosocial skills necessary to allow one individual to assume sensitive responsibility for other adults. Empathic leadership only looks like self-aggrandizement until one tries to do it. In all three Study cohorts mastery of Generativity tripled the chances that the decade of the 70s would be for these men and women a time of joy and not of despair.

• *Keeper of the Meaning:* Mastery of this fifth task is epitomized by the role of the wise judge. Again, Erikson obliquely refers to the importance of this task, but in his writing he assigned parts of the task to Generativity and parts to Integrity. Generativity and its virtue, *care,* require taking care of one person rather than another. The role of Keeper of the Meaning and its virtues of wisdom and justice is less selective. Justice, unlike care, means not taking sides. The focus of a Keeper of the Meaning is on conservation and preservation of the collective products of mankind — the culture in which one lives and its institutions — rather than on just the development of its children. Some people call such a dispassionate approach to life by the elderly stodgy, but that is to miss the point. As Erik Erikson suggests, there are dialectical tensions to every development task — Intimacy versus Isolation, Generativity versus Stagnation. And so with Keeper of the Meaning, the danger is rigidity. Put differently, to preserve one's culture involves developing concern for a social radius that extends beyond one's immediate community. This is not a trivial distinction. We can all appreciate the difference in social maturation between the partisan and successfully generative Ronald Reagan who called the other side "the Evil Empire" and a wise leader like Abraham Lincoln, who did his utmost to heal and to forgive the wounds of civil war.

The generative individual cares for an individual in a direct, future-oriented relationship — as, for example, a mentor or teacher. In contrast, the Keeper of the Meaning speaks for past cultural achievements and guides groups, organizations, and bodies of people toward the preservation of past traditions. The organizers, judges, and guardians of the Olympic Games play a very different role from the Games' more generative coaches. In addition, the former have a lot more gray hair. Matriarchs, genealogy mavens, and antiques refinishers are all exemplars of what is involved in becoming a Keeper of the Meaning. Clearly such caretakers are not superior to caregivers. The distinction is only that a seventy-year-old is usually better at being a Keeper of the Meaning than a thirty-year-old.

To expand on Erikson's concept of a "widening social radius," let me invoke the simple and culturally universal example of grandparents. Who has not known at least one seventy-year-old woman who was able to be closer, wiser, more empathic toward her grandchildren than she ever had been in the prime of life toward her own children? Grandfathers may need canes and false teeth and grandmothers need bifocals and hearing aids. But they, and they alone, elicit a special trust from grandchildren and teach them meaningfully about the past.

• *Integrity:* This is the last of life's great tasks. Erikson described Integrity as "an experience which conveys some world order and spiritual sense. No matter how dearly paid for, it is the acceptance of one's one and only life cycle as something that had to be and that, by necessity, permitted of no substitutions."[20] If care was to be the virtue of Generativity, Erik Erikson suggested that wisdom was the virtue of Integrity. "As for the final strength, wisdom, we have formulated it thus: wisdom is detached concern with life itself, in the face of death itself. It maintains and learns to convey an integrity of experience in spite of the decline of bodily and mental function."[21]

•   •   •

Admittedly, some individuals, often due to great stress, tackle developmental tasks out of order or all at once. Alexander the Great, General Lafayette, Napoleon Bonaparte, and Joan of Arc were inspirational and generative leaders in their twenties. William Osler, one of the greatest physicians of all time, did not confront the task of Intimacy until he married at age 40 — well after he had established his career as a brilliant professor of medicine and as the most generative physician of his era. Ludwig van Beethoven enjoyed a brilliant committed career, but never enjoyed Intimacy. Adult development does not follow rigid rules.

Nevertheless, the usually sequential mastery of these tasks through Keeper of the Meaning has been documented for both the Terman and the Harvard samples[22] and for the Inner City sample through Generativity.[23]

Of course, there are many differences between women and men; but with the passage of decades both genders appear to follow Erikson's sequence of expanding social radii. In a recent review of three longitudinal studies of women's development — from the University of Michigan, from Mills College, and from Smith College — between ages 30 and 60 women increased both in Generativity and in confidence in their power and authority.[24] Indeed, the authors found "evidence that some aspects of women's well-being (positive relations with others; personal growth) are somewhat better than men's at all ages, and none are worse."[25] Once again careful longitudinal study gives the lie to William James's — and Sigmund Freud's — pessimism about adult development.

I must close, however, with a caveat. One life stage is not better or more virtuous than another. Adult development is neither a footrace nor a moral imperative. It is a road map to help us make sense of where we and where our neighbors might be located. It also contributes to our "wholeness" from which our word "health" is derived. In old age there are many losses and these may overwhelm us if we have not continued to grow beyond ourselves.

* * *

Thirty years ago I used the life of Harvard Study member Adam Carson, whom I had interviewed in 1969, to illustrate mastery of the sequential tasks of Identity, Intimacy, Career Consolidation, and Generativity.[26] Having reinterviewed Adam Carson in 1997, I wish now to use his life to illustrate his subsequent maturation from Generativity to Keeper of the Meaning to Integrity.

Adam Carson was a Harvard Study member who became a physician. Carson and his father were interviewed while Carson was still in college. Both shared the same nervous tics. They both cleared their throat compulsively. Repeatedly his father scratched himself around the head, and Carson scratched himself around the neck. Half a century later when I reinterviewed Adam Carson, he had none of his father's nervous tics. He was now a mature septuagenarian, very much his own person. What had happened in the interval?

• **Identity:** As the above suggests, Adam Carson's adolescent struggle to separate from his parents was prolonged. At nineteen he had not fully differentiated himself. His parents described Adam Carson to the Study as a model child. His mother said that "from the minute he was born Adam has been completely perfect as to conduct, ambition, and everything. . . . Adam has been the one that I asked to do things because I have always known he would do them and do them as though he were delighted. . . . He has always been thoughtful and cooperative in the home. You would almost have to build a trophy room for the prizes he has brought home. . . . He is emotionally the most mature young person I have ever had contact with."

Carson's father admitted to the Study that from 16 to 18 his "perfect" son had become "a bit of a hell-raiser." He didn't know the half of it: for young Adam Carson had secretly acquired a motorcycle, a string of sexual conquests, and a skill at dancing that was so proficient and so pleasing to him that he considered abandoning medical school and becoming a professional dancer.

Perhaps as a result when Carson was 19, the Grant Study psychiatrist saw him as "giving an impression of considerable mental energy . . . his affect was vital, rich, happy, and colorful."

Adam Carson's brief respite from the tight control of his childhood was short-lived. By age 25, in all aspects of his life, Carson justified his father's boast that his son "was leading a planned existence . . . he has his emotions beautifully under control." Carson went to Harvard Medical School and interned at Massachusetts General, did postgraduate work at the Rockefeller Institute, and then returned to teach and do research at Harvard, claiming that he preferred research to private practice. But a Study physician who had been most impressed with him as an adolescent dismissed Dr. Carson, at 28, "as not a very broad-dimensioned person in my mind." Professional ballroom dancing had been Carson's idea, and he had abandoned it. Medical research was his father's idea.

• *Intimacy:* Adam Carson married at age 22. His wife provided him with conventional, almost sisterly, intimacy. At 26, true to the ethic of the nuclear family, he wrote, "I treasure my marriage above everything else in the world. I get tremendous happiness from it." But his marital adjustment changed over time. Dr. Carson had married an ascetic wife who was suitable for him as an immature 26-year-old "caterpillar," but she helped shut off his quest for Identity prematurely. Thus, at 29, the anthropologist described Carson as "gangly and awkward, young and adolescent . . . dependent on his family . . . unsure and terribly concerned with following the established pattern." Psychological testing showed "a superficial guy, a passive kind of dependence on circumstance, unsure about his own fate and passively awaiting it. There is a constant rejection of women and their sexual charms . . . seeking out the socially acceptable in order to avoid private emotion." As Carson matured, his passionless marriage degenerated into a series of angry, repetitive conflicts. By age 38 he was so depressed over his marriage that he was considering suicide; but consciously, as the interviewing psychiatrist noted at the time, he could only experience "depression, not as an emotion, but as a sense of fatigue." In other words, Carson could not yet feel his emotions. Nonetheless, lasting for fifteen years, his marriage had met the Study's minimal criteria for intimacy.

• *Career Consolidation:* Although Dr. Carson's research productivity was scanty, his career, again, met the Study's minimum criteria for Career Consolidation. At 36 he wrote to the Study, "I have given up practice completely . . . work consists almost entirely of research [commitment] . . . work fills me with constant ever increasing pleasure which private practice never did" [contentment]. Finally, he became an associate professor of medicine with tenure at a famous medical school [compensation and competence]. However, adult development does not stop with high school graduation. This badge of acceptance of academic tenure brought Dr. Carson little satisfaction, for over time he was evolving.

• *Generativity:* In 1967, when I met Adam Carson for the first time, he was 47, and a very different man from who he had been at 29. Now divorced and remarried, when he looked back on his first marriage, he recalled, "I felt that she was a rattlesnake and would do something mean and awful." It was not that he didn't know his own mind at age 26, but over time Carson had changed. In describing his general mood, he still said, "I'm chronically depressed, I think." But now his depression was clearly an emotion, not a "sense of fatigue." Indeed, Adam Carson was anything but fatigued. For a man who had gone through a divorce and now considered himself happily remarried, he had if anything too much energy. As he said, "I'm very highly sexed and that is a problem too." He proceeded at that point to tell me a very colorful story about his recent romantic entanglements.

His career focus had also changed, for he had returned to private practice. This once mousy researcher had evolved into a charming clinician. His dramatic office looked out over Boston's Charles River; he appeared suave, untroubled, kindly, and full to overflowing with the pleasure that he derived from his generative interactions with the patients in his private practice. And I, as a 33-year-old physician, saw Carson as a very broadly dimensioned person indeed. Admittedly, both the observer and the observed are products of adult development; I was still struggling to develop a career, and Carson had moved on to caring for the wider community.

Having made major changes in both his marital and his professional life, Dr. Carson had also come into a new relationship with his parents. At 28, Dr. Carson had said of his father, "I resemble him but he betters me in every respect." In fact, Dr. Carson was then hard at work at the research that his father had prescribed as the road to greatness. But Carson's father, a lawyer, labored in no such ivory tower. He was actively involved in a glamorous private practice that brought him into a close working relationship with his clients. At 47, Carson had ceased to do what his father said. He now did as his father did — immersing himself in the lives of those he served professionally. Thus, he was no longer constrained by his father's admonitions but, rather, inspired by his father's example. Behavior is so much more important than words.

In his shift from research to private practice, and by resigning from the academic hierarchy to become his own person, Carson realized that "I was forging something for myself that was of me and for me." His care of patients was, he explained to me, "more of a natural talent." Research had always been an effort. Yet, Dr. Carson's interests did not extend very far beyond his immediate world. Even by age 50 his family, his patients, and his church were as far as he saw. The national turbulence of the 1960s was beyond his ken. He was a wonderful physician, but perhaps not a very broad-dimensioned citizen.

• *Keeper of the Meaning:* By age 65 Adam Carson had not remained where I, his 33-year-old interviewer, had left him. His interests in medicine had broadened far beyond simple patient care. He had become concerned with the traditions of medicine and their ethical basis. As chief of his hospital's medical staff, he had mastered the generative issues of institutional responsibility. Caring for individual patients now had to compete with administrative work, attending meetings, and serving on committees. Carson was again teaching medical students, but his focus was no longer the molecular biology of his youth. Instead, he now taught medical students how to achieve rapport with their patients. He also taught students to take patients' histories, a critical facet of medicine as old as Hippocrates. Adam Carson had become a Keeper of the Meaning.

Yet, Dr. Carson's involvement with the world beyond his own hospital was still limited. He had reached that stuffy rigid side of late middle age that makes the imaginative young throw up their hands in despair and *Hamlet* audiences rejoice when Hamlet's rapier rids them of Polonius's pompous platitudes. On one occasion Carson remarked that his biggest worry in the past year had been trouble with the foundation of his summerhouse. But even he had to laugh at such a parochial worry and add, "That's not profound, spiritual, or medical." Asked what his greatest satisfaction had been in the past year, Dr. Carson continued, "We found a way to fix the foundation." His plans for retirement were equally pedestrian. "I wouldn't just sit around," he insisted, "I'd do something." He explained that he might spend more time sailing or maybe get a job selling real estate. Then, suddenly, he again laughed at himself. "Can golf, bridge, and senility be far behind?"

The only glimmer of hope that Carson would not disappear behind the gated walls of a retirement community seemed to reside in his involvement in the Episcopal church, where his activities put him in touch with a broader world of ideas and values. He was the chairman of his church's Social Concerns Committee. He had conducted a symposium on the role of spirituality in medicine and another symposium on ethical dilemmas in patient care.

Finally, at age 70, having found a young man to take over his practice, Adam Carson retired. "I don't miss the hospital," he wrote, "because I had begun growing something that I loved four years before." The garden that he cultivated was the Hastings Institute, a world-renowned foundation devoted to medical ethics. Dr. Carson had substituted a new passionate involvement in international medical ethics for his lifelong, equally passionate involvement with his beloved patients. Instead of puttering about fixing the foundations of his cellar, he now traveled the world in order to advance medical ethics. In short, he became less involved with his "hometown" and more concerned with the world. "I have become very interested in the nature and sources of ethics and morality. In the local environmental forum where I volunteer, I am responsible for a whole day's program entitled Ecological Philosophy. . . . For the past four years I have been working almost full-time in the environmental movement in my local area. This means board meetings, organizing courses, writing, speaking, field trips." Dr. Carson lived on a small planet, and he meant to take care of it.

Adam Carson's most important activity was fund-raising for the Hastings Institute. To do this well, he had taught himself how to be competent not only in ethics and fund-raising, but also in accounting and the computer. Dr. Carson had become perhaps more open to new learning than any septuagenarian whom I interviewed. Fascinated with mastery of new software, he wrote with pride, "I know things that people my age know nothing about." Yet while he was busy fund-raising, Adam Carson, the former adolescent trophy winner, explained, "I always let everybody else take the credit." Septuagenarians can do that. Adam Carson had also gone from caring for test tubes at age 27 in order that he might satisfy blind ambition to caring for the globe at 77. Years before Watson and Crick discovered the double helix, Adam Carson at the Rockefeller Institute had done research on DNA — the magical substance that converts structure into process and that transmutes inanimate organic chemistry into life. Now, Carson was spending what remained of his life forging bioethical rules to govern the responsible use of DNA — the powerful genie that he had helped to set loose. Without the young there would be no progress; without the old there would be no culture.

• *Integrity:* I interviewed Adam Carson again when he was 75. Adam Carson acknowledged that the hardest part of his life was that he tired so easily. The enthusiasm that Adam showed in talking about his day-to-day activities was limited by the fact that age, metastatic prostate cancer, and chemotherapy often made him feel exhausted. Episodic fatigue and bouts of sorrow are part and parcel of old age, but they do not preclude feelings of excitement and joy. With excitement Carson told me that he had met the man who had cloned the human embryo. He now had had time to explore New England and to venture to places on the globe where he had never been before. As he had been at age 18 and at age 47, at age 75 Adam Carson had become once more "broad-dimensioned."

Spiritually, Dr. Carson had become closer to a Shinto priest or a Lakota shaman than to the busy Episcopalian vestryman that he had been in midlife. "I have no sense of a personal God," he wrote, "but I do believe in some sort of Creative Power. . . . It would be good to start out with respect, if not reverence, for the endlessly creative cycle of life . . . rather than the miracle of any individual life. All living things have ethical standing, including, but not limited to, humans. . . . It behooves each of us . . . to work for the integrity, stability and beauty of that web of being which allows each of us a brief sense of oneness with the splendors of creation. . . . Each of us was born of this earth, nurtured by it; and each of us will return to the earth." Dr. Carson had come a long way from worrying about summerhouse foundations.

Erikson suggests that one of the life tasks of Integrity is for the old to show the young how not to fear death. Thus, I asked Dr. Carson about the effect of his prostate cancer on his life. He explained that whenever he had a sudden pain, he could never know if it was "simply old age or a metastasis . . . but I am a fatalist, when it comes it comes." He pointed out that in his need to take hormones to suppress the spread of his cancer there was "a suicide device. If my wife dies or I get too lonely, I just stop the medicine and let a thousand metastases grow." He said this whimsically, as a play on ex-president Bush's "thousand points of light" speech, rather than dramatically or sadly. And as he closed the interview, Adam Carson reassured me that the happiest period of his life was now. Dying need not beget fear.

In worrying about the whole planet, Carson had by no means lost his capacity for intimate care. As the interview progressed on his lovely garden terrace in Dover, Massachusetts, the sun began to set and the air grew chilly. Carson suddenly interrupted himself and said, "I am going to bring out a sweater for you, George, so you won't have to sit there wondering if you can have a sweater." As in 1967, I was again flooded with understanding of why this man's patients must have loved him.

*　　*　　*

But as with all of us, Dr. Carson's mastery of each life task was imperfect. Human development consists of grays, not blacks and whites. Toward the end of our interview, like a proud student still showing prizes to his Grant Study "parents," Carson suddenly blurted out, "Let me get some exhibits." He proceeded, rather sheepishly, to bring out a beautiful bound leather volume ensconced in a lovely silk-covered presentation box. In the book were at least one hundred letters from grateful patients. For his 70th birthday, Carson's wife had secretly obtained their addresses and had written to his longtime patients to request personal letters to commemorate their long relationships with their beloved physician. The letters that came back were deeply caring, often with photographs pasted to the bottom. Carson turned to me and said, "I don't know what you will make of this, George, but I have never read them." His eyes were filled with tears. The depth of his feeling, his obvious attachment to his patients, was deeply moving. Yet I was stunned by his inability to let himself fully enjoy the fact that his patients had loved him back. He blurted out; "I can't bear to talk about this."

On the one hand, if Adam Carson was still bringing prizes home, now the prizes were human, not inanimate. Now he knew that the prizes were for him . . . and not for his mother or the Study. On the other hand, if Carson could be a good friend to others, he still had difficulty in allowing others to be a friend to him. He could not bring himself to immerse himself in the letters that his patients had lovingly sent to him and that he so lovingly treasured. Even in late maturity Carson still did not fully comprehend that grief never kills and that grief can only be healed by remembering lost loves. But none of us is perfect; there is always room for further growth.

Put differently, Dr. Carson had a failing common to many professional healers. Unable to accept his own needs to be dependent, he could be a much better friend to others than he could let them be to himself. It was a sign perhaps of his maturity that he could now finally let his wife take a little care of him; but he still took pains to be independent, pains to bring me sweaters.

No, Adam Carson was not the perfect oldster that I wanted him to be, anymore than he had been the perfect youngster of whom his parents dreamed. But I shall close with a letter that in 1981 Dr. Carson's wife had sent to the Study: "To me Adam is the most remarkable, patient, and considerate man I have ever met . . . very generous. I am truly amazed that Adam is such a wise, healthy man. His sensitive judgment and insight into people is remarkable. He is very intuitive. . . . I feel you are the one person that knows how lucky I really am. He gives so much to all his patients, friends, and family."

Fifteen years later, warm in his sweater and having known Adam Carson for thirty years, I agreed.

•　　•　　•

Twenty-five hundred years ago Confucius anticipated the last thirty years of Adam Carson's life. "At fifty, I knew what were the biddings of Heaven. At sixty I heard them with a docile ear. At seventy I could follow the dictates of my own heart; for what I desired no longer overstepped the boundaries of right."[27] As the next three chapters will spell out in detail, mastery of three tasks, Generativity, Keeper of the Meaning, and Integrity are critical to achieving a graceful and satisfying old age.

Emotional Maturation: The Development of Increasingly Adaptive Coping Mechanisms

Old age is not all beer and skittles. We all know that with aging, nerve conduction is less rapid and our reflexes are slower. Forty-year-olds do not make good shortstops, and commercial airlines retire their pilots at 60. After 75 our eyes, ears, memory, and joints begin to limit our activities. As I write this chapter, Dr. Adam Carson is dying of prostate cancer. Nevertheless, throughout life we heal ourselves through involuntary (unconscious) coping mechanisms. And, if our brain stays free of disease, we are able to use these mechanisms more gracefully at 75 than we did at 25.

Long ago Plato understood that a wise "charioteer" was needed to balance the pull of his two horses, "Desire" and "Obedience." Too often over the next two thousand years, however, the more people thought about it, the more important the paradigm of intellect over emotion, obedience over desire, became until it culminated in Marxist and Skinnerian belief in utter obedience and rationality to the exclusion of emotion. But Plato's view is proved right by long-term follow-up. We ignore desire and emotion at our peril. The sweet rational Enlightenment of the French Revolution worked for about a year; then all hell broke loose. By ignoring the "desire" of greedy capitalism for decades, disciplined Marxism, too, has failed. In recovery from alcoholism, Alcoholics Anonymous, with its attention to the "language of the heart" and its wise use of humor is, at least arguably, more effective than the more rational cognitive behavior therapies.[28,29] We all need to balance obedience with desire.

But how? Certainly, the sweet emotional freedom preached by the Woodstock generation has worked no better than dour rationality. We must go back to Aristotle and Plato to find the Golden Mean, the wise charioteer, the delicate synthesis between passion and reason. This psychic balance is not achieved through willpower or police. It is achieved through involuntary mental regulatory mechanisms that are largely unconscious.

A test of successful living, then, becomes learning to live with neither too much desire and adventure nor too much caution and self-care. None of us want to be like the health nut who in hopes of living to 100 gave up Havana cigars, scotch whiskey, French cuisine and, finally, Italian romance. He kept giving up his passions until by age 30 he could no longer tell if he was still alive. Rather, successful aging means giving to others joyously whenever one is able, receiving from others gratefully whenever one needs it, and being greedy enough to develop one's own self in between. Such balance comes not only from following Erikson's orderly sequence of life tasks but also from employing elegant unconscious coping mechanisms that make lemonade out of lemons.

Let me draw attention to some relatively maladaptive, involuntary coping mechanisms: *projection, passive aggression, dissociation, acting out, and fantasy.* We often associate such coping strategies with adolescents and with personality disorders. With *projection* unacknowledged feelings are attributed to others. *Passive-aggressive* individuals turn anger against themselves in a most annoying and provocative manner. The capacity of theatrical people to *disassociate* themselves from painful emotion and to replace unpleasant with pleasant affect, as if they were on stage, is familiar — occasionally even engaging. In real life when individuals use *dissociation*, however, we scorn them as being "in denial." *Acting out* obscures ideas and feelings with unreflective behavior such as tantrums and impulsive conduct. Schizoid *fantasy* replaces real human relationships with imaginary friends — a habit chilling to others.

Put differently, these maladaptive coping mechanisms (or "immature defenses," as I shall call them) are not only the stuff of which adolescent coping and personality disorders are made; but they can be reframed as "sins." Those behaviors eliciting social disapproval include: self-absorption and masturbation (*fantasy*); sadism, masochism, and cutting off one's nose to spite one's face (*passive aggression*); prejudice and injustice collecting (*projection*); delinquency and child abuse (*acting out*); and, finally, binge drinking and "what, me worry?" insouciance (*dissociation*). All of these mental mechanisms soothe the user over the short term; all eventually leave the user worse off than before.

We must remember, however, that adolescence is, one hopes, a self-limiting disorder. With time, immature coping evolves into more adaptive coping strategies (or "mature defenses," as I shall call them.) Examples would be *sublimation, humor, altruism,* and *suppression.* Such strategies appear moral as well as adaptive; and as we shall see in chapter 7, they make an important contribution to healthy aging. (See Appendices B and C for a more detailed glossary of these mechanisms and how they were scored.)

Healthy septuagenarians use these more mature mechanisms more often than do 20-year-olds. With his earthy chauvinism, Freud quipped, "The young whore becomes an old nun." In more politically correct language, with time the young, sexually exploitative, acting-out Italian aristocrat becomes the altruistic St. Francis of Assisi. Thus, as a child grows up, the annoying, covert sadism of playing *passive-aggressive* practical jokes on others can evolve into the mature *humor* that permits people to laugh at their own misery rather than at the misery of their victims.

In short, with the passage of time adolescent jerks can evolve into paragons of maturity. Such maturation, however, requires emotional development, years of experience, and a seemingly miraculous capacity to internalize others. It also takes the continued biologic evolution of our brains, whose connecting pathways — especially those integrating desire and reason — continue to mature past age 40.[30,31]

Sublimation involves a kind of psychic alchemy; the pain of childhood becomes transmuted in the mature artist's masterpiece. A less grandiose example was provided by a Study member who wrote, "I have twice the sex drive of my wife. We adjust ourselves by varying our sex play to suit each other. We believe that lovemaking should be practiced as an art!"

Mature *humor* allows us to look directly at what is painful. Humor permits the expression of emotion without individual discomfort and without unpleasant effects upon others. Humor requires the same delicacy as building a house of cards — "timing is everything." The safety of humor, like the safety of dreams during sleep, depends upon motor paralysis. We see all, we feel much; but we do not act. Miraculously humor transforms pain into the ridiculous. But, alas, many *New Yorker* and *Punch* cartoons are opaque to the young.

When it is used to transform conflict, *altruism* involves getting pleasure from giving to others what we ourselves would like to receive. For example, although victims of childhood sexual abuse often mindlessly abuse children themselves (acting out), alternatively and transformatively, such victims work in shelters for battered women and in support groups or hotlines for abuse victims.

Suppression (stoicism) has none of the deep humanity of altruism, sublimation, or humor. Indeed, suppression is often regarded by psychotherapists as a failing, not a strength. But when used effectively, suppression is analogous to a well-trimmed sail; every restriction is precisely calculated to exploit, not hide, the winds of passion. Both the stoic and the "in denial" Pollyanna note that clouds have silver linings, but Pollyanna leaves her umbrella at home. Both repression and suppression, for time present put desire out of mind. But the next day when the time is ripe, only suppression remembers. Thus, Sigmund Freud regarded the postponement (suppression), but not the forgetting (repression), of gratification as the "hallmark of maturity."

These four mature coping strategies are not only associated with maturity, but they can be reframed as virtues. Such virtues can include doing as one would be done by (*altruism*); artistic creation to resolve conflict and spinning straw into gold (*sublimation*); a stiff upper lip, patience, seeing the bright side (*suppression*); and the ability not to take oneself too seriously (*humor*). These latter behaviors are the very stuff of which Victorian morality plays are made and they provide antidotes to narcissism. Indeed, these coping strategies often seem quite conscious until one tries to employ them on purpose. If only through willpower we could always remember to count to ten before we speak our mind and to laugh at our own pricked vanity, life would be much easier.

*   *   *

If only through willpower we could emulate the late-life adaptive style of Terman Study participant Susan Wellcome. When we first met her, she was 76 and appeared a perfectly ordinary gray-haired, somewhat overweight old lady. Her dress seemed to hang on her body like a chintz flour sack. By the time we left the interview, Susan Wellcome had become transformed into the grandmother whom I wished I might have had, and her dress flowed as regally as a Hawaiian queen's muumuu. In other words, in two hours Wellcome evolved from an unremarkable blue-collar widow who had let herself go into a wise woman who inspired my wife and me with a positive zeal for old age. Wellcome epitomized this chapter's epigraph; she had "that within to show the alchemy of life that has made gold from dross" — and for this there were many she was glad to thank. Susan Wellcome was open to the world. There was nothing but an unlatched screen door between her living room and the working-class Akron Street on which she lived. In every other Terman woman's home that my wife and I had visited, the elderly women were somehow protected from life outside by gated communities or by locked doors and security systems. But Susan Wellcome lived on her urban street as she might have lived in a grass hut in Tahiti.

When we arrived, Wellcome was on the phone. Somehow she managed to be courteously attentive to her caller while warmly waving two strangers into her living room. Then she went back to the telephone and finished her call in a crisp but involved fashion. While we waited, we noticed cats wandering in and out of her cluttered living room; we admired the horse brasses on her well-used fireplace, and we listened to the old clock that ticked on the mantelpiece flanked by many photographs.

That first minute of the interview served as a metaphor for Wellcome's life. Simultaneously, she could welcome the outside world in and yet remain attentive to her own needs and those of her friends. Soon there was another telephone caller to whom she explained that she was going to be busy with the local orchestra in the evening and could not come to dinner. Once again, the world had entered her living room, and she entered the world. Indeed, on the morning that we had arrived, the seventy-six-year-old Wellcome had already been to the polls to vote.

Once the interview began Wellcome could not help revealing that she had had a mother who surely ranked as one of the meanest in the Study. Asked what she would do differently if she had her life to live over again, Susan Wellcome exclaimed, "I would have had brothers and sisters — and a new mother!" Our question had been crafted to reveal alternative career aspirations, but Wellcome put first things first. Susan Wellcome's mother neither enjoyed cooking nor did she teach her daughter to cook or sew. At the same time, she tried to prevent her daughter from taking any initiative and labeled young children "little stinks." As an only child, Wellcome grew up believing that her mother hated children. Wellcome told us that the worst thing her mother had done to her was "telling me that she wished that she had never had me."

Her mother had pushed her five-year-old daughter, Susan, into vaudeville, but kept all her daughter's earnings for herself. In order to evade child labor laws, she made her daughter lie and say that she was six years old. Worse still, raised in a fundamentalist religion, Wellcome "knew" at the time that both her dancing and her lying were sins. She also "knew" that it was a sin to be angry with her mother. In short, her mother had blighted her daughter's mastery of basic trust, autonomy, and initiative — the three developmental tasks of childhood that many besides Erik Erikson regard as essential in order to begin life.

For a child a rational solution to such a conflict was simply not possible. Thus, in her early years Susan Wellcome defended herself against her mother and her own life through passive aggression. She could defeat her mother only by defeating herself. As Wellcome explained to us, "My parents wanted me to be great," but she would not gratify them because "my parents wouldn't let me be independent." Thus, having been a musical child who had danced professionally on the stage, Wellcome became an adolescent described by a teacher as "exceptionally awkward and her sense of rhythm is poor." On meeting Susan Wellcome a Terman Study psychologist wrote, "I never would have suspected that she had made a public appearance in her life." Her teacher had commented that "her companions are very fond of teasing her." The defense of passive aggression both diminishes the self and invites abuse by others.

Early on, Wellcome's mother, recognizing that her daughter had a photographic memory for music, tried to exploit that gift too. She pushed her daughter to play the piano, but would not let her play Bach. Wellcome was allowed to play only pieces like Strauss waltzes that her mother thought "pretty." So, in another effort to sabotage her mother, Wellcome gave up the piano altogether. "I wanted to get out of her jurisdiction!"

At the University of California at Berkeley, Susan Wellcome continued to rebel by defeating herself. Unconsciously, she may also have been inhibited by the fact that she was attending college after her father had completed only the seventh grade. For the first time in her life she got low grades. In addition, although Wellcome believed that nurses were only "highly specialized slaves of the doctor," in defiance of her parents she resigned from

Berkeley and went to nursing school. In other words, instead of getting openly angry, she spat into the wind. How would she ever create a self that was worth passing on? How could she ever become generative and age gracefully?

In her twenties three important events happened to Susan Wellcome that allowed her involuntary coping strategy to evolve from rebellious adolescent martyrdom to mature empathy and patience (a.k.a. altruism and suppression). First, Wellcome found a mentor with whom to identify. Second, she learned to accept her anger toward her mother as healthy, rather than to regard it as a sin. Third, she initiated a loving marriage that was to last for more than forty years. These events created three of the most valuable catalysts for maturation of defenses: taking beloved people inside, honest recognition of affect, and being safely held. In the 1920s few of the Terman women found mentors; after all, their mothers had only just been given the vote. But when we asked Susan Wellcome if she had ever had a mentor, she replied without hesitation and no little reverence, "I had a French teacher." This teacher of a romance language not only attended Wellcome's church and thereby softened her harsh religion, but was also a dressmaker so skilled that she could sew dresses without a pattern. As a result of such teaching, Wellcome boasted, "I was much better at French and at sewing than Mother." Her French teacher also taught her to cook and encouraged her in many other activities in which, her mother had always warned her, "You might get hurt."

When her beloved French teacher and surrogate mother died, Wellcome's real mother, with characteristic meanness, prevented her daughter from attending the funeral services. Asked how she had coped with the loss of her mentor, Wellcome replied with simple candor, "I was very unhappy." But strengthened inside through the internalization of a woman who had really seemed to love her, Wellcome dealt with her grief by quitting the hated nursing school and "taking music up as a remedy." Rejecting her mother's piano, she turned to the violin so that she could play in the orchestra at church — and at her father's lodge. Although both furious and depressed at the time, "I fell madly in love with the violin." And so, with friends her own age, Wellcome organized a string quartet.

Adam Carson and Susan Wellcome came from very different families. (Carson's father loved him not wisely but too well, and Wellcome's mother seemed to love her not at all); nevertheless, both had to mature into mid-adulthood before they could embrace their "natural talents" as their own and before they could fully master Eriksonian tasks hitherto uncompleted. At 30 the character of neither Carson nor Wellcome had been "set in plaster." When we asked her how she had changed in equanimity since age 40 (a standard question), Susan Wellcome replied, "I used to feel sorry for myself, and I don't anymore."

At this point in the interview Susan Wellcome jumped up impulsively and exclaimed, "I think pictures always make things clearer." She showed us a picture of her adored French teacher. In contrast to some Study members, Wellcome gave every person she discussed a first name and illuminated her narrative with pictures. She always connected her prose to her passion. True, her living room was cluttered, but it was cluttered with totems and symbols of old attachments. Maturity consists in part of preserving the memory of old loves; for holding on to those we have loved is one way that our defenses become better able to serve us. Half a century had passed; but Wellcome's sewing table, her violin music stand, and the picture as well as the memory of her French teacher filled the room. Recent copies of *Quilter's Newsletter Magazine* covered her coffee table. Her French teacher's sewing lived on. In memory the dead remain immortal.

When she was 27, Wellcome had a thyroidectomy for goiter. After the operation she experienced an epiphany. In her own words, "An inhibition to rage toward my mother seemed to have been removed along with the [thyroid] gland. For the first time I could talk to my mother without feeling I was suffocating." For the first time she could acknowledge to herself that she had had an unhappy childhood and that she had hated her mother and felt claustrophobically dominated by her. From then on, altruism could replace passive aggression as a means of tempering anger. Susan Wellcome managed to transmute the dross of spiteful martyrdom into the gold of loving service.

Her emotional growth was also catalyzed by a happy marriage. At 29 Wellcome wrote to Lewis Terman, "I always put my husband and baby first in everything. I never feel sorry for myself. . . . I had never been happy until I got married." And at 40 she told the Terman Study that although she knew she fell far short of her abilities, "raising the boys is all pleasure." For biology flows downhill. Giving to her mother drove her crazy. Giving to her children brought her joy. She also regarded being intellectually gifted "as a gift from God"; and gratitude is almost always more fun than spite or regret. The career that Wellcome consolidated was that of housewife.

In response to the question: What held your marriage together for forty-two years? Susan Wellcome replied with disarming simplicity, "Well, we were in love." On her previous questionnaire she had written the Terman Study that "my husband's death still brings active tears of grief after five years; but I try to remember the forty-two wonderful years that we had together and go on with my life." She and her husband had camped together and sailed together in a boat that he had built with his own hands. When her husband became blind, she read to him daily; but her altruism turned such work into play. The old vaudeville performer in her enjoyed mimicking each book's different dialects. Once more dross became gold.

At 44 Susan Wellcome returned to nursing — this time not as self-punishment, but because she felt grateful to life and wanted to give something back. At 47 she was again able to enjoy playing the piano, in the form of "passing it on." Now, in her own living room, she could enjoy teaching other women on the same piano that she had been made to play as a child. Wellcome also played the piano for a women's evening exercise class which, as she pointed out, was mainly dancing. To Wellcome the piano and dancing were no longer signs of exploitation; they had become vehicles for her Generativity.

Perhaps the clearest example of Wellcome's use of altruism and the virtue of the Golden Rule was that she developed a special interest in helping women who were in prison — an unusual interest perhaps for a nurse, housewife, and a musician, but understandable in a woman who for twenty years had longed to get out of her mother's oppressive "jurisdiction."

When we interviewed Susan Wellcome at 76, her husband's pool table still dominated the center of her living room. But in the transmutation of her grief, the table was currently covered with a board so that she could also use it as her sewing and cutting table. On weekends, however, the sewing was put away and her husband's pool table helped her to find new boyfriends. She used the table to play pool with neighborhood adolescent boys. These, of course, were the same sort of "young punks" from whom other Terman women protected themselves by deadbolts and gatekeepers. Sometimes the 76-year-old Wellcome could beat the teenagers at pool, but competition for Wellcome was exciting only if it were turned into play. For sublimation lets you express the strongest of passions — even the anger that suffocated you as a child — if you can but transform it into play. The verb *compete* comes from *competere,* to seek together.

Maturity for Susan Wellcome also included a number of steps in spiritual development. The altruism of her church work was as important to her as was the sublimation available through her music, her pool table, and her sewing. As a child she had belonged to what was called "the Christian Church." The Catholics in her class had teased her for her self-importance in belonging to *the* Christian Church. Her parents in turn tried to teach her to hate the Catholics. Projection and prejudice are not adaptive defenses. Nor is drawing religious circles that keep others out. Like Adam Carson, Susan Wellcome saw maturity as giving up the religion of childhood for one that you developed yourself — one that included everyone. With maturity her social radius expanded.

At age 15 Susan Wellcome had gone surreptitiously to a service in an Episcopal cathedral. The lush Episcopalian service had much greater appeal than her own dour fundamentalist church. When in her 30s she moved with her husband to Akron, Ohio, she became confirmed in the Episcopal Church. Gradually, she advanced from the women's council within her own church to become a member of the Akron Ecumenical Council and then a member of the Ecumenical Executive Committee for Ohio. This council included most of the Christian churches in the state. She began drawing spiritual circles that drew others in. There were nine people on the state committee. Most were clergy. Susan Wellcome was the only woman *and* the only member without a college degree.

Ten years ago Susan Wellcome had started out as secretary to the Council, and in order to advance the ecumenical movement she had learned to type. This was an act of generosity, for she had attended Berkeley, where for a college woman to learn how to type was considered demeaning, dangerous, or both. More recently, a man had taken over her secretarial duties. Now she edited the newsletter. She proudly gave us two copies, one of which included two articles by her. Like many of her fellow "Termites," as they called themselves, Wellcome had dreamed of becoming a novelist, but now she was satisfied with being a newsletter editor. Her husband's pool table served yet another purpose; she used its broad expanse to send out her ecumenical mailings.

Altruism is doing for others what they need, not what you want to do for them. Perhaps only one person in a million becomes a good novelist; but after age 60 this college dropout, blue-collar housewife, and self-taught typist had a long list of publications to her credit and a multitude of honors for her ecumenical work. The most recent interfaith dialogue that she had organized concerned how the different denominations regard the Virgin Mary. Recently, her Council had been reaching out to the Greek Orthodox Church.

Susan Wellcome described her involvement with the World Council of Churches as "my small effort to support healing the rifts of four hundred years. It has given me tremendous satisfaction." She again jumped up to show us a picture of the priests and ministers with whom she worked. She explained, "We all go out together and have a Japanese meal because one of the priests is fluent in Japanese. They are like brothers" — the brothers for whom she had always longed. Once again dross had become gold.

Asked what she had learned from her children, Wellcome instantly replied, "Oh, a lot. It was such a joy to discover that they knew things that I didn't." As an example she described her son William telling her that he was going to take part in a puppet show. When she offered to help him sew the puppet costumes, he explained that he did not need costumes; he was going to be in charge of the lighting. "So I thought, he was doing something I knew nothing about — how wonderful!" She had also learned a lot about the visual arts from her son Mark, a graphic artist.

Asked for her definition of successful aging, Susan Wellcome replied that successful aging was "not thinking about it or talking about it. . . . What I don't care for is someone who wears eye shadow. They aren't fooling anybody." No, she did not even want to begin to think about being old; "I have too much to do." True, Wellcome had physical ills; but the point was to get over them and not to feel sick.

Besides, she assured us, she had plenty of money — and money left over to give to charity. "It's not fair for me to hoard it all." She boasted that she had even gotten a refund from the Internal Revenue Service because she had given so much of her money away. In actual fact, her retirement income consisted only of her husband's Social Security and his pension from being a university carpenter. But if you take enough people inside, it is easy to feel rich. And despite her low income and her simplicity, her life was full of adventures. Over the years, despite her working-class upbringing and income, Wellcome had made three trips to Europe.

If that were not riches enough, Wellcome had two sons. But as she explained to us she was also close to one former and two current daughters-in-law. And she had three grandchildren, two of whom were now married to spouses to whom she also felt close. By the same alchemy that made her feel rich from a Social Security check, her adaptive math added up to telling us that she had TEN children of her own. With such adaptive accounting practices, of course she felt rich!

Asked whom she would feel the freest to inconvenience — a question that often baffled the Harvard men — Wellcome explained that she had neighbors on three sides of her with whom she was close. One man came over to fix her mantelpiece clock, and another friend put on a magic show so that she could entertain the neighborhood children. Susan Wellcome had also kept friends from the Akron Mother's Club that she had helped to found during her sons' preschool years in Akron. The club had continued to meet every month for forty years. Asked how she replaced such old friends when they died, Wellcome explained she had made a lot of younger friends in her churchwomen's group. She again pointed to the photographs on the mantelpiece of her young clergy "brothers." Put more crassly, as her elderly lady friends died, she replaced them with charismatic middle-aged men and teenage pool sharks!

Wellcome's life revealed that mature septuagenarians could still play. With mature defenses the inner conflicts of adults are played out in the real world, but such play transforms the world in ways that can be inspirational.

* * *

However, maturation is not an inevitable consequence of aging. After all, drought can blight ripening wheat; a bad cork can destroy the future of a fine Bordeaux; and shin splints can transform a future Derby winner into a worthless nag. A certain amount of good luck is involved in growing old without accident, disease, or social catastrophe.

What happens when adults' defenses fail to mature? What happens to people who ignore all of Erikson's life tasks? Human maturation, after all, depends upon brain development that continues unencumbered into middle age. Any organic insult to the brain can destroy or reverse the normal maturational process and leave the individual an insecure youth forever. In our study the most common such insults were alcoholism and major depressive disorder.

In Bill Loman's case it was alcoholism. Bill Loman was not a happy man, but he concealed it under the stiff upper lip of upper-class formality. Thus, at 57 he chose to be interviewed in his law office, not his home. On the surface he struck me as younger than his 57 years. He was handsome and his good looks were made even more so by his easy smile. There was little left of his former boarding school accent, however, for most of the time he talked like the tough, well-educated New York City trial lawyer that he was. At his best, he looked like a tanned, fat-cat politician with exquisite grooming; and despite his tight lips, the interview was pervaded by his sense of humor.

His unflappable exterior, however, did not reflect mature defenses; it was a social mask. Underneath, Bill Loman was insecure and unable to make eye contact. He struck me as incapable of letting other people into his life. Instead of enjoying the interview, he acted like an unhappy adolescent being grilled. "I don't think I'd have joined the Study if I knew it was going to last so long," he grumbled. Throughout our interview he fiddled with a bayonet letter opener. He sharpened it and gestured with it, as topics became painful. But his feelings were rarely verbalized. Throughout the interview there was a pervasive sadness and wistfulness. Despite an income twenty times higher than Wellcome's, he took no vacations, involved himself in no civic activities, and had no exciting relationships with the opposite sex. There was no one in whom he had ever confided. Like his namesake, Arthur Miller's famous salesman Willy, despite a rich network of acquaintances, Bill Loman after almost sixty years had "nothing in the ground." For he had let nobody in.

But Bill Loman's life had not always been that way. True, his father had committed suicide when his business failed in 1929. But Loman had grown up with a mother who was proud of him, who loved young people, and who saw her son as getting on well with other children. His brother, also in the Study, became generative and successful.

In addition, Loman grew up in a "true Virginia manor house, with its white columns, its boxwood, its gardens and the broad rolling plains, which sloped away to the distant Blue Ridge Mountains." His family also maintained a twenty-room house in New York City, with sixteen servants and eight cars. Loman was close to his brother and spoke warmly of his mother. At St. Mark's boarding school Bill Loman had been a senior prefect and captain of the football team. At Harvard he was elected to the most prestigious college club and graduated magna cum laude. College descriptions of Loman included "unspoiled by his wealth," "well-poised and very attractive," "rather mature."

In World War II Loman's record was also exemplary. He won three battle stars for active participation in the Battle of the Bulge and the crossing of the Ruhr and the Rhine Rivers. His commanding officer described him as "intensely loyal, collected and cool under most trying conditions . . . sense of humor never deserts him." He was promoted to first lieutenant and then captain. In summing up the 25-year-old Loman's record the Study director remarked, "It might very well be that this boy could go quite far." After the war Loman returned to Harvard Law School and finished in the top tenth of his class. He went to New York to practice corporation law. There he was elected to the very best clubs and spent his weekends playing golf and bridge with other members.

But there was another thread running through Bill Loman's life that first made itself manifest in college. This clubbable man spent his weekends drinking. In college he had experienced three- and four-day episodes of "depression" — probably alcohol related — and saw the world as a "very sorry place." The college psychiatrist saw Loman as "undependable, careless, self-centered, and evasive." Since Loman's sense of duty was very great, these derogatory comments probably reflected the psychiatrist's reaction to Loman's heavy use of alcohol. In the military, too, Loman recalled, "I spent most of my spare time drinking and chasing women." Indeed, perhaps the greatest responsibility Loman was to have in his entire life was, at age 24, in the months after V.E. Day, being officer-in-charge of all the liquor supplies for American troops in Europe!

After the war, during law school, because he already recognized that he could not have even one drink without going on a binge, Loman dared to drink only on weekends. By age 30 he had established a pattern of drinking heavily from lunch on Friday through Sunday evening. He was abstinent during the week, but he took frequent sick days, especially on Monday, to recover from hangovers. Loman worked in a series of New York law firms where he was a modestly successful but unhappy litigator. Until she died when he was 60, Loman lived — at least on weekends — with his mother. Intimacy, Career Consolidation, and Generativity were not to be his. He worked largely for his personal clients, to whom he felt responsible and whom he met through his extended family or through the elegant clubs to which he belonged. During his entire legal career he was discontented and undercommitted, and believed he was undercompensated. Unlike most lawyers in the Study he worked only a forty-hour week and daydreamed of retiring at 55. Several Study lawyers were still working happily at 75.

Loman took part in no civic activities, was not close to his nieces or nephews, and gave little to charity. During the same period his intellectually less gifted but more abstemious brother was a smashing success in his law career. His brother built a successful family and was active in civic participation.

From 20 to 30, Bill Loman acknowledged he had had "casual sexual relations with several women, but became emotionally involved with only one or two." At 30 he proposed to one of these women. Although she turned him down, they remained closely involved for the next quarter-century. However, they neither lived together nor depended on each other.

From 20 to 30 Loman's defenses had been relatively mature. From age 50 until his death Loman's defenses were largely projection and passive aggression — the same immature defenses that with time Wellcome had replaced. For example, at his age-56 interview Loman acknowledged, "I live partially with my mother . . . an extraordinary woman." However, Loman claimed that the reason his girlfriend would not marry him was that she lived with *her* dominating mother. Such externalization of blame was scored as projection. When pressed Loman admitted that his girlfriend's reluctance to marry him might have been due to his binge drinking.

Asked how he had fought with his girlfriend, at first Loman denied conflict; and, then, as he sharpened his bayonet letter opener on his trousers, he grunted, "I just wouldn't come around to see her for a couple of weeks." When he was 53 his girlfriend's "dominating" mother died, and she married someone else. Indeed, it was not until five years later in response to the question "What heavy blows have hit you the hardest?" that Loman finally acknowledged to the Study that it was "the marriage of a girl with whom I had had a close relationship for twenty-five years." Up to then he had kept his relationship secret from the Study. Asked to whom he turned to in unhappiness, Loman always replied, "I turned to me." Other Study members used the Study as a willing witness to their difficulties. Altruistic Susan Wellcome was always willing to call on her neighbors for help.

All his adult life observers were astonished by the narrowness of William Loman's focus. For example, his greatest personal satisfaction, he explained, "was mastering an extraordinarily difficult legal question." As an example he told of his success in litigating a family trust in order to make his already rich relatives still richer. But it was not a basic lack of social skills that hampered Bill Loman's community involvement and kept his social radius small. Rather, in developmental terms, Bill Loman had never really left his mother's home. More or less continually tipsy, he lived within the protective matrix of his mother's country house and his exclusive social clubs. He never lived intimately with another person.

Despite an income that had gradually grown to $350,000 a year, Loman gave only 1 percent to charity — to his already rich boarding school. He took no vacations and never developed any new hobbies or intellectual interests. His brother sadly revealed to the Study when Loman was 50 that he had developed no new friends. At age 65 when asked, "What is your most satisfying activity?" Loman answered, "None." Although he was the titular head of his small law firm, by the time he was 67 the firm had shrunk to a single lawyer, himself. He was the opposite of Generative. Finally, as he grew older he did nothing to preserve his cultural heritage. Unlike many unhappy Study men and women who if socially isolated could rely on strong religious affiliations, Loman went to church once a year — on Christmas with his mother. Alcohol abuse interferes with finding spiritual solace.

After our interview in 1982 Loman's alcoholism continued to progress, but for decades he had kept it a secret from his physicians. What allowed him to "control" his drinking was "a sense of duty drilled into me by my family and St. Mark's. . . . You can't just let everything go. . . ." Besides, his alcoholism did not affect his liver, only his life. When he was 30 both he and his girlfriend were already worrying about his alcohol abuse. When he was 40 the police (three D.U.I.'s, with damage to others) and his mother and brother were worried. By age 50 he had needed detoxification. At age 60 he was regularly having fifty drinks a week. He would go on binges when he would drink a quart of whiskey a day for five days, only to be rescued by the fact he became too ill to drink more. He had his first seizure caused by alcohol withdrawal at age 65. After that he had made repeated unsuccessful efforts to go on the wagon.

At his death Bill Loman was still working forty hours a week, for "I would be bored if I retired." But Loman worked until his death only because he had acquired none of the proper tools for retirement. He could not play. Despite reasonable health he no longer attended any of his clubs. He could not create. He could not give. His social network had steadily shrunk. He could not learn new things. Unlike most of his Harvard cohort he had not even begun to master the computer. His losses had never been replaced. Among his friends and relatives there was not a single person of whom he could say his relationship was "intimate, we share most of our joys and sorrows." Not surprisingly, he saw the present as the unhappiest period of his life.

Bill Loman's lack of progress and satisfaction with his life could also be seen in his Harvard class reports. The last time he told his classmates anything about himself was in his twenty-fifth reunion report. Then he emphasized his military career, a period that ten years later he was to report as the happiest time of his life. After age 30 his life was simply not worth communicating. From his thirtieth through his fiftieth class report — the years in which most Harvard men describe grandchildren, civic responsibilities, and concerns about the world — Bill Loman said nothing. By his fifty-fifth annual report he was dead. For Bill Loman aging had reflected only decline. As will be demonstrated again and again, money has relatively little to do with successful aging; and alcohol abuse has a great deal to do with unsuccessful aging.

• • •

Like the concept of adult maturation, however, articulating how we adaptively and unconsciously modulate the painful thoughts and feelings produced by difficult people and painful reality is a relatively new development. The concept of involuntary psychic adaptation was original to Sigmund Freud in 1894.[32,33] Unlike many of his ideas, Freud's schema of what he chose to call "defense mechanisms" has more than stood the test of time.

The fact, however, that Freud, as I do, called them defenses should not connote anything pathological. Rather, defenses, even maladaptive ones, are a cornerstone of a positive effort to adapt.

Defenses have more in common with the behavior of an opossum vigorously and alertly playing dead or with a grouse seeming to nurse a hurt wing in order to protect her babies. Such smoothly functioning actions are a sign of health. Such mechanisms are analogous to the involuntary grace by which an oyster, coping with an irritating grain of sand, creates a pearl. Humans, too, when confronted with irritants, engage in unconscious but often creative behavior.

Of course, involuntary coping does not always produce pearls. The elegant involuntary clotting mechanisms that we employ to stanch a nosebleed and the equally involuntary but ingenious immune system that we use to heal the flu are usually our friends. But clotting mechanisms can function maladaptively and plug a coronary artery. Or immune mechanisms can function maladaptively, attack our knee joints, and cripple us with rheumatoid arthritis. It is the same with our mental mechanisms of adaptation. The less adaptive defenses like projection can leave us worse off than before. Thus, whether we deploy adaptive or maladaptive defenses can have far-reaching consequences.

The relative adaptability of our defenses is not the product of social class; it is not a product of IQ; and it is not a product of years of education.[34] It has nothing to do with the color of our skin or our mother's schooling. Rather, the ingenuity of defenses is as democratic as our sex lives and our ability to play pool. And it has everything to do with increasing age.[35]

The concept that involuntary coping mechanisms like projection and delinquent "acting out" may mature into altruism and sublimation, however, is a very modern concept that has evolved only in the past forty years.[36–38] For such transformation becomes visible only through the vantage point of the prospective study of lifetimes. Once such studies are available, the evidence that defenses could continue to mature into late midlife seemed clear in all three cohorts of the Study of Adult Development.[39] Such maturation of defenses over the life span has been confirmed by several other investigators.[40–42] For example, in studying the members of the Baltimore Longitudinal Study of Aging, Robert McCrae and Paul Costa believed that in older individuals a consistent picture emerged. As the Baltimore Study members grew older, they became more forgiving, willing to meet adversity cheerfully, and less prone to take offense and vent frustrations on others. In other words, with maturity altruism increased and projection decreased.[43] Finally, a recent sixty-year follow-up of the same cohort that Erikson had studied in 1940 offers convincing evidence — at least for the Berkeley Institute of Human Development cohort — that men's and women's mental health actually improves as they enter their later years.[44]

Finally, the continued maturation of defenses can be demonstrated in the Harvard cohort into old age. The maturity of defenses for 67 Harvard men had been assessed by interview and by recent questionnaires at about age 50. Their adaptive styles were contrasted to the adaptive styles of the same men assessed by recent questionnaires and an interview at about age 75. Information available to the assessor at each age was kept from the other assessor. Over the intervening twenty-five-year period the mechanisms of altruism and humor had *increased* significantly. Use of suppression (a mature defense that had increased dramatically between adolescence and midlife), reaction formation (an intermediate defense epitomized by Shakespeare's line "The lady doth protest too much, methinks"), and all "immature" or maladaptive defenses as a group (for example, projection and passive aggression) had *decreased* significantly. The relative overall maturity of defenses had clearly increased for 19 of the 67 men. For another 28 men their defenses at age 50 were already so mature as to render significant increase not possible. For 17 men maturity of defenses stayed essentially the same. For only 4 of the 67 men had defensive styles become clearly less "mature" with age. One such man suffered from Alzheimer's, two suffered from alcoholism, and one man was so ill that he died shortly after his interview. It is only disease, not old age, that interferes with the maturation of our coping processes.

• • •

In sum, the lives of Adam Carson and Susan Wellcome demonstrate that aging involves processes far more vital than mere decay. At 75 Adam Carson and Susan Wellcome could carry out behaviors of which most 25-year-olds are incapable. The next four chapters will expand upon the importance of social development to aging well. Chapter 7 will underscore the importance of emotional development to healthy aging.

CHAPTER THREE

THE PAST AND
HOW MUCH IT MATTERS

Woe to the man whose heart has not learned
While young to hope, to love, to put its trust in life
                                        Joseph Conrad, *Victory*

I said — Then, dearest, since 'tis so,
Since now at length my fate I know . . .
                My whole heart rises up to bless
Your name in pride and thankfulness!
Take back the hope you gave, — I claim
                Only a memory of the same.
                        Robert Browning, *The Last Ride Together*

Once more I ask the question: to understand old age should we listen to Robert Browning's optimism or do we need a writer with a more somber view of reality? As before, the truth lies somewhere in between. Conrad is right to point out that in old age a warm childhood is our friend, and Browning is wise to remind us that it is better to have loved and lost than never to have loved at all.

In short, our childhood colors our old age in two ways. First, there are the complex ways in which a chain of events is launched in childhood that allows the child to develop trust, autonomy, and initiative. This chain of events allows a child's hope, the child's sense of self, and the child's self-efficacy to forge the relationships and social supports leading to self-care and an enriched old age. Conrad's prediction of woe to those who have not learned to trust comes true again and again. Psychiatrists tell us that unhappy childhoods lead to "orality" in adult life. But orality is only a metaphor for hungry hearts that have not learned when young to hope and love.

Second, there are the sleeper effects to which Browning refers. These are deep childhood attachments that through chance and tragedy were lost from view, but which, many decades later, memory may bring to light again. Recovery of and gratitude for these lost loves can be enormously healing.

Assessment of Childhood Environment

How did the Study assess the quality of the Study childhoods? There were several rules that we observed in order to minimize bias. First, lest hindsight influence judgment, the research associates responsible for rating each man's childhood environment were kept ignorant of the fate of the men after adolescence.

Second, each man's childhood was assessed by at least two raters. Rater reliability was excellent[1] and the validity of their ratings was supported by the ratings of a senior child psychiatrist (see Appendix D). Third, these childhood ratings depended not only upon psychiatric interviews obtained when the men were in college (or in junior high school) but also upon interviews with the parents of each Study member. Fourth, the ratings referred to in this chapter were made between 1970 and 1974. The good news was that these raters were informed by major theoretical advances in childhood development since the initiation of the Study in 1940. The bad news was that the relatively inhibited childhoods of men who grew up in the 1920s and 1930s were judged by members of the "Woodstock," post-Vietnam generation who had grown up under the more permissive mores of Benjamin Spock.

To control for this historical drift the Study employed another check. The 1970–1974 ratings made of the Harvard men's childhoods were contrasted with similar ratings made by raters in 1940. Two-thirds of the time, a rating of a "warm," "so-so," or "bleak" childhood made in 1940 agreed exactly with the rating made in 1970. In only two instances did a middle-aged rater born circa 1910, with the pre-Spock mores of the 1940s, call a childhood "warm" (top quartile) while a baby boomer rater of the 1970s called the same childhood "bleak" (bottom quartile). In only two instances did the 1940 rater call a childhood bleak and the 1970 rater call it warm.

To prevent a judge's idiosyncratic view of any single facet of childhood from carrying undue weight, five separate facets of childhood were rated in the following terms:

- Warmth and stability of home atmosphere
- How warm and encouraging (i.e., conducive to basic trust) and how conducive to autonomy, initiative, and to self-esteem was the boy's relationship with his mother?
- With his father?
- Did he have siblings? If so, did he enjoy supportive relationships with them?
- Would the rater have wished to grow up in that home environment?

Each facet of childhood was rated superior (5), average (3), or poor (1), and the scores of the five facets were combined to make a rating that ranged from 5 to 25 (see Appendix D for a more detailed description). Childhoods in the top quartile were called warm, and its members *the Cherished*. Childhoods in the bottom quartile were called bleak, and its members *the Loveless*.

•   •   •

Often happy childhoods have enduring qualities that last for generations. Such was the family of Judge Oliver Holmes, who had enjoyed one of the warmest childhoods in the Study. On the Childhood Rating Scale he received a score of 23 out of a possible 25. The important people in his life had always brought him pleasure, and the virtues of his parents endured unto the third generation. Oliver Holmes's childhood was blessed. No one in his family was known to be afflicted with nervous or mental disease. His aunts and uncles were nurses, music teachers, and YMCA directors. Holmes's parents, although prosperous, spent little money on themselves. They had no servants and modest furniture. Instead they gave their children "private schooling, expensive music lessons, private skating lessons, etc." But Mrs. Holmes never stood over the children and made them say their prayers. Rather, as she explained to the interviewer in 1940, "I felt that religion must be taught by example rather than by words. Oliver was always cooperative and reasonable and almost never had to be punished. He has a delightful sense of humor."

In grammar school, Oliver Holmes got in frequent fights with other boys. Twice he was knocked unconscious, once with a rock. But ever the optimist, having been felled by the rock, he afterward had reassured his parents, "Thank God, the other fellow got the worst of it." It is easier to be the Quaker that Holmes became as an adult if your parents accepted your assertiveness when you were a child.

What had struck the social investigator most about Judge Holmes's mother was that she was "a rather serious person with a great deal of kindness and gentleness. . . . During the interview Holmes's younger brothers were in and out of the living room, playing football on top of us, aiming BB guns at our heads, but it didn't take Oliver's mother long to have the situation well in hand. I would call her a wise person, an intelligent mother, and calm in emotional makeup."

Judge Holmes's father had worked his way through medical school to become one of the leading orthopedic surgeons in the United States. His wife described her husband to the social investigator as follows: "His fellow physicians don't see how he can be so genuinely concerned about his patients. . . . He has so much sympathy for people who are ill and in trouble." Holmes himself described his father as "generous and never encroaching on a person's individuality." The Study psychiatrist was impressed with Oliver Holmes's "very clear and vivid description of his family."

The Holmeses were always a close-knit family. At 50 Holmes wrote, "My parents gave me wonderful opportunities," and in response to the Study question "When were you best friends with your parents?" Holmes replied, "Never better than now." After Holmes completed law school his father bought him a house in Cambridge. His parents lived fifteen blocks away, and his wife's parents lived even nearer; for just as Holmes greatly admired his father, his wife had admired her father.

At age 65 Judge Holmes described his brother's family as "So nice that one would have to be a stone not to enjoy it"; and at 77 he wrote, "I'm proud of my children; each of whom is a superb person." Asked what he would most like to give to his children, Holmes replied, "I'd be delighted if I could give my children as much as they give me." (At a dinner in honor of Holmes's father, I got to meet the third Holmes generation, now grown with children of their own. They were wonderful too!)

The Holmeses had recently sold their large house and now lived in an ungated retirement complex with absolutely beautiful grounds. The living room was enhanced by a dramatic twenty-five-foot cathedral ceiling whose soaring chalk-white walls were covered with maybe twenty of Mrs. Holmes's very good watercolors. The room was also filled with photographs of the children and grandchildren, a working fireplace, and an upright piano in active use.

Judge Holmes himself was now a tall, slightly balding man. In appearance, he first reminded me of a distinguished but uptight professor of neurology I once knew, but the longer he talked, as the depth and complexity of his humanity came through, the more his appearance reminded me of Solzhenitsyn. Many years before, continued contact with Holmes had wrought a similar transformation in the mind of his Vienna-born interviewer. She had often taken a rather dim view of New England WASPs, but Judge Holmes was different. In 1980 she had summed up the 60-year-old Holmes: "He seems to care for others and has a marvelous ability to see the goodness in others without ever losing sight of reality. He was thoughtful; he laughed at times; his eyes filled up with tears; he displayed a whole range of emotions — all of them appropriate. Because his personality is so vibrant and he is so full of good feelings, he became better looking as my time with him passed."

Holmes continually focused on the positive side of people, not as someone who saw the world through rose-colored glasses, but in the way that a loving parent sees a child. Both Judge and Mrs. Holmes, who took such pleasure from their children, were also able to make me, the interviewer, feel very comfortable. Although the interview lasted three hours, they never betrayed impatience. They often laughed; and when they did so, it was with a laughter that came from the belly and was in no way nervous or social.

I began our interview by asking if the purchase of their old house, which Holmes's father had bought for him after law school, had seemed like pressure to keep him in Cambridge. Holmes assured me that he and his wife had carefully considered Philadelphia, New York, and Washington, but they had both really wanted to live in Cambridge. Rather, of his father's gift, Holmes exclaimed, "It was a nifty thing." His wife, Cecily, asked, "Can I chime in? If not, I can be quiet or I can find something else to do." I told her it was fine if she helped with the interview. So Cecily chimed in, "We wanted our children to go to Shady Hill [a Cambridge private school], and it was a great house for raising a family."

To achieve such familial geographic unity in late-twentieth-century America was not easy; but having parents who were "generous and never encroaching on a person's individuality" probably helped, and having a mother who understood that boys will be boys — even when the social investigator from Harvard College came to call — must have helped too.

Many people equate mental health with being dull, stodgy, and boring; but another of Judge Holmes's gifts was his ability to achieve stability and preservation of sameness without a hint of stodginess. On the one hand, Oliver Holmes had belonged to the Harvard judo club and to his house debating team; on the other hand, he had also belonged to the pacifist society. Later, his vacation travel, too, like his remaining close to his parents, conveyed stability without stodginess. Borneo and Morocco were not for the Holmes family; instead they returned repeatedly to London, Paris, and, especially, Block Island. They had never summered anyplace but Block Island, off the Rhode Island coast, but Holmes had always derived extraordinary pleasure from each destination. The Holmeses had played bridge with the same three couples for forty-five years, but I imagine that around the bridge table there was more affection and good conversation than banal chit-chat to stave off boredom.

Put differently, Holmes was a study in contrasts. In college he had been characterized as "well-integrated" and "pragmatic" — the hallmarks of future conservatives; and yet he was one of the very few "soundest" men to be also categorized as "cultural," "verbally fluent," "sensitive," and "ideational" — the hallmarks of future liberals. Although Holmes remained a lifelong Democrat, his grandchildren attended the same private school that he and his children had attended. "I used to admire great statesmen — Wilson, FDR, Stevenson," he explained to the Study, "but I've come to admire Mozart and Bach more. For I have become skeptical of political change and have gained respect for the vision and craftsmanship of the great artists."

Oliver and Cecily Holmes had met in the third grade. At first, to Holmes, she was "an attractive and mysterious creature," to whom he did not pay much attention until the eleventh grade. Then, "I was in love. There it was." The future Mrs. Holmes had at first been more skeptical. Although in high school Holmes was class president, Cecily had always seen him as shy. Besides, she explained to me, "I was having a good time. . . . Maybe in my subconscious I had been attached to Ollie, but I didn't fall in love with him until junior year in college." Cecily Holmes admitted, however, that "Ollie Holmes" was the man to whom she always compared all of her other beaux. They married just before Holmes left for military training; and as best the Study can tell after fifty years of prospective study, they lived happily ever after. Long, happy marriages have a lot in common with successful aging. They are hard work. Both require a healthy dose of tolerance, commitment, maturity, and a sense of humor.

After nine years of marriage, when asked to give a sketch of the person he most admired, Oliver Holmes had nominated Cecily. He described her as "pretty and moderately aware of it, very artistic . . . sweet-tempered and patient . . . not especially rational, approaches matters intuitively with a nice combination of sensitivity and common sense — possessed of a devoted husband." At 62 he described his wife as "darling with the children . . . she has been a great support to me. I hope that everyone can have a marriage as good as mine." Then, his eyes welled up with tears.

At 65 Judge Holmes saw his feelings of love for his wife as "much deeper than at the beginning" and categorized his marriage as "extraordinarily happy." At age 77 he confided, "As life gets shorter, I love Cecily even more." Indeed, during our interview Judge Holmes expressed more tenderness toward his wife than any Harvard Study husband that I can remember. And it all started in third grade. Stodgy? I think I would choose another term.

I asked Holmes if his wife had helped him in his political campaigns for election to the judiciary and he blurted out, "Oh, George, she was a brick! She was marvelous." As a duet they then told me funny stories from the campaign trail from which I got a sense of their mutual pleasure in working together. What was it like, I asked Judge Holmes, being home for lunch; and Cecily burst out laughing. She made it clear that she understood my reference to "I married him for richer or poorer, but not for lunch." Holmes's response was, "I look forward to weekends. . . . I just love my three days with Cecily." Together they would go on little adventures. "We had just a lovely day together two weeks ago"; they had driven up to Vermont to look for covered bridges. Cecily interjected, "Or we will go to the movies."

I asked how they depended on each other. Holmes said, "I depend on Cecily for her love, confidence, and judgment. . . . I depend on her for pleasure. I have more fun with her than with anyone else. I depend on her for comfort when the future is uncertain." Cecily added that she depended on Ollie for his "devotion and leveling me out. . . . He was such a devoted father. . . . We have fun together. We are simpatico." And all this happiness began when they both grew up in happy families.

When I asked how they collaborated, they told me about their Block Island garden. "We plan for it. We buy for it. We garden in it." Together, they had painted all the rooms in their summerhouse. Later, I asked, if with his move to a retirement apartment, he missed his Cambridge garden. He responded with, "George, you do put your finger on it!" Actually, at the retirement home they had been allotted an attractive plot of land in which to garden, but their main gardening efforts were in June and September on Block Island. Holmes explained they did not go to Block Island in July and August because in summer they gave their house to their children. They tried not to overlap in summer because, like their own parents, in winter they lived only about a mile apart from their children in Cambridge. I asked if the children helped with the garden. "We don't want the kids to take care of the garden," was Holmes's immediate reply. "They have other things to do." Good boundaries make close families.

I asked them how they fought. They both laughed. They were clearly delighted with my question, and their enjoyment was contagious. I thought of Holmes's mother laughing at her sons playing football in the living room. Judge Holmes volunteered, "I go into a complete sulk. I can tell when Cecily is provoked. I find it hard to deal with. I can't bear to be confrontational. I don't want to join the issue . . . but we have to resolve it . . . and so we finally talk it through." His wife said, "Ollie will say something funny . . . and break the ice." One time she had poured coffee on him by mistake, and Judge Holmes accused her of doing it on purpose. "He was so angry!" Cecily exclaimed with delight. By this time Holmes was chuckling. Another time, Cecily said, "I threw a sieve at him!" Holmes replied, "I caught it"; Cecily's conciliatory response had been "Pretty good catch." Clearly, the Holmeses knew how to fight; a sieve, after all, is a much gentler missile than a frying pan — and easier to catch. At the end of the interview Cecily showed me two pictures in matched silver frames, their engagement picture and a picture of them at their fiftieth wedding anniversary. They looked happy in both.

To grow old successfully you must learn from the next generation. Thus, I asked Holmes what he had learned from his children and he responded as if I had posed the simplest question in the world. "Different things from different children. From Judy I learned how resilient, warm, and what an outgoing a person she is. . . . If you let yourself be vulnerable, things will work out. . . . I've learned about love from Judy.

"From Janet I've learned how self-discipline and artistic interests can be combined together. I don't usually think of those as going together. . . . Mark is a saintly young man. Mark is working in an inner city ministry. . . . Saintly is a strong word, but I know of no one who is *more* committed to helping helpless people. . . . His generosity of spirit is awesome. I learned dedicated idealism from Mark."

Then, good lawyer that he was, Judge Holmes summarized what he had learned: "Resiliency from Judy, creativity from Janet, and unselfishness from Mark." He then added the caveat, "By saying that I have learned from them, I don't mean that I can match them." I could understand why his children were all glad to live nearby. Having been a well-loved child, Judge Holmes never forgot that biology flows downhill.

Judge Holmes was conscious of using his emotions to make up his mind; and he understood the difference between his intellectual decisions and his emotional decisions. Seventeen years earlier his interviewer had written, "When Holmes was having trouble in making an intellectual decision, he was usually swayed by his emotional decision." Real wisdom requires that care and justice walk hand in hand. In a wise man Judge Holmes said he would look for "detachment combined with passion."

At 78 Holmes still worked forty hours a week. He did not go into the office on Mondays, but he often worked at home on legal briefs. The other four days he worked from 8:00 A.M. to 6:00 P.M. Fridays he would sometimes leave early, at 5:00 P.M. He did take off all of June and all of September to garden on his beloved Block Island, and this May he and Cecily were going to France. In his private law firm, due to his experience as a judge who had specialized in appellate cases, he was basically a lawyer for lawyers — "A great treat." His model for growing older was his father, who had worked until age 85, but he acknowledged that at 80 he might retire entirely. Unlike most Harvard Study men, Holmes listed six "intimate" friends with whom he shared "joys and sorrows."

Judge Holmes's health was spectacular. He engaged in calisthenics five times a week, and he was able to do everything that he wanted to do physically. Then he added, "There are some things that I no longer want to do. . . . Tennis and squash bore me." At age 78, he took no medicines; and he had not spent a night in the hospital for at least thirty years. Once a year he saw the doctor for his prostate. "He admires its size." (Since during the interview Judge Holmes had had to get up three times to urinate, the way he put his only medical problem was characteristic of his humor — or what his college interviewers had called his "whimsy.")

Because Holmes had never admitted physical symptoms under stress, I asked him what he did when he got a cold. Instead of the usual cheerful spin that Holmes had put on my other questions, after a moment's hesitation, he waxed eloquent. "I think I'm going to die. . . . Cecily eventually tells me that I'm going to live." Cecily burst out laughing. "She tells me to read something and take advantage of the free time . . . but I'm sure that the firm will fail in my absence." And so he would hungrily consume books, fruit juice, and vitamin C. "And sleep," Cecily chimed in. "He's a very good sleeper."

Were his dramatic colds psychosomatic? I asked. Holmes answered frankly, "They come along when I push too hard." Like his comfort with tears and anger, this happy and well-beloved son, this responsible and venerated judge, had no problem acknowledging that being childlike (not childish) could be healing. In short, although his health was wonderful, his capacity to feel monumentally sorry for himself over colds was as inspired as was his capacity for spending long vacations on Block Island and in Europe. He might still be working at 78, but he also remembered how to play.

What was Judge Holmes's prescription for successful aging?: "Share Socrates' love of the search, while knowing no answer will be found. Exercise the little gray cells (Hercule Poirot), work and love (Freud). Show respect for and try to care for the planet. . . . Don't dwell on the past except when blue and then only to remind oneself that those problems that seemed insurmountable often weren't. Try not to worry about the future. It's not over, 'til it's over."

In some ways Holmes's life seems too good to be true. Arguably, his life was the most successful in the Study.

Links Between Childhood and Old Age

Only recently have studies of normal development survived the three or more decades needed in order to follow well-studied children into maturity, let alone into old age. Such prospective study has demolished many cherished assumptions. For, in retrospect, adult outcomes can always be explained. In psychological biography hindsight permits all the pieces to fall obediently into place. By choosing illustrative single case histories, I can prove any point I wish. As explanation I can use the crazy aunt, the rejecting mother, the clubfoot, or the bad neighborhood. In actual fact, however, although we all "know" that childhood affects the well-being of adults, recent scientific reviews reveal that such explanations are rather less important than we thought.[2, 3] For every Oliver Holmes who confirms such explanations, there is an Anthony Pirelli who confounds them.

For example, when the childhoods of the best and worst aging outcomes in the Harvard Study were compared, there were few differences. When identified in advance, rather than in retrospect, fingernail biting, early toilet training, even that old standby the cold, rejecting mother, failed to predict either emotional illness or bad aging. Remember Susan Wellcome. Birth order, childhood physical health, the distance in age between the subject and the next child, even the death of a parent, proved relatively unimportant by the time the men were 50. True, at 18 infant/childhood problems of some kind (for example, phobias and marked shyness) were recollected by the parents of virtually all the men who as adults became mentally ill. However, these same problems were also recollected by 60 percent of the parents of men who remained healthy. Orphans, by the time they were 80, were as likely to be happy and in the pink of health as those whose parents lovingly watched them graduate from high school.

In cross-sectional studies, one of the most powerful correlates of successful aging is income, but among the three Study samples emotional riches seemed far more important. In addition, aided as the men were by white skin and the GI bill, financial success seemed much more a reflection of mental health than a consequence of social class or parental privilege.

Even among the Inner City men the story was the same. Good mental health, good coping both as children and adults, warm friendships, admired fathers, and loving mothers predicted high income. In contrast, dysfunctional families and fathers on Welfare did not predict future income. Perhaps the best summary statement is, *What goes right in childhood predicts the future far better than what goes wrong.*[4]

Again, there is a common assumption that alcoholism results from an unhappy childhood. Such an assumption is based upon retrospective evidence. After the fact, both alcoholics and their clinicians blame bleak childhoods. But the prospective evidence suggested that memory reverses the cart and the horse. The men who became alcoholics had childhoods that did not differ from those of social drinkers, but the childhoods of alcoholics were sometimes altered after the fact to fit the theory. However, the childhoods of men whose parents were alcoholic were decidedly unhappy.

Expressed differently, *unhappy* childhoods become less important with time. When the lives of the men whose childhoods were most bleak — the Loveless — were contrasted with men whose childhoods were the most sunny — the Cherished — the influence on college adjustment was very important. By early midlife, childhood was still significantly important, but by old age the warmth of childhood was statistically unimportant. A warm childhood, like a rich father, tended to inoculate the men against future pain, but a bleak childhood — such as with a poverty-stricken father — did not condemn either the Harvard or the Inner City men to misery.

When the Harvard men were middle-aged, the evidence suggested that childhood environment genuinely affected the men's physical health.[5] For at age 53, more than a third of the 23 men with bleak childhoods, the Loveless, already suffered from chronic illnesses like hypertension, diabetes, and heart disease; 4 had died. Among the 23 men with the warmest childhoods, the Cherished, all were living and only 2 were chronically ill.

Such positive association between childhood and physical health, however, did not persist. By age 75 there was little relationship between the quality of childhood and objective physical health. At 80, four of the 20 Loveless men from the Harvard cohort (5 would be expected by chance) were among those with the best aging outcomes. Again, for every 8 Loveless men from the Inner City cohort who aged badly, 5 aged very well. In short, Joseph Conrad was not always right.

·　　·　　·

Four findings, however, did confirm Joseph Conrad's bitter prophecy. First, the Loveless were more likely to be labeled mentally ill. Second, they found it difficult to play. Third, they trusted neither their emotions nor the universe. Fourth, the Loveless often were relatively friendless for all of their lives.

The first of these findings, that bleak childhood environment predicts mental illness in adult life, can surprise no one. A warm childhood protected against mental illness, and this in turn protected against being among the Prematurely Dead or the Chronically Ill. Of the 56 Harvard men with Cherished childhoods, only 4 were ever depressed; only 4 felt both sick and unhappy by the time they were 80; and only 6 (a third as many as would have been expected by chance) were among the Prematurely Dead. The Harvard men classified as Loveless were three times more likely and the Inner City Loveless were 2 times more likely to die from unnatural deaths (i.e., from accidents, suicide, cirrhosis, lung cancer, and smoking-related emphysema) as were the Cherished. The Loveless, believing that they belonged to no one, failed to remember the old song's advice to "Button up your overcoat/When the wind is free."

By age 50, 80 of the Harvard men had met Study criteria for mental illness (significant depression or alcohol or drug abuse). Forty or fully half of these mentally ill men were dead by age 75. In contrast, 111 men had been unusually free of psychological distress. Of these men, only 12 — just one man in six — had died by 75. The Terman women were not included in these comparisons because the Study lacked objective information on their physical and mental health.

. . .

Second, men with unhappy childhoods found it difficult to play at 45 and at 65. Compared to the Loveless, the Cherished were five times more likely to play competitive sports. They were also five times more likely to play games with friends and, like Oliver Holmes, to take full and enjoyable vacations.

. . .

Third, the quality that seemed most clearly to link a warm childhood with a sunny old age was a sense of comfort and acceptance of one's emotional life. The mistrust and the dependency instilled into the Harvard men with bleak childhoods plagued them all of their lives. In adult life they maintained the greatest mistrust of the Study. Although in reality the Study of Adult Development did little to assist its members, the Cherished, like Oliver Holmes, consistently viewed the Study as helpful.

At midlife the men were asked a number of true/false questions.[6] Many of the questions distinguished men who thirty years later in old age would be classified as the Happy-Well from those who would be classified as the Sad-Sick. Many questions also distinguished men who thirty years previously had been classified Loveless from those who had been classified Cherished. There were eight true/false questions at age 50 that were highly correlated with both past and future; these questions linked childhood with old age. "True" answers to all eight of these questions reflected discomfort with emotions and were indicative of loveless pasts and the unhappy futures that led to feeling physically and mentally "sick" in old age. "True" answers to the following four true/false questions suggested that the men at age 50 might be too defended against their emotions:

- Others have felt that I have been afraid of sex.
- Marriage without sex would suit me.
- I have had a difficult sexual adjustment.
- Sometimes I feel numb when I should be feeling a strong emotion.

"True" answers to the other four questions suggested that the men might experience their own needs and emotions as too overwhelming.

- I have sometimes thought that the depth of my feelings might become destructive.
- I sometimes fear that I will wear people out.
- People usually let you down.
- Sometimes I feel I am a considerable strain on people.

The Harvard men who 30 years previously had been deemed Loveless were *three times* as likely to answer "true" to these eight questions as were men deemed to be Cherished. The Harvard men who thirty years later would be classified as aging the worst were *three times* as likely to answer "true" to these eight questions as men classified as aging best (see Appendix E).

How does a family give a child permission to experience emotion? Perhaps the fact that Mrs. Holmes allowed her two younger sons to act up in the living room was a coincidence. I don't think so. The mastery of aggression is as delicate an ego-balancing act as is the mastery of sexual intimacy. It affects future major life tasks of adulthood: Intimacy, Career Consolidation, and Generativity.[7] Nor is the mastery of aggression a developmental challenge that is confined to women. The Inner City men who failed to achieve Career Consolidation at 50 and those who comprised the Sad-Sick at 70 were three to four times more likely to have reported when interviewed at age 47 that they handled anger either through explosive outbursts or by burying it deep within themselves. In contrast, three-quarters of the Inner City men with stable work commitments and three-quarters of the men who at 70 were among the Happy-Well reported at age 47 graceful and attenuated ways of expressing anger. Harvard men who never achieved successful or gratifying careers also revealed a lifelong inability to deal with anger. It makes all the difference in the world if when you are young your parents tolerate and "hold" your sadness, your love — and your anger — or if instead they treat your emotions as misbehavior.

•   •   •

The fourth and cruelest association of bleak childhoods was its correlation with friendlessness at the end of life. The Cherished were three times as likely at age 70 to enjoy wide social supports. The Cherished not only had warm relationships with both parents when young but were likely to appear charming, extroverted, and energetic thirty years later and to be rich in friendships 60 years later. In contrast, one man's parental home was so inhospitable that even the charming social investigator remarked that upon visiting the house that she had felt decidedly unwelcome.

At 47, the same Harvard man who had spent the first twenty years of his life in that loveless environment confessed, "I don't know what the word *friend* means."

Does Depression Cause Physical Illness: Fact or Fancy?

There is something romantic in all of us that wants the soul to control the body, just as there is something romantic about the operatic heroine dying of a broken heart. It is exciting to believe that the brain affects the immune system and that, to play on words, if we are made to feel in-valid when young, we may become invalids grown old. It is heartwarming to believe that we can mobilize our own bodies to fight tumors and that if we think only positive thoughts, we may live in joy until 100. When I tell you that of the sixty-two best outcomes among the Harvard cohort only one man ever endured a serious depression before 50 and that, proportionately, fifteen times as many of the sickest, most unhappy octogenarians had experienced a serious depression before 50, your ears may prick up. Then, when I remind you that only 4 of the Cherished but 11 of the Loveless developed major depression in adult life, you may not be surprised. For is not that what Joseph Conrad predicted?

When romantic bias is involved, however, unusually careful scientific caution must be exercised. For, as with other examples of mind over matter, there are many alternative explanations. Thus, before considering what allowed the Cherished children to age as well as Oliver Holmes, and what led the Loveless to age poorly, remember the difference between association and cause.

In trying to understand what links depression to late-life poor physical health there are a number of suspects: depression per se, alcohol abuse, smoking, poor self-care, chronic illness, and unhappy childhood. Which of these possible contenders are real culprits, and which are merely innocent bystanders or themselves a victim of risk? A sixty-year prospective study helps to answer these questions.

First, in studying adults who lost their mothers when young, investigators have found that orphanhood per se had remarkably little long-term effect.[8] Statistical exceptions come only when the same hereditary illness that killed the mother also afflicts her child. In other words, when orphanhood affects old age the causal culprits are genes more often than deprivation.

Second, it is quite true that depression is *associated* with cancer. However, the more careful the study, the weaker the evidence becomes that depression is a primary cause of cancer.[9] The cancers most associated with depression are cancers of the lung and gastrointestinal tract — in short, the sites most affected by alcohol and cigarette abuse, both of which are common among the depressed.

Third, if physically ill individuals also suffer from depression, the likelihood increases that they will bring their physical illness to medical attention, thereby inflating the apparent association between depression and disease. Conversely, good mental health often makes it possible for the physically ill to cope without obvious distress, incapacity, or recourse to physicians. If you do not visit your doctor when you are happy, how is he or she to know that happy people become physically ill too? Finally, it is depressing to be physically ill; and physical illnesses like certain cancers and strokes on the left side of the brain cause depression for purely biological reasons.

In raising alternative possibilities I am not suggesting that the mind does not affect the body. There are excellent studies demonstrating causal links between depression and some physical illnesses. I only wish to instill reasonable doubt that it is depression, per se, that is the cause of poor health in old age. Rather it is the heavy smoking and the poor self-care that accompanies depression that are the major culprits.

Rewriting History

Sometimes old age is made bearable by forgetting the bad stuff. We all spend our lives reconstructing our biographies to make our present more harmonious. For example, from Plato's day until the present the old have maintained that as teenagers they were more respectful of their parents than their own adolescent children are to them. Sometimes, then, the past does not matter, because it is fiction.

At age 78 we asked each of 40 Terman women whom we interviewed, "Do you believe society has given you a fair chance to achieve your potential?" At the end of their lives 39 of the women accepted full responsibility for their often stunted careers. For example, one Terman woman replied tentatively, "I think so. I have had every opportunity. I must be lazy." Yet, as a child her outstanding trait had been "perseverance."

A second woman felt she had lived up to her full potential, which was "much smaller than this study would show." In fact she had an IQ of 154, had made straight A's at Berkeley, and had been elected to Phi Beta Kappa. Among her many gifts was the ability to memorize anything by reading it through once. Interested in art history, she had graduated with honors but, instead of pursuing her own career, she had worked as a medical secretary to put her first husband through medical school. Next, she worked for ten years as a Stanford departmental secretary, for which she was rewarded with a $50 per month pension. I felt sure that no male janitor at Stanford had been treated as shabbily. But the outrage remained mine, not hers. At age 40 such selective amnesia on her part might have seemed like denial, but at 78 such refusal to assign blame protected her from resentments and the poor-me's. Complaining at 78 would not have made the world any less sexist. Life, today, is always easier if you accept yesterday. But the fact remained that society had treated the Terman women badly.

•   •   •

When reinterviewed at age 67, one Inner City man was asked about how his parents had supervised him. He earnestly replied, "Oh, they really made [us] . . . go to school and back in that era, you know in elementary school, you would go home for lunch.

My mom would have a hot meal waiting for me. And I would spend an hour or so with her, then I would go back to school. No foolish stupid buses or these cold, dumb lunches that they give you today. My mommy took care of these things. Didn't let the State worry about it. Maybe that's probably one of the reasons I have a lot of resentments toward liberals; I don't want to get into no political thing with you, but I don't like liberals. The left liberals especially." The interviewer asked, "Was your family poor?" "Ah, no," came the answer. "I would say we were probably lower middle class back then."

The original record revealed that when this man was one year old the Society for Prevention of Cruelty to Children (SPCC) had been called in. They noted that the subject had rickets (a disease of malnutrition) and "the house was dirty and in disorder." When he was 7 his mother was on Welfare with multiple drunken arrests; when he was 10 the SPCC was again called in to find "no lunch provided by mother" and the "house in chaotic condition." When he was 16 the interviewer noted that his parents "harped on how little aid they were getting from Welfare." Selective amnesia at 67 allowed him to feel in control. He needed no help from liberals, now; he had never needed help from liberals.

Recovery of Lost Loves

There is a distinction between privation and deprivation. Privation means never having loved or been loved. This leads to psychopathology. Deprivation means losing those whom we have loved; such deprivation leads to distress, not illness. To lose someone whom we can remember having loved and been loved by produces tears, not patienthood. As Tolstoy wrote, "Only people who are capable of loving strongly can also suffer great sorrow; but this same necessity of loving serves to counteract their grief and heals them. . . . Grief never kills."[10] Thus, when we are old, our lives become the sum of all whom we have loved. It is important not to waste anyone. One task of living out the last half of life is excavating and recovering all of those whom we loved in the first half. Thus, the recovery of lost loves becomes an important way in which the past affects the present.

Since it is far easier to talk of loss than of taking people in, psychotherapists sometimes emphasize present grief at the expense of helping clients to remember past loves. Counselors sometimes forget that the psychodynamic work of mourning is often more to remember lost loves than to say good-bye. The primate brain is constructed to retain, and not relinquish, love.

During the course of living, too, we often "discover" forgotten loves. No one whom we have ever loved is totally lost. That is the blessing, as well as the curse, of memory. Grief hurts, but does not — in the absence of conflict — make us ill. What is more, just as rivers expose buried geologic strata, so may the erosion of living uncover life-saving memories of love, formerly obscured by pain, resentment, or immaturity.

•　　•　　•

Consider the example of Martha Meade, who after age 65 became an archaeologist of her past life courtesy of psychotherapy and poetry. I arrived at her house on a rainy day late in autumn. Meade had protected herself against the San Francisco chill with a cashmere turtleneck sweater, a brown knit cardigan, a brown skirt and sensible shoes. I had told Meade that I had read her valuable book on psychotherapy with great interest. She reciprocated by saying that she had read my book *Adaptation to Life* with great interest. We had both looked forward to meeting each other. She briefly introduced her husband to me, and then, unlike the Harvard men, she sent her spouse upstairs. At 75, wives were often surprisingly dominant and independent; in contrast, husbands often welcomed their wives into the interviews for support.

Martha Meade was a small woman who laughed easily. The longer I talked to her, the less I experienced her discursive speech as tangential and the more I found myself talking to a sensitive — and highly intelligent — artist. Throughout the interview I was never bored, for I always sensed passion was just below the surface. She was by no means the psychologically healthiest woman that I met in the Study, but joy, laughter, excitement, were all present during the interview. All were harnessed and in their proper place.

Like many people who have had many hours of psychotherapy, Meade was very interested in her own associations and inner workings, but she was not self-centered. She talked about herself because as a social worker and psychotherapist the internal life interested her, but she was just as interested in her friends' achievements, in her husband's vulnerability, in what her sons and her patients had taught her, and in what my wife might be doing at that moment in Russia. In spite of the seriousness and the chronic nature of her past psychological distress, she had a wonderful capacity not to take it seriously. I asked Meade, a gifted clinician and more recently a gifted author, what was the most responsible job that she had had. In response she exclaimed, "Ha!" and then pointed out that she had caught me trying to place her in a hierarchy. "How can I answer such a ridiculous question? . . . The biggest achievement of my life has been to be free to be myself." That was what she had worked on consciously all of her life. "That is the pinnacle of the whole thing. . . . I started off as a mouse." As a child there were so many things that Meade could not do for herself; her role within her family had caused her to develop characteristics of dependence and submissiveness.

"I could not afford to alienate the adults upon whom I depended; and so I could not allow myself to say or do anything that would make people angry at me. . . . I walked a constant tightrope, effacing whatever aspects of myself might upset the careful balance I was maintaining, hardly daring to breathe at crucial moments." Within the family dynamic, Martha Meade was not supposed to be angry with anybody. She wasn't allowed to offend her mother without having to beg her forgiveness. Fortunately, she had found in her husband a committed "feminist." He was impressed with what she did, was proud of her achievements, and also balanced the checkbook. Her ability to achieve, she explained, would not have been possible without her husband, "who was handed to me on a silver platter." For women, as well as for men, spouses could sometimes heal dysfunctional childhoods.

Along the way Martha Meade received many hours of psychotherapy — psychotherapy that had helped her to condemn her mother for making her a mouse. She discovered that her phobias and panic states were brought on by a rising sense of anger. It was mastery of freer emotional expression, not Prozac, which permitted her panic states to recede. (Admittedly, it takes different strokes for different folks.)

After retirement Meade had planned to paint, but instead she found herself writing more and more poetry. She had taken a course on "family sculpture" (a form of psychodrama) and then put her own family sculpture into verse. "This was my second analysis. . . . I was galvanized." She tried to describe her family sculpture, in which her mother and father and sister "and I and a cat were on an isolated island in the Pacific." She placed the time when she was seven. "It was just there." The wonderful thing, Meade told me, was that now when she got anxious, she would write poetry. She could memorize it and recite it back to herself if she awoke upset in the night. She suggested that her poetry, not psychotherapy, had made her "symptom-free."

Martha Meade described poems occurring full-blown in her head. She had just written a poem about her mother, who had died ten years before. She began by telling me that people who knew her mother for a long time grew to hate her. Indeed, the difficulty in her family was that everyone got angry at everyone else, and what had always disturbed Meade was her own ambivalence toward her mother. At this point Meade became so moved she momentarily stopped talking. Her affect was much more like what happens to an artist in the act of creation, or a patient deep in therapy, than simple grief.

On the one hand, Martha Meade was furious that her mother

had turned her into a "mouse" by refusing to tolerate any aggression or assertiveness on her part. On the other hand, Meade was clearly very involved with her mother. She suddenly remembered back to two people whom she had asked about her mother — these two women had said her mother was a very special person. They told her that her mother had walked like a "queen," had "loving eyes," and should have become famous. Then Meade added, "My mother didn't know her own worth. [I suspect she wasn't clear whether she was talking about her mother's aborted career or her own.] Everyone loved my father. I adored my father. I had a towering transference towards my father." But Meade then associated to the memory of her friends observing that her father had held her mother back. Her oldest high school friend, Margery, had been one of the women who pointed out to Meade that her mother was special. All her high school friends who had survived remained very admiring of her mother. Meade's life narrative was changing before my eyes.

Meade then boasted to me that her mother had adored Thoreau and Emerson and read very modern books on subjects like "trial marriage." The more Meade reminisced, the more real love and admiration toward her mother came through. The woman she described sounded so different from the one who had guilt-tripped Meade in her wish for independence and had turned her into a mouse. Returning to her mother, Meade said, "We are very much alike, but I'd never admit it." After her mother's death she had been unable to have anything to do with her mother's possessions. I asked her whether this was from "grief or ambivalence." Meade retorted, "I'll have to live another hundred years to answer that."

As we talked, Martha Meade became increasingly full of energy and joy; for poetic archaeology has its own very special rewards. As she grew older, Meade explained, the quality of her life went down; but there were "a lot of compensations. . . . These are the happiest years of my life." Later, when I asked her what her dominant mood had been over the last six months, she said,

"It's obvious — I've been happy." From age 10 to age 70 there had been little evidence of such contentment in her question-naires. I suspect that finally to be able to openly acknowledge love for her mother — and herself — played a role in this trans-formation.

* * *

When he was 18, Ted Merton — who in chapter 1 had reminded me that the old were "interesting" — had told the Study: "I am sorry that my family was so terribly strict with me from the ages of 5 to 12. . . . My family sat on me, but they can't be blamed for it because they were brought up in 1890 New York. . . . Dad and I have never gotten on very well. . . . He has done nothing that I consider a father should do for his children. . . . Mother hasn't exactly made up to us for Dad's shortcomings. . . . Mother hesi-tates and evades facts; wait till Miss Gregory [the Study's family interviewer] tries to pin her down."

As predicted, Mrs. Merton described the Merton home life to Miss Gregory as "happy and united . . . the two boys are close to their parents . . . she [Mrs. Merton] feels that they have done a good job bringing up their boys." Lewise Gregory, a discerning woman, described Mrs. Merton as "one of the most nervous people I have ever met. She is a past-mistress in self-deception." A child psychiatrist reviewing Ted Merton's record thirty years later saw his childhood as among the bleakest in the Study. At age 46 Ted Merton sadly affirmed his earlier statements and wrote laconically, "I neither liked nor respected my parents. A friend of mine," he added, "when she met my parents, was just aston-ished at how limited and shallow they were." Thirty more years passed and Merton observed, "I think my parents' self-esteem de-rived from show. In their living room was a Steinway grand piano that neither parent could play."

Merton had been cared for in all the wrong ways. Throughout his childhood, a succession of chauffeurs had driven him to school, and Merton had often been kept from playing with neighborhood children. But his parents' overprotectiveness did not extend to caring for him themselves. Until Merton was 6 he ate his meals, alone, in his playroom. From age 13 on, he was conscious of an urgent need to escape this parental stranglehold. Surely, if Joseph Conrad was always right, Ted Merton at 76 should not have become my "cordial" friend, guiding me to feel more positive about old age.

The sea change began at age 33. During his hospital training Dr. Merton became infected with subclinical tuberculosis. Seven years later, following a broken engagement, he was hospitalized for fourteen months in a veterans' hospital with pulmonary tuberculosis. Uneasily, I asked how he coped with an event that for most young men would have been devastating. Referring to it as "that year in the sack," he replied, "It was neat. I could go to bed for a year, do what I wanted, and get away with it." Later, he confessed, "I was glad to be sick. My poorly met dependency needs found an acceptable harbor." For him his illness had been akin to religious rebirth. He felt there was divine intervention. "Someone with a capital 'S' cared about me," he wrote. "It made me feel that I was nutty for a while, but in the Catholic Church it's known as Grace."

Ten years after Merton's illness an intuitive child psychiatrist blind to his outcome was asked to rate his childhood. After acknowledging it as one of the bleakest in the Study, she noted an exception to the general barrenness: up to age 5 Merton had had a close relationship with his nurse. She wondered if someday that nurse would not provide a source of strength. The psychiatrist seemed to be onto something, for I believe that the healing function of "that year in the sack" had been to put him again in touch with his multiple past caregivers. In any case, like Lazarus, at 34 Ted Merton arose from his sickbed, became an independent physician, married, and grew into a responsible father and clinic leader. His enforced invalidism from age 33 to 34 catalyzed over the next five years his mastery of Intimacy, Career Consolidation, and Generativity.

Over the years Dr. Merton has tried to help me understand what took place. In reference to his cameo appearance in *Adaptation to Life* as Godfrey Minot Camille, he wrote at age 66, "Whoever it was who talked of my attachment to a nurse maid didn't then know of Pearl. She was a person in my infancy whom I rediscovered in my more Kleinian hours [i.e., his psychoanalysis] in 1981 and 1982. I have reason to believe she was a warm, caring woman. My mother spoke of her as "Pearl, the dirty girl." I found [my memory of] her by following the trail of associations to abalone and mother-of-pearl which were very affect-laden for me. Whatever her role, and that of her successors in trust, I know also that I absolutely loved my teachers. Some of them cared about me too . . . sent there [to school] to be properly educated, I learned about proper loving." Much later he wrote:

> Is it the re-finding of the love that matters? Or is it the chance to re-celebrate and to re-celebrate again and again the bond that holds? An image comes to mind — the empty wine bottle used as a candlestick. The wine may have been the initial warmth in life, but once it is gone only the cold and empty glass bottle remains — until in memory we re-light the candle of conviviality, and as it drips, it transforms the symbol of the warmth that was spent into a differently shaped, differently colored object — alive with new warmth. Early loves may be "lost" because they were taken for granted and never reinforced by review. Recollection and retelling have a way of making them increasingly visual and real. It is the visual perception that's particularly effective when it comes to learning.

Years passed and Merton continued to demonstrate his capacity to recover hope and strength from such "cold and empty glass bottles." At 65 he wrote of one such memory of his father. First, he reminded me, as if I could forget, that "empathy was not my father's strongest suit." As a boy Ted Merton had climbed a cherry tree to look at the blossoms. He lost his balance and fell twelve feet to the ground. Instead of being comforted, he was spanked for disobeying his parents; they had told him not to climb the tree. Nevertheless, a few days later his father picked the young Merton up in his arms:

> Once beneath the shimmering canopy of the cherry tree, my father pulled a small branch towards me and let me hold it in my fist while we traded glances and smiles. Before he drove off to work, he used his pocketknife to cut a sprig, which he put in a tumbler of water, placing this on the little table where I ate my meals. . . . I knew I was both understood and forgiven. . . . This was my first mystical experience.

How much, I wonder, does our spirituality and faith depend upon our recovery of lost loves? The devout reader may feel free to answer back, "No, our recovery of lost loves comes to us through the grace of God." In the grand scheme of things, I suspect, I and such readers agree.

Almost a decade later, at Dr. Merton's forty-fifth college reunion, I asked him what he had learned from his children. Merton replied, "I haven't stopped learning from them." Appreciating that his answer was too facile, he thoughtfully added, "That's a tough question. . . . Isn't that a whopper?" I was disappointed; I had felt sure that he was going to come up with a more profound response. Two days later he came up to me in Harvard Yard just before I was to give a talk to his reunion class. Tears in his eyes, Merton blurted out, "You know what I learned from my children? I learned love."

Still another decade passed and this time I came away from our interview confident that Ted Merton was aging well. At 77 he was in love; he was still playing squash; he was actively involved in community life; and he was nurturing a beautiful garden. Beside his chair were a picture of his daughter and her husband, and a picture of him and his son climbing in the Alps. In addition, he had translated his interest in genealogy into discovering a whole network of his father's cousins with whom he had formed new real relationships. In a sense, through active archaeology of his past he was still creating the family that he never had. He was still mining memories of time past to invest in time future. In both his genealogical research and in his renewed religious involvement Merton had found fresh ways to get strength from his father. As with Meade his discoveries depended in part on psychotherapy and creative writing.

CHAPTER FOUR

GENERATIVITY: A KEY TO SUCCESSFUL AGING

> My twelve children are my greatest joy. Between them they
> have given me thirty-six grandchildren and four great-grand-
> children. I have a very close relationship with them. I see them
> very often and there is always some family activity going on.
> Frederick Hope, a 67-year-old Inner City Study member

In all three of our samples the mastery of the Eriksonian task of Generativity was the best predictor of an enduring and happy marriage in old age. Surprisingly, among the Terman women, mastering Generativity, not Intimacy, was the best predictor of whether they reported attaining regular orgasm.[1] In addition, one of the more exciting Study findings was that after 70 the marriages of generative Study members got still better. For example, one 78-year-old Harvard Study member exulted to the Study, "Our marriage keeps getting better. Phyllis and I are at the age when what life we have left together is like the last few days of a great vacation. You want to get the most out of them, so we want to get the most out of our togetherness."

However, Generativity is not just about marriage. Generativity provided the underpinning of successful old age. Consider the quote from a 76-year-old Harvard man who had objectively enjoyed one of the best childhoods in the study — his father's alcoholism not withstanding. In addition, despite divorce and remarriage at 52, at 76 he enjoyed one of the best marriages and one of the sunniest outlooks on life in the entire Study. He wrote: "I have been greatly blessed. I had an incredibly happy childhood, school years, college years and career. I loved my own business, I love my five children and both wives. . . . Sure my father was an alcoholic, but I loved him and stuck with him and helped get him into AA. I'm sure I could drum up some problems but I guess I forgot them. I don't give a damn if I am remembered for anything. I've enjoyed my life and had a hell of a good time. I'm most proud of those times I've helped others."

Generativity involves taking care of the next generation. Thus, one of the basic rules of Generativity is to appreciate that biology flows downhill. Parents should look after children. To be pushed into vaudeville at 5 to look after your mother, as was Susan Wellcome, can be soul destroying. To be a generative parent enriches everyone. One of the Harvard Study men, himself the product of a caring family, wrote of the first half of his adult life, "From twenty to thirty I learned how to get along with my wife. From thirty to forty I learned how to be a success in my job, and at forty to fifty I worried less about myself and more about the children." At 78 his adaptation to aging is brilliant. In terms of his adult development, this Harvard Study man had spent the first two decades of adulthood collecting a self through mastery of the twin tasks of Intimacy and Career Consolidation. He then spent his subsequent years giving away the self that he had collected. He gave not only to his own children but also to countless other adolescents. His career developed from distinguished professor to dean of a small college. He not only looked after students but, as he matured, he also looked after the young faculty.

In contrast to their successful Terman Study brothers, many of the Terman women gave themselves too "selflessly" to their parents and their husbands at too young an age. They did not experience Wellcome's epiphany. Their own selves shrank as a result. I once made a study of men and women admitted to a medical-surgical hospital to understand the underlying psychological reasons why they came to the hospital — "at this time."[2] No women were admitted to the hospital from the exhaustion of caring for multiple young children, but several women were admitted from the exhaustion of caring for ailing parents. Biology flows downhill.

Confucius, Moses, and King Lear would all disagree. For what I am suggesting threatens patriarchal society. Must not children honor their parents and care for them in their old age? No, that was the very premise that made *King Lear* a tragedy. Health, adaptation, and the biological imperative all argue quite differently. The old are put on earth to nurture the young — not vice versa. True, we may marvel at the stability of Chinese family structure, just as we may marvel at the stability of antebellum Virginian society. Slavery and patriarchy fosters social stability — but not adult development. To sacrifice the young Chinese bride to the care and feeding of her mother-in-law stunts the growth of all involved.

If creativity puts into the world what was not there before, so selfless Generativity, too, puts into the world more than was there before. But when Generativity is attempted before its appointed hour, it may fail. We can give ourselves away only after our selves are formed. Wheat must be ripened before it can make bread. Of course, as we reach middle life we should help our parents help themselves. But we should help our parents out of gratitude and not at the cost of our own development. If we are to go down with the Titanic, let us give our places in the lifeboat to our children, not our parents.

•   •   •

In his illuminating *Outliving the Self,* John Kotre sums up the task of Generativity succinctly: "To invest one's substance in forms of life and work that will outlive the self."[3] This quote was mirrored in the life of the Inner City father of twelve, Frederick Hope, whose quote provides the epigraph for this chapter. Review of Hope's 1940 record revealed that he had remembered his childhood correctly. True, his uncles and aunts were delinquent or alcoholic or mentally retarded; but his parents were not. They had lovingly cared for him. With an IQ of only 90, Hope repeated one grade in school; nevertheless, the child psychiatrist saw him as "a very well adjusted personality with a good sense of responsibility." He had been tenderly cared for and so he could afford to be grateful to life. All his life Hope had worked as a truck driver. "I love it. Every day is a challenge." At 65 he had found his friendships, his family, his job, his hobby (golf), his community service, and his religious involvements all "highly satisfying." (To be rated in the Study as *subjectively content* Study members had to find only two of these six areas "very satisfying." See Appendix 1 for a more complete description. Hope had been very satisfied with six. At 63 when asked to rank life tasks reflecting social development in order of importance to him, Hope ranked "passing on the past — its traditions, its culture, its environment — to my grandchildren" (i.e., Keeper of the Meaning) first, and "fostering adults younger than myself, coaching the next generation" (i.e., Generativity) second. At 67 Hope's physical health was in the top fifth of all those in his Inner City cohort.

· · ·

The family life of Gwendolyn Havisham of the Terman Study had been very different from the life of Frederick Hope. When we asked her for an interview, she was initially reluctant and then blurted out with real outrage, "You don't expect me to come to Stanford!" Of course not. And so my wife and I arrived on time at her small San Francisco house. To our surprise she greeted us warmly. With a deep laugh about how difficult parking was in the city, she sat us down in her living room.

Gwendolyn Havisham was one of the best-dressed women in the Study. She wore a stylish green suit, a very good ring, and an artfully placed brooch. Her trim ankles were set off by expensive patent leather shoes. Her laughter, twinkling eyes, and general manner were charming and conveyed an aristocrat who was very much in the world. Initially, I was impressed with her cultivated diction, her aura of education, and the gaiety in her eyes. However, that was the high point of the morning. The interview was dominated by the banality of her answers, as if they came from an empty fortress. Her past history suggested that ever since World War II she had spent her life not getting close to anybody lest they upset her. At the end of two hours we realized that she had completely eluded us. She had escaped without touching us or being touched. Without letting others in, we do not grow.

Her house was reminiscent of that of her namesake, Miss Havisham, who in Charles Dickens's novel *Great Expectations* kept her house exactly the way it was when she had been abandoned on her wedding day. Gwendolyn Havisham's house, too, was very dark, beautifully furnished, with a fine Victorian piano, good Oriental rugs, old sets of books on the shelves, and good Chinese and Japanese scrolls and screens along the wall. But there was no sense that anyone else had spent much time in the house for thirty years.

Being interviewed was not Gwendolyn Havisham's cup of tea. Selfishly, she did not wish to contribute to the Terman Study. She did not wish to reveal any more of herself than she had to. Asked what she had done postretirement, she replied guardedly, "We run a thrift shop; it's like playing store." She also belonged to a musical club that put on a concert every two weeks, and she belonged to a women's club. She was like a train conductor reciting the stops. The thought that she might enjoy one activity more than another, or even that she enjoyed any of them, was impossible for her to entertain.

Asked when her family life was the happiest, Havisham replied that there was no one time and added with affectless banality, "I was fortunate to have had a very nice family." But now she was 78. Asked whom she could count on to help her, she replied, "No one." Her close friends had all died. Asked if there was anyone to replace her friends who died, she said there was nobody like the old friends. Then sadly she added, "My friends are all so busy; they are bringing up their grandchildren." Asked how she kept in touch with the younger generation, Havisham acknowledged that she had an artistic niece who never paid any attention to her, but who sometimes used her house "for a bed and breakfast." She had another niece who was a dancer and who had come out with her boyfriend to vacation at her summerhouse. She gave neither of these nieces' names. There was no sense of attachment and no photographs. Indeed, the only photograph in the entire downstairs was a picture of her mother. None of her friends had names — only her cat, Tabitha.

Miss Havisham had been born in the house next door, and her grandmother had lived in her present house. Before that, her family had lived across the street, in a rather grander house. In 1905 her grandfather had died imagining that his wife was left secure, for he had left her a number of lucrative second mortgages in bustling San Francisco real estate. The very next year the San Francisco earthquake and subsequent fire rendered all of the mortgages worthless. But Havisham still grew up amidst wealth.

After graduating from Stanford University Gwendolyn Havisham taught flower arranging. During the war she worked for the Office of Censorship "until I got tired of reading other people's mail. . . . You got an insight into how people lived in other parts of the country." Havisham often spoke of herself as "you." After the war "I got into the rag business. It was fun and interesting." She said this in a gloomy and depressed way. Even calling it the "rag business" had a sense of forced gaiety. In New York she had worked for a "dumb woman with very good taste" selling bridal dresses. Her job was to greet the customers. Finally, "she fired me . . . then I realized that my mother was not well."

So in her thirties Gwendolyn Havisham came home to live in her parents' house to look after them and had remained there ever since. Her life with her parents had been stable and selfless. She had taken such good care of her parents that now she would die without social support. Asked over her long life what man had most touched her heart, she replied, "I can think of no one." When she had lived in New York, she had met a third cousin. "I fell for him, but it didn't last very long . . . there were men that you'd fall for for a short time." It seemed she had never fallen in love in the first person.

She explained that after World War II, the parties and the upper-class San Francisco social structure that she had taken for granted vanished. Her mother had developed Alzheimer's, and she had had to watch her constantly to keep her from escaping. Her father would spend long days downtown in San Francisco and leave his daughter and wife alone. Finally, father and daughter found Havisham's mother a rest home. After this, Havisham would pick her father up at his San Francisco law office and drive him out to see her mother every other day or so. That was her life. "I didn't want to go to work."

Asked what her most responsible job was, she shrugged, "I duck responsibility when I can." She had had enough responsibility looking after her mother. Now she kept house for her parents' ghosts. Asked if society had allowed her to live up to her potential, she said that the question would have been relevant only if she had had to do things. "I've never had to do anything." Asked what she liked best about herself, she laughed charmingly and replied, "I've never thought of liking myself." A pity.

Asked how she spent time with friends, she said that she kept house and looked after Tabitha, her pussycat. She also went to her Berkeley music club, where she was only an associate member. This meant that she listened and other people played the piano. "My mother bought me a beautiful cello. But I was not the musical one." The cello was still leaning against the wall in the dining room — perhaps had for fifty years. For a long time she had been trying to make up her mind whether to give the cello to Berkeley for some impoverished college student to play. But with so little self, it was hard for her to give anything away.

The hollowness of Havisham's life began to pervade the interview. It was as if she had lived out her life as a charade, and despite her charming laugh and sense of humor, nothing was important. Unlike some Study members who triumphed over barren lives with a deepened spiritual life (see chapter 10), Havisham's spiritual life, like William Loman's in chapter 2, was non-existent. As a child she had wanted to go to Sunday school because she wanted a pretty hat. After her mother bought her the hat, she went to Sunday school for a month, then stopped. Her father was a nominal Unitarian, and he had gone to church until he found out that the minister was "an out-and-out Communist." He had never gone back, and neither had his daughter.

Asked if any book had touched her, she said no, "I've never been a great reader." Asked who her favorite artist was, she waffled between "old masters" and "some contemporary art." When pushed to name a single artist, she very reluctantly said, "I used to like Rubens." Asked what music touched her, she said the night before she had heard a Rachmaninoff concert. "It was familiar, it was fun. If you can hear it, it becomes part of you." Even though she said all this with a bright, birdlike manner, my wife and I remained unconvinced. It was their real-life behavior that rendered what our interviewees *said* convincing or unconvincing.

As we reflected over her entire life, Havisham's most skilled job was in her early 20s, when she lectured to ladies' groups about flower arranging. For a young woman with a high intelligence and a Stanford education to teach flower arranging was graceful. It was safe and socially acceptable, but there were certainly issues of the Great Depression that had caught other privileged young people's attention. Havisham had been selfish in all the wrong ways. It takes mastery of the earlier "selfish" tasks of Identity, Intimacy, and Career Consolidation to develop our selves so that in midlife we have something to give away to the next generation.

Gwendolyn Havisham had never seen a psychiatrist; she had never been seriously depressed; and there was no evidence that she abused alcohol. During the course of the interview and in reviewing her entire record, the only hint of mental illness was that her doctor treated her with low doses of thyroid. (Before the development of effective antidepressants, depressed women were often given low doses of thyroid.) Havisham had lived out her life as a diligent daughter without bothering anybody else, or even being very bothered herself.

•   •   •

Consider the contrasting life of Inner City member Bill Dimaggio. His family had been in social class V. As a child he had had to share a bed with his brother in an apartment without central heating. His father had been a laborer who became disabled when Dimaggio was still a teenager. When he was 16, his mother died. With a Wechsler Bellevue IQ of 82 and a Standford reading IQ of 71, Dimaggio completed ten grades of school — with difficulty. As we measure intelligence, Bill Dimaggio was only one half as smart as Gwendolyn Havisham.

Nevertheless, at age 50, Bill Dimaggio was a charming, responsible, and committed man. If he was short and noticeably overweight around the midsection, he still retained much of his youthful vigor. His face was expressive; there was a twinkle to his eyes; and he conveyed a good sense of humor and a healthy appetite for good conversation. While maintaining eye contact, he answered the interviewer's questions directly and frankly.

By consenting to be a continuing part of the Study, Dimaggio told the interviewer, he felt that he was contributing something to other people; unlike Havisham he felt that this "little thing" was important. For the last fifteen years Dimaggio had been working as a laborer for the Massachusetts Department of Public Works. He said that several years before, a position had opened for a carpenter, and even though he did not have any carpentry skills, he was able to get the position by seniority. He had learned the necessary skills on the job. Of his work he said, "I like working with my hands." Indeed, he had always enjoyed working with wood; and he pointed out how he had redone the inside of his own house, rebuilding door frames and putting up cabinets. He took special pride in his role of maintaining some of Boston's antique but historic municipal buildings. Like Frederick Hope the truck driver, Dimaggio the carpenter loved his work. Asked how he handled problems with people at work, Dimaggio replied, "I'm the shop steward in the union, so they lay off me. I'll stand up to them if I feel I'm right"; and so if he felt that certain jobs were dangerous, he would not allow his men to work on the job. Under union rules, management would listen to him. In short, he had learned to speak with authority.

Over the last year, Dimaggio explained, his bosses had been trying to get along better with him. Because he had become one of the few really experienced men on the job, he noted, "They depend on me more." Management also depended on his experience to help teach other men. Put differently, after the age of 40, IQ as measured by a school-oriented test like the Wechsler Bellevue Intelligence Test does not count for much. It is what you have learned along the way that matters.

If he had his life to live over again, Dimaggio did not think that he would do anything differently. Dimaggio at work took pride in his job, enjoyed it, and saw himself as enhanced by it. However, he continued, "It's only a job. I'm more concerned about my wife and kids. Once I leave work," he added, "I forget about it." He was too concerned with family matters to worry about work when he got home.

"I have had more time for my children than my father had for me," he told the interviewer. He described taking his sons fishing and taking them to all sorts of places as they were growing up. "We spent a lot of time together." He explained that his own father — chronically unemployed — had never had time to take him fishing or go out with him very much. In other words, if you need help with community building, ask a busy woman or a busy man.

When asked what he felt his greatest problem had been with his children's growing up, Dimaggio replied with a smile, "Do you have about six months?" Becoming serious, he added, "Being worried about drugs." He knew that his children smoked marijuana; and he said he could accept that. But if both parents seemed somewhat tolerant of their sons' smoking marijuana, they would not let them smoke in the family house. They were accepting of the fact that their youngest son had moved in with his girlfriend, and they made no moral judgments about that. They chalked this up to "him being very immature," and they felt that he would become more mature as time went on. A vital ingredient of Generativity is hope, but such hope is only possible if one's mind can encompass the concept of adult development.

At various times, Dimaggio joked with his wife with ease and animation. Indeed, the interviewer was moved by the affection that they held for each other. When Dimaggio was asked to describe his wife, she tactfully left the room. He then yelled after his wife that if she didn't come back, he would tell all the bad things and not the good things. This inarticulate man then proceeded to offer the interviewer a simple string of words: "sweetheart . . . very understanding . . . everything you want in a wife . . . she loves to talk and argue and I like this." Dimaggio said that probably what pleased him most about his wife was her "sense of humor — without it we couldn't have survived."

What bothered him most about his wife, Dimaggio revealed, was that she seemed to be smoking more lately, and "I want to hang on to her as long as I can." On family disagreements, Dimaggio said, "We don't settle them readily, but we don't let them overcome us." He explained that when he and his wife had arguments, they did not last very long. "We don't hold grudges." Again, he mentioned using a sense of humor to help take the bite out of arguments and disagreements. Besides, each realized that they were different from the other, and so they tried to respect the other's opinions and not force their own upon the other. Asked whether he turned to anybody in times of trouble, Bill Dimaggio replied, "We turn to each other." His wife then chimed in, "Bill is my best friend." Referring to the number of deaths they had had in the family over the last couple of years, he said, "We try to comfort each other." If results from the Study can be generalized, Generativity, commitment, tolerance, and humor seem the four key ingredients to a contented, long-lived marriage.

The Dimaggio couple's whole social life was involved with visiting relatives. As they put it, they were "very into family." Bill Dimaggio's greatest ambition in the next ten years was to see his children living independently. The capacity to accept such a generative balance between care and letting go requires intrapsychic maturation. Being forced to reflect — to observe oneself from a different vantage point — a person begins to take pause and wonder again. Such self-reflection can never be imposed by society or culture. It comes from within — as does looking where one is going or learning to walk — but, like walking, respect for another's autonomy is a complex balancing act that develops in its own time.

Bill Dimaggio belonged to the Sons of Italy. He had been quite active in that organization and he regularly helped out with Bingo night, which meant running games for the large number of women who came on Wednesdays to play. He and another member, a friend of his, regularly cooked for the club on Saturday morning, when the club hosted a lunch for members. Dimaggio said he liked to do the cooking; he liked the feeling of people being happy with his food. Through the Sons of Italy, Dimaggio also did volunteer work in community activities. For example, on the Fourth of July he helped host a big party for the kids in the neighborhood, with games and refreshments. Indeed, he was active in various club activities for children held throughout the year.

In addition, Dimaggio and his wife had also signed up to work for one of the candidates for mayor who was challenging the old-guard city boss, and he expected to donate his time to campaign for him in the coming election. Finally, Dimaggio was quite active in the "Council of Organizations," which was a sort of umbrella organization for all the charitable clubs in Boston's North End. Thus, this socially and intellectually limited schoolboy had matured into a leader of leaders, a wise man, and a Keeper of the Meaning.

The interviewer closed his report, "Dimaggio maintains a close relationship with, and a healthy interest in, people around him. He is tolerant of those who are prejudiced, but he is not compromising of his own principles. On the whole, he is a quite mature and interesting man." There was no difficulty with the raters agreeing that Bill Dimaggio was generative. You do not need to attend Stanford or Harvard or have a high IQ to engage in community building. Nor do you need to choose between Generativity and the alternative goals of a contented career and family commitments.

.   .   .

My interview with Frederick Chipp, a retired Phillips Exeter schoolteacher, revealed a man whose whole life was permeated by Generativity. At 78 he still had never troubled himself with becoming a Keeper of the Meaning. Being generative was just too much fun. In response to my request for an interview in 1997, 75-year-old Chipp explained that he would be getting in from a sailing trip the day before, and he would be going out to sea four days later. But it would be just fine if I came by at 2:30 on Tuesday afternoon. His enthusiasm and warmth over the telephone were palpable.

I arrived ten minutes early. His wife was still in the middle of lunch but went outside to find her husband. Chipp was on his knees weeding his vegetable garden with his 18-year-old granddaughter. He had on khakis, an inexpensive polo shirt, and sneakers. They were both laughing and covered with mud. He washed his hands first; and, then, still in his deeply stained khakis, he ushered me into the sunroom for our interview.

The Chipps' Boothbay, Maine, "compound" consisted of several houses. One was a boat shed where one adult child used to summer. A second was a house that Chipp, as an impoverished schoolteacher, had built with his own hands. A daughter and her children were summering there. Upstairs in the Chipps' house, a house that formerly belonged to his parents, another daughter and her children were summering. There was an easy sense of back-and-forth interchange in the Chipp family. Each of his children had privacy, but they shared many meals together. And the grandchildren were as numerous as the Chipps' fruit trees. The Chipp home was not expensive but was nevertheless quite beautiful. It was a simple shingled Cape with a white picket fence, large rooms, and light coming in everywhere. The Chipps lived well, but their retirement income of fifty thousand a year was modest by Harvard Study standards. Chipp's income was below that of several Inner City men. You don't get rich teaching school and educating four children. At 75 Fred Chipp looked extremely handsome. Without being narcissistic, he was charismatic, masculine, vital, and extraordinarily relaxed. The sunroom opened onto a large dining room furnished with New England antiques and surrounded on all four walls by a relative's beautiful oil paintings. In the study were a grand piano, a good deal of music, and more of the gifted relative's paintings. The kitchen was small and low-tech; but the laundry room was enormous and filled with freshly washed, neatly stacked piles of clothes belonging to myriad laughing children and grandchildren. Even laundry becomes beautiful when it captures the activity of a happy family.

Fred Chipp explained that that morning he had spent his time spraying his apple trees, caulking his twelve-foot Beetle Cat sailboat, and helping his brother next door with his gardening. Then, like any grandfather, Fred Chipp started to reminisce and tell stories. He told me that last December he had put on cross-country skis, skied from the house down to the beach, climbed into his Beetle Cat, sailed for two hours on the midwinter ocean, and then skied home. Clearly, it was his idea of bliss. Remembering the past made Chipp happy. Unlike Miss Havisham, he liked being interviewed; he enjoyed giving to the Study.

Asked the most important thing that he did during retirement, Chipp replied, "It's the sailing." It was through sailing that he, as a retired schoolteacher, continued to spend time teaching young people lessons of value. "I love teaching them [his eleven grandchildren] sailing skills. I am in a boat every day." I asked Fred

Chipp what for him was the most difficult part of retirement. He replied, "Not enough time to do what I want to do." He said his granddaughter had asked him what books he read, and he had realized that he did not have time to read very many books. He still read twenty magazines and always read the *New Yorker* "cover to cover." But Chipp and his wife also read to each other; they were two-thirds through the novel *The English Patient.* He said he liked the novel so much that he had bought copies for each of his daughters. Even the usually solo act of reading he carried out in relationship.

Fred Chipp had none of the adolescent, childish qualities that often go with prep school teachers. He was very matter-of-fact and did not use humor. He wasn't interested in gossip or small talk. He made no effort to be liked, but at the same time there was almost a saintly quality about him. He conveyed a warmth that made me trust him and want to tell him of my life even as he told me about his. But he did not pick up on things that I revealed about myself. He was a teacher, not a psychiatrist. Rather, he conveyed a spiritual and serious sense of the importance of life as a whole. But Chipp was not a man to spend time in introspection. Instead, his life was entirely devoted to a world of relationships. Without being particularly extroverted, he was enormously committed to the human beings whom he cared for.

Fred Chipp had taken from his parents and had given to the next generation. He told me that his oldest daughter had written a still unpublished novel that had won second prize at a literary contest. He got up and brought me the manuscript. With pride he told me that he had worked hard with her on editing the book before she submitted it. I asked Fred Chipp about his own writing. He explained that he had never had the time; "teaching is too important." As he talked, it became clear that he viewed his life's work of teaching youngsters to write as an almost sacred vocation. In his freshman year at Harvard he had taken an exciting writing course with Wallace Stegner, but that was the spring that France had surrendered to Germany. Chipp believed that there were more important things for him to do in the world than cultivate his own interest in fantasy. Instead, he enlisted in the United States Navy. During the battle for the Solomon Islands and in subsequent Pacific invasions, he experienced heavy combat. Then, for the next forty years, he had taught school in the winter and had taught sailing in the summer. "Encouraging others," he explained to me, "was more important than doing it myself."

Asked what he disliked most about retirement, Chipp explained that he missed his colleagues. He went out of his way to stay in touch with them, for "I get spiritual sustenance from talking shop." Because of his own eleven grandchildren, he did not miss his pupils. "Teaching is an almost total human commitment. It is wonderful to help someone acquire skills. . . . I see it on Grandparents' Day visiting my grandkids at school. . . . Teaching starts a whole process of exploring." Small children know how to play, Chipp explained, and "the adult in education has to remember how to do that." Because of other commitments in their lives, however, he noted that it was hard for adolescents and grown-ups to remember how to play. That was a great loss. Chipp had not forgotten how to play; and with great pride he next gave me a copy of another daughter's published book encouraging parents to go adventuring with their children, especially in the outdoors.

I asked Chipp what it was like "being home for lunch." He said he and his wife led different lives. They had different passions, and "I do not impinge on her work," but there were things that they shared. They had supper and breakfast together, but they ate lunch separately. I asked how he and his wife collaborated, and he pointed to their many gardens. His wife did "the planting and harvesting, and I do the heavy labor." And, "We go walking together." Every day they walked together for three miles. This year they had gone camping for two weeks in Florida with three daughters and eight grandchildren.

I asked Chipp how he and his wife depended on each other. He choked up, fought back tears, and looked off into space.

"Gosh," he blurted, "just by being there. If she goes first, it would be pretty traumatic." At their fiftieth wedding anniversary, Chipp had dug out the diary he had kept at 16. In it he had described his future wife as "simply swell." That was the year he and his wife started sailing together. The first time he had met his future wife, Chipp went home and told his mother, "I met the girl I'm going to marry." He admitted that it had taken him a few years to convince his wife; but "I've lived happily ever after from then on." Tomorrow, sixty years later, they would spend two weeks sailing together. "I do the skilled and the nautical parts. I take charge — it's just instinct." His wife preferred the aesthetics of sailing. As Chipp said, they led different lives. But Erikson would have noted that they had no trouble with intimacy. Every year they also went canoeing together in Nova Scotia for two weeks. Solemnly Chipp told me, "That is important time." They also played tennis singles together. His wife used "drop and dunk shots, and I hit the ball harder. We are dead even." The previous night they had played "three-generation tennis." They had played two sets; both sets had gone to seven/five. "Everybody won. . . . I played twenty-four games. I have a lot of energy."

I asked Chipp to tell me more about his energy, and he grunted, "It's genetic." When I suggested that that was too easy an answer, he admitted that his parents had not been particularly athletic. However, keeping so active "gives me a chance to do things with my grandchildren." He then reminisced that all his grandparents did with him was play backgammon. I pushed Chipp on what there was in his family besides genes, and he explained that he had come from a family of "people who savored life . . . who put everything in human context." His aunt was his role model for growing older. She had been one of the first women to graduate from Johns Hopkins Medical School. After 65 she had been very active in running an orange grove in Florida. When she was 88, she went to buy medicine at a senior's discount; but to be sure she was really over 65 the pharmacist had asked her for her driver's license.

I observed that his commitment to family and his involvement with family were outstanding. Chipp again shrugged. "It goes back to my mother." Her farm had been in the family for twelve consecutive generations. Chipp boasted to me that during the Boothbay Harbor Fourth of July parade his granddaughter had ridden in his mother's wicker baby carriage. In other words, his granddaughter's great-grandmother's baby carriage was still in the family four generations later. Happy families, like bank accounts left to compound interest, build on themselves. But the roots of Generativity are certainly complex. Such roots extend far beyond good genes or a happy marriage or my ability to analyze them. It probably helped that Chipp came from a family that had loved "gardening" the same farm for twelve generations. It also probably helped that Fred Chipp, like Susan Wellcome, could not keep people outside. Twenty-five years before, I had interviewed Fred Chipp at the Exeter dormitory where he lived. Then, his wife and children had kept interrupting our interview. Now they no longer intruded; but, instead, their laughter and animated kitchen conversation provided the background music for our interview. Now the interruptions came from Chipp's two-year-old grandchild, Posie. She came frequently in and out of the sunroom for cuddles and for unconditional admiration. She also needed to have her tummy scratched and to discuss her "ouchies" with her adoring grandfather. Chipp was in excellent health. He slept well and at 75 played tennis and continued downhill skiing. I asked him if he took any medicines. He did; he took one aspirin a day. He also had "a pesky ankle" that swelled up "now and then," and sometimes he had trouble with his foot but that went back to a high school injury. At age 75 nothing else was wrong. Asked what he had had to give up as a result of aging, Chipp admitted that he had given up running marathons. Now, as he approached eighty, he only ran "half-marathons." I asked what his dominant mood had been during the past year. Chipp exclaimed, "Buoyant . . . enthusiastic . . . wildly so!"

After the interview, Chipp showed me his vegetable garden,

his flower garden, his apple trees, the marsh through which he cut his trails, and the house (quite an impressive house) that he had built entirely by himself except for a mason who built the chimney. The self-built house was cozy and conveyed a sense of "elbow grease."

I drove home from my visit delighted and filled with admiration. The overall effect was a stunning sense of familial harmony in which the older generation cared for the younger. Twenty-five years ago when I interviewed Chipp, he had seemed quite ordinary and forgettable. But in the intervening years, like a great Bordeaux, Chipp had aged so as to become full-bodied and richly memorable. Viewed from the perspective of a fifty-year study, the maturation of great human beings becomes as miraculous as the birth of a child.

What Have You Learned from Your Children?

Erik Erikson noted, "The fashionable insistence on dramatizing the dependence of children on adults often blinds us to the dependence of the older generation on the younger one."[4] Thus, after the age of 65, we asked both the Harvard men and Terman women, "What have you learned from your children?" Some septuagenarians could only relate what their children had learned from them; few of such individuals had mastered Generativity or were aging well. I asked Frederick Chipp what he had learned from his children. "Times change," he replied, "and your children help you make adjustments." He had learned that the idea of living together before marriage "makes very good sense, but in 1960 it would not have crossed my mind." I asked him to be more specific about what he had learned. Chipp wasn't stumped the way many men were by my question, but he became very serious and thoughtful. He looked past me in his characteristic way and replied, "All of my daughters helped model the different lives that were possible for American women living in the Liberation Movement." His mother had seen the entire world as being "just her children and her garden"; whereas, he said, watching his children's different lifestyles had helped him adjust. It was his daughters who had taught him how to guide Phillips Exeter Academy to become coeducational. He had had to learn that bringing in girls was not for the purpose of making school life better for boys but for making life better for women. His daughters also mentored him in dealing with "my female colleagues and getting on their wave length."

Paradoxically, the Study members who learned most from the next generation had been also the most successful at caring for them. Successful aging requires continuing to learn new things and continuing to take people in. In King Lear, one tragic flaw — and he had several — was his inability to learn from his children. Not only did he fail to take in Cordelia's gentle wisdom, but also he failed even to understand Goneril's simple statement of fact: his knights were too many, too greedy, and too badly behaved. His response to his daughter was, ". . . thou liest: My train are men of choice and rarest parts." In reality, he had saddled his daughter with a hundred rowdy oafs.

For many of the less generative men and women in the study the question "What have you learned from your children?" was overwhelming, even ridiculous. Asked what he learned from his children, one man said he probably couldn't answer that question. "I have been pretty good friends with them," he waffled, "and they have been pretty good friends with each other." He hemmed and hawed that some of the things that his son used to complain about "we see him doing with his children. . . . They do have an influence . . . it's too hard to answer."

In contrast, another Harvard Study member, Frank Wright, who will appear in the chapter on retirement, responded to my question about learning from children, "Oh boy, it is hard to say . . . probably an awful lot, but I don't know." Then without breaking stride, he easily gave me clear, affectively balanced answers. His middle child, Derek, "the one who usually looks as if he's not reacting, he was the first person to teach us as a family how to hug." Nobody in Frank Wright's family or his wife's family had hugged each other until Derek modeled it for them. Now they all hugged each other — a lot. He added, with pride, that his son was singled out as being one of the ten best family doctors in Virginia. "I also learned a lot from my son Arthur. . . . He delights me. He is the most like my father. It was wonderful to have him close by this past winter." Arthur had taught him a lot about music.

Nongenerative men and women were simply incapable of allowing the role of familial giving to be reversed. When asked the question, several Study members repeated the question back with astonishment to be sure that they understood. Then they told us what their children might have learned from them. Some of the answers were sadder still. When asked what she had learned from her children, a very unhappy woman replied, "I'm glad I only had one. I'm not the mothering type."

The majority of generative men and women, however, understood the question, for they had mastered the reciprocity involved in caring for and in learning from children. One woman echoed Frank Wright above. She told us that she had grown up without touching; and yet both her grown sons felt comfortable coming up to her and hugging her. "I hadn't known what I was missing." Another woman answered that from her children she had learned "freshness of outlook. . . . We are each made up of all the people we have come in contact with." In a very simple way she had summed up the quality which I believe is most crucial for successful aging. That quality has already been illustrated in chapter 1 with Anthony Pirelli's gift of allowing the healing hope, strength, and experience of others inside.

• • •

Anna Love can serve as a model of both Generativity and learning from children. But she also served as a model for Anne Morrow Lindbergh's dictum: "The seeds of love must be eternally resown."[5] Anna Love was a widow with short gray hair, dimming vision, too much weight, and arthritic hands. But she was anything but sick. She still adored life with a passion. Throughout our interview she took great pleasure in boasting to me about her children. She would catch herself, saying, "That's pride, and the church says we're not supposed to be proud." Then she would go right back to being proud.

Anna Love's life had not been free of tragedy. Her parents had been poor. Like her, her father had been a brilliant but poorly educated high school teacher. His dream had been to teach classics at a university instead of math at small rural high schools. But it was not to be. Anna Love, too, went to a poor college and had taught in dangerous inner city schools where she had been physically assaulted. Ten years before our interview she had lost her husband, and now she was growing blind.

Anna Love had just moved to a retirement community. She had decorated her living room in a Japanese style and there was a sense of sunny simplicity everywhere. There were three treasured paintings on the wall, a colored photograph of her husband, and two blown-up photographs of her children. On her coffee table were a clump of artificial irises and a *Good News Bible.* In front of her house was her pride and joy, her bright yellow Volkswagen Rabbit. She was the only one of her elderly friends who could still drive, and she loved playing chauffeur to her social set.

I asked Anna Love if as a math teacher she had ever had a mentor. She paused for a moment and then replied, "My dad, in teaching. . . . I never would have made it through geometry without my dad." She explained that he was a wonderful teacher. He taught high school math in Leadville, Colorado, where he stood on the porch and took loaded revolvers from the young men as they came to school and put them on his desk. He gave the revolvers back to the students after school; the dangers of this frontier town were still real. She added that her mother had been a mentor, too — "in the field of motherdom and love. . . . I had a lot of good people who cared about what I did." Now Love had a 93-year-old friend who might also qualify as a mentor. "She smiles and she never talks about other people's faults." Asked to describe her career identity, Love, like Chipp, answered, "I have been a teacher all my life." For Love, Generativity came early; in the high school where she taught, at age 25, Love was made dean of women. Over the years she had also done a lot of counseling. Even at 78 she had found a neighborhood child to tutor. Asked what legacy she would leave behind, Love answered, "I leave four wonderful children with their families." Like Chipp, Love felt no need to become a Keeper of the Meaning. Care was too much fun.

I asked Anna Love how she had combined her teaching career with raising four children. She said she had fought for paid leave for teachers when their children were sick. Her child had had scarlet fever; she had stayed home to look after him. The principal had docked her salary; she confronted him and finally won her point. Then, when she moved to the Berkeley school system, she had had to fight the same battle over again. Again she won. In other words, this woman who always saw the positive side of everything, who seemed a little crass and boastful, when it really mattered could use her aggressiveness to win important social battles. Anna Love could harness her passion, while Gwendolyn Havisham could not even admit that hers existed.

Anna Love said she would get all her four children off to school before she went to her own teaching job. When she came home from school, she would put all the papers she had to grade on her desk. Then she would go downstairs, give her children snacks, feed them supper, and coach them with their math. She would be sure that she helped to get them to their after-school activities, for all of her children had been active in Scouts, and all had had music lessons. "Then, after they were in bed — and usually everything was quiet by nine or nine-thirty — I picked up my stack of books; I made a big pot of coffee; and I graded all my geometry and trigonometry papers." All of her children had chores, and they would help her with the housework. "We were a team." But what was clear in the Love family was that biology flowed downhill.

Asked for her most important current activity, Love replied, "Through my church, sharing myself with others and helping others." Thus, her bright yellow Rabbit stood poised outside her apartment door for errands of mercy. This evening she was going to take a neighbor supper. "If I don't do something every day to help someone else, then I feel very badly at night." She said she had just driven a friend to the doctor, and she was going to look after her daughter's three young children while her daughter and husband went away for the weekend. Feistily, however, she explained that she had made it clear to her daughter that she was not going to be "her baby-sitter." What she wanted was "one half day of Luke a week." Luke was her ninth grandchild; he was the youngest and geographically the nearest; he also had a special place in his grandmother's heart. "He inspires me and makes me happy. He's a humdinger!" Such different language from Miss Havisham's telling us without emotion, "I was fortunate to have had a very nice family."

Anna Love's marriage of forty years' duration had been one of the sustaining strengths of her life. The only difference that she would have made in her life would have been "to have met my husband ten years sooner . . . but I am happy with my life. . . . Before we married we agreed that we were both equal in rights." She often out-earned her husband. The chief focus of their collaboration was in their church and in the children's after-school activities. They would work on church and school projects together. They both had loved watching the children develop. I asked how her marriage changed over time. In their last fifteen years, especially after the children left home, she stated, "Our relationship became closer and closer." They did a lot of hiking on the beach together, and "he could read my emotions and I could read his. . . . We were very happy together, very happy."

Asked how she had coped with the loss of her husband, Anna Love exclaimed, "Oh, it was hard! I did not feel I was going to live after he died. . . . All the flesh went off my bones. . . . I needed more from God and from church fellowship." She had asked for greater faith, and she had received it, a blessing that she saw as a gift from her church fellows and from God. Where human community ends and one's Higher Power begins is not always easy to discern.

Then Love shifted gears. "At that time, the little girl you just met was having her first baby." (Her daughter Judy, Luke's mother, had stopped by only a few minutes earlier.) Love's eldest son had brought his grieving mother to see Judy and her new baby, and "that was the beginning of my healing. . . . Judy was grieving her daddy — oh, she loved him so. And I had to be a strong mother to help her and to help myself." By this point she was crying. "I even moved over to his side of the bed to sleep and I still do." She started to apologize for her tears, then she remembered her wise 93-year-old mentor, who assured Love that she, too, had continued to cry for her husband even after fourteen years. Besides, Love explained, after she cried she always felt relief.

I asked Love what she liked best about herself. She explained that she made things and gave them away. Next she associated to her husband's "treasures." He had had a collection of one hundred rare books on early California history. Every time she went to visit one of her children, she would take two or three of their father's books as a present.

Owing to poverty neither Anna Love nor her father had been able to attend graduate school, but Love had made sure that her children could enjoy brilliant careers. The mean IQ of her four children was 155. But so was Love's; and so, I suspect, was her father's, for not everybody in Leadville, Colorado, aspired to teach university classics. Love knew that she was not supposed to boast about her children, but each one of her children had attained a graduate degree. "I know it, and I keep thinking about it." She said this with joy, and in such a way that her boasting was not at all irritating. Her older daughter was a superior court judge in Oregon; her older son got his Ph.D. at Harvard and had realized his grandfather's dream by teaching classics at the University of Michigan. The second son was dean of a small medical school, and Judy, with a master's degree in special education, was a schoolteacher working with dyslexics.

I asked Anna Love what she saw of herself in her children. She replied, "They are all positive; they all love life." All of her children believed in the work ethic, "to enjoy one's work." She joyously related that she had friends in all the places where her children now lived. Thus, when she visited her children, she could have lunch with these new friends. She went to great lengths to stay close to all of her grandchildren, and she visited all of her geographically scattered children once or twice a year. "The girls are wonderful mothers, and the boys are good daddies."

Asked how she replaced her friends as they died, Love explained that as soon as she arrived at her present retirement home in Palo Alto, she had been invited to a birthday party. Within a month or two she had organized a "gang" of twelve friends. Acknowledging Love as their leader, they would have lunch with one another almost weekly. They would study the Bible together, and go out to dinner too. In Berkeley, however, she still had two "dear friends," both of whom were bright, active career women in their thirties. "Why they fell in love with me I don't know, but I fell in love with them." She still talked to them often by telephone. "My doctor tells me I'm going to live a long time. He says I have a lot of youth in my body. I hope so. I love life." Havisham could fall in love with no one; and only her cat, Tabitha, had a name.

To the provoking question "What have you learned from your children?' Anna Love responded as if it were an opportunity, not as an annoyance or a puzzle.

> Gee, from John, the oldest one, I'm learning more about how to get along with people and how to see something good in everyone . . . that's what I've learned from my oldest son, patience and loving people — find something good in them.
> From Clarinda, I think she's taught me to be somewhat passive. To be somewhat thoughtful before you speak is good. From

this little one, Judy, that was here just now — she's not little but she's just a baby [age forty years] and she said, "Mom, don't call me the baby." That's why I did it in front of you, because I knew what she would say. She is so jovial, so warm. She makes me smile, and I have to smile more sometimes than I do, because I forget to smile. She sings. She makes me sing with her. I love to sing, but I don't do it anymore when I'm here alone. I wish I would. I used to sing when I did my housework. They're all just an inspiration to me.

Inspiration, after all, is a metaphor for how we take other people inside. Through our lungs, through our guts, and through our hearts.

CHAPTER FIVE

KEEPER OF THE MEANING

> *. . . And then the justice,*
> *In fair round belly with good capon lin'd,*
> *With eyes severe, and beard of formal cut,*
> *Full of wise saws and modern instances;*
> *And so he plays his part.*
>
> Shakespeare, *As You Like It*

With advancing age personality becomes more sharply defined. Some call such definition character, and others condemn it as rigidity. When organic brain disease is absent, the mental rigidity of old age is often the result of having discovered satisfactory choices, not lack of imagination. The novelist May Sarton at age 70 realized, "I am more myself than ever before." A gerontologist, Carol Ryff, wrote, "It might even be speculated that personality is the realm compensating for loss in other spheres."[1] In my youth I learned that I liked Brie and Bordeaux, and that I did not like goat cheese and rosé wines. The narrowness of my menu, then, is a function not only of stodginess, but of experience. Nevertheless, such certainty can irritate friends and relations. William James did not mince words when he wrote, "Old-fogyism . . . is the inevitable terminus to which life sweeps us on."[2] But besides developing a more sharply etched character, what *is* the role of 60- to 70-year-olds in society? Certainly not to perpetuate the species.

With advancing age, sexual differentiation becomes less sharp. As they grow older, women grow facial hair, and men's beards grow more slowly. Women may become flat-chested; their voices deepen; their facial features sharpen. The estrogens that may have once inhibited dominance decrease. The breasts of old men grow, their faces soften, and the testosterone that may have once facilitated dominance decreases; in women it increases.[3] True, with "eyes severe" old men can be gruff, impatient curmudgeons — but there also is a pervading gentleness. The legendary gentleness of grandfathers was captured by Francis Ford Coppola in his movie *The Godfather,* in which Marlon Brando, retired Mafia don, now plays sunlit games in the garden with his little grandson. Perhaps much older men may appeal to younger women precisely because they can let themselves become more gentle and nurturing. In contrast, young men can become as wary of and combative toward matriarchs as they once were toward their own fathers. Thus, an extraordinary fact about the Study men was that in old age they often got to manifest a more caretaking side. Former Rotarians who once hunted and fished now wore pastel-colored jackets and volunteered to push wheelchairs down hospital corridors. With age, men who once had driven relentlessly toward the future became interested in genealogy and conservation. At age 59 a former corporate president told the Study of his new duties: "Chairman of State Chapter of the Nature Conservancy, Chairman of the Planning Committee of the Mystic Seaport Maritime Museum, Trustee of the Rhode Island Environmental Trust." Stodgy, perhaps, for a man who had once shot lions in Africa — but better for the environment.

Passionate as he was about retaining his own macho masculinity, Ernest Hemingway admitted, "At a certain age the men writers turn into old mother Hubbards. The women writers become Joan of Arc without fighting."[4] Contrary to popular belief, however, prospective studies reveal that menopause, per se, does not alter the personality of women.[5]

Nevertheless, in one prospective study women at age 27 had scored much lower than their husbands on a scale attempting to measure goal-oriented, organized, practical, confident, and realistic behavior. Between 50 and 60 the wives, if anything, scored a little higher.[6] In reviewing twenty-six different societies cultural anthropologist David Gutmann (1987) noted that in fourteen of them the women became dominant in old age, twelve showed no change, and in none did male dominance increase.[7] In our own culture the causes of such marital dominance shifts are many: maturity, change in hormone production, and retirement. Sometimes the cause is a newly liberated wife who with her absorbing career outside the home now needs a househusband.

•   •   •

Nevertheless, be they male or female, the old have an important role to play. Generativity is only one role that adults play. Carl Jung poetically speculated, "A human being would certainly not grow to be 70 or 80 years old if this longevity had no meaning to the species to which he belonged. The afternoon of human life must also have a significance of its own and cannot be merely a pitiful appendage to life's morning."[8]

Simone de Beauvoir tells us why the old are important in Bali:

> The elderly men work little: they talk and chew betel. But they have many duties — they direct the village assembly, practice medicine, tell tales, and teach the young poetry and art. And they also often take the ducks out into the fields. They play an important part in the religious ceremonies. There are some very old men and women who are excellent dancers. They go into trances and speak as oracles. The old have a very important role — both male and female, for the distinction between the sexes disappears with age. Their opinion is asked on every subject.[9]

Among jackdaws and chimpanzees a similar respect for age occurs. The young are unable to alert their fellows, but the alarms of the elderly are taken very seriously.

•   •   •

If the virtue of the task of Generativity is care, a drawback to care is that it requires paying special attention to one person rather than another. In contrast, the virtue inherent in the task of Keeper of the Meaning is justice; for justice involves a more non-partisan and less personal approach to others. Society needs dispassionate judges as much as it needs passionate trial lawyers. If the task of young adults is to create biological heirs, the task of old age is to create social heirs.

In part the shift from Generativity to Keeper of the Meaning is a function of increased experience; and in part it is a function of decreased physical stamina. It takes less energy to be a caretaker than to be a caregiver. Perhaps it was the extraordinary vitality of Anna Love and Frederick Chipp that permitted them at 75 to still specialize in Generativity.

Generativity is different from Keeper of the Meaning in another way; for being generative is more likely to win us love than being a justice. We love and we need our partisan managers and our team captains; but we shout, "Kill the umpire." Referees and judges need thick skins and gray hair in order to survive. Thus, the passage from Generativity to Keeper of the Meaning may be difficult for those who wish the cheering crowd. Being needed, however, is a luxury that the young allow the middle-aged, but it is a luxury that wise grandparents, and certainly wise great-grandparents, learn to relinquish.

Old people, however, even if they become set in their ways, grow more understanding and perhaps more aware of who they are. Erikson writes, "Those in late mid-life describe both themselves and their aged contemporaries as more tolerant, more patient, more open-minded, more understanding, more compassionate and less critical than they were in their younger years."[10] Erikson then goes on to quote from the septuagenarians whom he studied. "Patience is one thing you know better when you're old than when you're young." "Now I can see both sides." "Nothing shakes me any more."

There is a certain peacefulness about becoming interested in genealogy, conservation, and history rather than meeting payrolls, running church rummage sales, and reining in teenagers.

One Study member wrote on reaching 65: "It's a brand new marvelous life for us and we love it. We no longer own a car or a lawnmower or a hedge clipper or a dog." Another wrote, "I'm not old and tired, just more selective." A third wrote, "We none of us have to pull our punches any more, but we can be forbearing — bear fools, if not gladly, and appreciate the absurdities of life." However, I am oversimplifying the distinction between the active task of the generative caregiver and the more sedate task of Keeper of the Meaning. Just as Intimacy and Career Consolidation can evolve hand-in-hand, so can care and justice. The line between being a caregiver and a caretaker is as vague as the boundary between green and yellow.

The downside, of course, of preserving the past is rigidity. A once clearly generative man described his increasing sense of alienation from the world and his lessening sense of personal control. As an aging senior law partner, he no longer felt needed. "I get discouraged by a good deal that I see and read. Individual morality, taste, and self-restraint have declined. The degree of theft in schools and in colleges appalls me. The degree of filth and wretched conduct in the movies disgusts me — and I am not a prude. . . . In general, I think life has become more crowded and less civilized than a generation ago. I think the vote for 18-year-olds is a mistake — it adds a volatile, unduly idealistic, and arrogant element to the electorate." In midlife he had been generative and a star of successful adaptation, but unable to share his wish to preserve past traditions with others, he fossilized. By age 70 he was dead.

Another Study member reported, "I am distressed at the weakening of our nearly ideal form of democracy by liberals, the disappearance of authority, the loss of religion, the weakening of family, immorality, and the disregard for the dignity of age." Of course, both men were partly right, but they would have been equally right in Shakespeare's day or in the Age of Pericles. To each older generation, the younger generation appears uniquely disrespectful. The problem was that rather than try to take responsibility for passing on their past, these rigid men choked on their own anger that their past was not being preserved by others.

In contrast, Peter Wiseman understood that the passing on of the past was his problem. He loved being 80. Wiseman had retired in 1982 from his job as a generative consultant to technology industries. But after age 65 he couldn't say no to a variety of volunteer posts, including: president of the historical society, chairman of the library board of trustees, and chairman of the board of selectmen. When he got remarried at age 74, he quit all of his volunteer positions, because he realized there was "more to life" than being so busy. However, he remained the honorary chair of the town's hundredth anniversary committee — a position he agreed to take because he was assured it wouldn't require any work, and he and his wife, together, became docents at the town historical museum.

Wiseman began to write down his memories only to discover that "no publisher would touch a single authored book of regional memoirs." So he decided to publish his memoirs himself. Asked if he was surprised to find himself a writer, he explained with obvious gratification that he was having a lot of fun. "Everyone who reads it seems to like it." Recently a woman had stopped him on the street to tell him that the book had moved her to tears. He had received a letter from a woman reader who had liked his book; later he received a second letter from her revealing that "recovery from heart surgery is slow, but your book is helping me every day." When you get a letter like that, he said, it makes you feel pretty good. Only the old can make the past come alive for the next generation. He is currently working on a second book, of Nantucket history from 1900 to 1920, which requires historical research. "One more thing I'm doing," he added, "is carving cedar roots." Long ago he and his father had planted cedar trees on the family farm. When cedar trees die and rot, he explained, they leave a hard root behind. He began collecting the roots and shaping them into sculpture. He pointed to about twenty abstract and polished wooden shapes from the very trees that he as a child had helped his father to plant. Again the old, replete with yesterdays, can make the past beautiful.

Since age 40 one Terman woman had been clearly generative. Most of her life she had enjoyed being a leader. Not only had she been a successful mother, helping her less intellectually gifted daughter to equal her own intellectual achievements, but she also had run a twelve-million-dollar social service organization. Then, at age 60, she had stepped back from doing casework with the elderly; she comfortably planned her retirement, and she began enjoying her grandchildren. In order to continue "keeping up with new ideas," she began studying California history. For the next fifteen years she became class correspondent of her Stanford class. She served on her town historical society board for six years and became its vice-president. In short, she became a village elder.

Between the ages of 64 and 68, another Terman woman became involved in conservation, in ecology, and in consumer protection for the elderly. She could write at 68 that she continued her old comptroller job half-time, but now as a consultant. "My advice is sought and followed, and more than adequately appreciated and paid." Her perception of her grandchildren was not as a source of emotional support, but as a source of pride, a not insignificant distinction. Put differently, mothers sometimes take pride in children as extensions of themselves; grandparents' pride in grandkids is more selfless and more fun for the grandchildren. At 72 she had become the "unofficial secretary" for her deceased husband's extended family of fifty people. She, too, had become a village elder.

*   *   *

But the conclusions of the Study about the universality of adult development are vulnerable to criticism. Remember that the individuals in the Study had the social advantages of education, intelligence, nondelinquency, white skin, and the GI bill. Cannot an environment of social stigma and prejudice be as great a handicap to adult development as the *genes for Alzheimer's disease, alcoholism, or major depression? Yes. Like bad genes, social stigma is a poison that keeps on corrupting and infecting. Cannot social injustice destroy the effect of good genes as insidiously as bad genes can destroy the effect of good environment? Not always. As with blighted plants, the forces of positive development remain at work beneath the surface, even if the results are not immediately visible.*

•   •   •

Maria was a Latina deprived even of her real last name because her father abandoned her in infancy and then died young under mysterious circumstances. She grew up in a Spanish-speaking household in Los Angeles and was subject to Anglo prejudice against Mexicans. Her fourth-grade teacher wrongly believed that Maria's English vocabulary was below average. In fact, it was in the top 1 percent of American schoolchildren's. But prejudice not only corrupts the honesty of the observer; it blames the victim as well. Thus, when seen from the vantage of the societally privileged staff of the Terman Study, it was Maria, not her teachers, who was criticized for not giving honest answers to the investigators. At age 9, so very anxious to please, Maria claimed that she had read all the books on the Terman Study book list, even the imaginary titles that Lewis Terman had added to check on the children's accuracy. To the Terman staff Maria was a liar. They could not put themselves in her shoes.

As a child Maria was so nearsighted that in order to read the school blackboard she had to sit in the first row. Yet her mother never had her eyes examined. The family already had enough troubles. Maria never progressed in school beyond high school, but she managed to graduate at 15. Instead of sending her to college, Maria's seamstress mother sent her daughter to work at 16 as a stenographer. Maria married, but her husband, like her father, disappeared to Mexico shortly after the birth of their daughter. Maria spent her young adulthood raising her daughter and looking after her mother. At age 37 she said the driving force in her life was "making Mother happy." Although the two courses Maria had hated most in high school were sewing and typing, she continued to work for the federal government as a clerk-typist until her mandatory retirement at 65. At 47 Maria advised the Study, "Working for the Federal Government stifles ambition and incentive, since women are undesirable employees with no possibility whatever for advancement." In 1960 her salary was still five thousand dollars a year.

Maria's first cousin, born just as poor as Maria, had the advantage of being born male and remaining in his own country, where his teachers could admire, rather than scorn, the fact that his native tongue was Spanish. He became a successful poet and a politician. Maria had to content herself with doing the cryptograms from the *New York Times*. Such cryptograms are far too difficult for the Harvard professor who wrote this book and, I suspect, for many of its readers.

At age 40 Maria earned a score of 141 on the Concept Mastery Test (an intelligence test for gifted adults that was biased in favor of the highly educated) and on which Stanford medical students and Berkeley Ph.D. candidates received an average score of 90. Thus, her fortunate genes continued to manifest themselves, but to no avail.

Until Maria was near death, her career aspirations continued to flit between being a dancer, a poet, and a surgeon. Probably she could have succeeded at all three. But owing to the stigma of being a Mexican, a woman, and a single mother in Los Angeles in the 1930s, Intimacy, Career Consolidation, and Generativity were not to be hers. Maria died of cancer at 70, more than fifteen years earlier than the average Terman woman. Was Maria's life a failure because she was without enjoyment of her paid job? Or was she a success because her career commitment was looking after her sick mother, raising her daughter, and ignoring the twentieth-century Western notion that individuals must become self-actualizing? At age 47 Maria answered the question and succinctly summed herself up: "economically and academically a failure . . . but not in family relationships." As I hinted at the start of her story, the forces of maturation can allow even the most disadvantaged to become Keepers of the Meaning. A year before her death Maria's multiple talents were finally recognized. At 69 she was made chairman of the board of trustees of the San Diego Brotherhood of Federal Clerks. She had become a matriarch and respected village elder at last.

*   *   *

Rigidity is sometimes difficult to distinguish from healthy conservatism. I have suggested that adolescents sometimes misjudge healthy justices because of their seeming rigidity. And clinicians and teachers sometimes dismiss the conservative young as rigid or uninteresting. Mark Stone was old before his time, but his life illustrates the importance of the societal role of Keeper of the Meaning.

At age 75, Professor Emeritus Mark Aurelius Stone, in his oxford-cloth button-down shirt open at the neck and his worn tweed jacket, looked very much who he was — a distinguished Ivy League professor on holiday. He appeared very young for his years, but his face was wooden and his facial expression rarely changed. For most of his life he had been a physicist, and a generative department chairman who deeply enjoyed teaching. Most recently he had become a Keeper of the Meaning — maintaining through his own unpaid efforts a scientific subspecialty that his university could no longer afford.

But I get ahead of my story. Originally, Stone had been an enigma to the Grant Study staff. Caught in their own prejudices, they initially saw Stone as a rigid and uninteresting nonentity. It was hard for them to appreciate that Stone's apparent failures lay not in him but in the eyes of his beholders.

Stone's maternal grandfather and great-grandfather had been tailors, but the latter was a tailor to whose shop Henry Thoreau and other nineteenth-century literary figures had come in order to converse. Stone's mother could not afford college, so before marriage she worked as a governess and a secretary. Stone's paternal grandfather was a missionary who found the means to send his son to Harvard. After graduating, Stone's father became a diplomat of great distinction. Stone's father had been assigned to the American embassy in Japan. The Study staff described Stone's mother as "a rather reserved individual and not particularly lavish with affection." Stone's mother explained to the Study family worker that her son had been a good-natured, active, normally social child. "There was never an easier child in the world to bring up. He never was naughty. If you explained a thing to him and why a thing was so, he saw the reason. Even as a child he had good powers of reasoning. He had no tantrums or rages as a child. I can't seem to remember any fears or anxieties. He got on well with other children. At 22 months of age he would put his blocks away, almost always with the red side up. At four he spoke Japanese fluently. . . . He was never influenced by social usage. I think he keeps things to himself a great deal."

Mark Stone finished third in his prep-school class at Andover. His grades at Harvard were almost all A's and his innate intellectual gifts were perhaps as formidable as those of anyone in the Study. The Study psychologist noted, "Performance on manipulative tests was outstanding for both dexterity and insight. Stone was able to accomplish the most difficult assemblies as speedily and easily as the simplest."

But, alas, Mark Stone's Rorschach responses were deemed "rather inferior." Worse yet, Stone had had the Philistine temerity to call the Rorschach designs "just ink blots." Thus he posed a conundrum to the earnest social scientists who studied him. Because of his equanimity in the face of stress, in the monthly case study conference one psychiatrist called him a "robot," and another piously added, "He has never had to suffer. I don't see how you can have lived without having suffered." A third psychiatrist thought Stone had a fundamental lack of ability to establish rapport with his fellow man. "He seems to be a rather constricted sort of person." The Study psychologist decided that Stone apparently did not have any creativity and would "work better under direction." Another judged that it was lucky that Stone was entering research "in view of how little he could offer to teaching." They acted as if Stone was a fossil before his time.

At last a sensible visitor to the staff conference lost his patience and demanded, "Why is it we all seem to dislike these successful people?" His remark gave another staff member the courage to chime in, "As far as I can tell from the history, Stone has always been this way, and I predict he will always be this way. He sees things pretty much as they really are." Like it or not, the Rorschach designs are just ink blots.

Fortunately, the Study staff kept a careful record of facts as well as the results of speculation and of projective tests. Mark Stone's freshman adviser wrote that he was "mature, self-possessed, able to make his own decisions." His graduate adviser described Stone, "as one of the best ten percent of all graduate students I have known." The wise Study internist wrote of Stone, "extraordinarily benign medical history, few problems and I really suspect none in spite of his quiet and reserve. Strong, silent man?" After forty years it has become clear that although the men's Rorschach results were often fascinating, they failed in any way to predict the future. However, the men's equanimity and stoicism — Stone's most salient qualities — turned out to be powerful predictors of future success.

In February 1942 the world was falling apart. Axis victory followed Axis victory. Stone's response to its effect on his own situation was, "There isn't much I can do about it, so it doesn't worry me." But later, when he had greater power to change things, he became more involved. He felt his contribution would be greatest in the navy, in which he served for two years. In the 1960s, as a liberal Democrat acting on his beliefs, Professor Stone left his cozy Ivy League nest and went south for six months to a black college in Mississippi to teach physics. By age 55 Mark Stone impressed his interviewer "as not an isolated scientist, but, rather, a man who was both easy to talk to, and who also was interested in others." But his interviewer was a social worker; and, unlike psychologists and psychiatrists, social workers are often trained to recognize individual strengths. Thus, she continued:

> He is interested in the Study and had cooperated fully over the years, but his prime concern seemed to be what had come out of all the data — how had it helped others? . . . He does not get very angry, and seems to internalize most of it. However, he has never had any of the psychosomatic symptoms associated with people who internalize anger. . . . He now drinks a glass of sherry when he attends parties, and drinks a glass of sherry each night of the weekend. He has never drunk much more than this.

In his university setting Stone had been consistently productive. Clearly generative, he worked hard with his postdoctoral students and wrote collaborative papers with them. But with age he also knew when to step down as chairman. He did not need to be generative forever. When Stone retired, his university had put on an all-day symposium in his honor. His old graduate students, even from overseas, returned, and there was a big dinner in his honor afterward. Even the emotionally contained Professor Mark Aurelius Stone exclaimed, "It was overwhelming." I asked him what had been the very best part. He replied how much it had meant to see his students, who had not always been outstanding in graduate school, return to demonstrate that they had had some "good ideas" in their careers. True, his most successful student had been disappointed when he (the student) had been nominated for but passed over for the Nobel Prize. But, then, most of us are not even nominated; neither are our students.

As a Monday morning quarterback I can poke fun at my Grant Study predecessors, but my own early judgments about Stone were no more astute. I, too, let my prejudices run away with me. For the thirty years that I have directed the Study I have always found the black sheep, the ones who did not return their questionnaires promptly, more fascinating than the diligent rule-followers. The former had often suffered from major depression and alcoholism, they told interesting stories on their Rorschach, and they had made countless visits to psychiatrists like me. They were introspective and discerning chaps — if a little self-absorbed — and I always looked forward to their tardy questionnaires. At 40 I preferred adolescent 55-year-olds to men who had behaved like sober judges even as adolescents. I, too, needed to learn to distinguish stodginess from mental health.

Mark Stone, bless his heart, always returned his biennial questionnaires. Indeed, he was always among the first to send his in. Instead of being grateful, I imagined him to be dreadfully boring and insufferably square. I was 60 years old before I met Mark Stone face-to-face. Finally, I could appreciate what an admirable man he was. But by then I was a little like Polonius myself. I had learned to value people who never exceeded the speed limit.

In his 70s, at great cost to himself but with no self-pity, Mark Stone looked after his wife, crippled for more than ten years with multiple sclerosis. Because his wife grew steadily worse, his behavior toward her, of necessity, became more that of a conservator than a generative spouse. During the same decade Mark Stone worked without pay in his special niche as emeritus professor in plasma physics. He still supervised graduate students, and he paid his laboratory expenses out of his own pocket. He also expressed his interest in conservation by taking special pride in trying to improve the beauty of his immediate suburban neighborhood. As a department chairman and a mentor to graduate students he had been a caregiver. Now at home and at work he had become a caretaker — a subtle but important difference.

When I asked Stone what he liked least about retirement, he looked very sad and replied, "Getting used to new things. . . . Once I get a routine it is not so bad." I asked him what about retirement was most difficult to master; again he acknowledged that it was "adjusting to new things." But he was not expressing stodginess; what this inarticulate stoical professor of physics was really telling me was that watching new and devastating symptoms of multiple sclerosis appear in his wife was tragically painful. Finally, as his wife's multiple sclerosis had progressed still further,

Stone had checked the present period as his unhappiest. But in a postscript he added that he didn't really feel he should call himself unhappy; "I just wish it hadn't happened."

Few men in the Study met the criteria for successful aging with as close to a perfect score as Professor Mark Aurelius Stone. At age 75 he was still writing original papers, and physics journals were still publishing them. He was still working with doctoral students, and his health was outstanding. Occasionally, he still played tennis; and since 1970 he had been in the hospital only once — for a hernia repair. He never spent days in bed from colds or flu. Although the average 75-year-old takes three to seven different prescription medicines, the only medicine that Stone used was over-the-counter "bag balm" for chapped hands. True, at 75 Stone had to give up his beloved squash to protect his back so that he could lift his wife as needed. Besides, he had been having trouble finding partners. "The young guys were too good," he admitted, and the men his own age were all too infirm to play.

Today, he remains a stoic. Asked what his biggest worries had been during the past year, Stone replied, "I don't worry very much." His greatest regret was, "Perhaps I should have planned things more. I seem to take things as they come more than most people." But taking things as they come was how for seventy-five years he had so successfully survived.

Are Keepers of the Meaning All Republicans?

As an optimist, a psychoanalyst, and a Democrat, I brought many prejudices to the Study. I have always been delighted when the Study confirmed them. One confirmation was that altruism really is more adaptive than paranoia. Another was that Mark Twain's cynical definition of marriage as "the triumph of hope over experience" was wrong. If you are willing to wait for the decades to smooth out the bumps, happy marriages really do exist. And finally, William James was wrong. Character is not set in plaster. Folks change and improve. Fine. That was the good news.

The bad news was that one of the real values of a longitudinal study is to shatter prejudices and superstition, not to support them. My own prejudices were no exception. One prejudice was that conservatives were not as loving and so would not age as well as liberals. (I forgot that Gandhi was a very bad father, and that John D. Rockefeller was a reasonably good one.)

The second prejudice was passed on to me by my very Republican grandfather. As he explained to me, if you are not a socialist before you are 30, you have no heart, and if you are still a socialist after 30, you have no brain. The facts of his life did not support his prejudice or mine. First, he remained vigorous and enjoyed life until his death at 86. Second, as a right-wing Republican he had backed Douglas MacArthur in old age, but he had also enthusiastically voted for William McKinley when young, and I, nearing 70, have already admitted to having never voted for a Republican president.

Perhaps my grandfather and I were exceptions. Thus, I looked to the Study of Adult Development to support my prejudices. Alas, sometimes folks did not change as much as I supposed. Sensitive "pink" editors of college literary magazines remain liberal and unconventional all of their lives. Pragmatic economics majors, who in college belonged to the Young Republican Club, in old age never veer from being proper conservatives. Politics are set in plaster. Thus, George Washington's own conservative and, I am sure, loving mother did not attend either of her son's inaugurations; she was too distressed by his liberal politics.

It was possible to chart the Harvard men's political preferences from 1940 to 1995. Every biennial questionnaire had asked questions about politics, and independent raters could place men along a political continuum from 1 = "red hot" socialist to 20 = a man well to the right of Newt Gingrich. The men were rated on what they did and how they voted as much as on the way they talked.

In the Harvard sample the liberals were more likely to be open to new ideas and to approve of the younger generation's long hair, protests, and use of pot. They were more likely themselves to display creativity, to use sublimation as a defense, to have had highly educated mothers, and to have gone to graduate school. The conservatives made more money, played more sports, and were less open to novelty both in real life and on pencil-and-paper tests. But at the end of the day such differences were not important.

In 1944 twenty-five personality traits, or characteristics, were assigned to the men.[11] These traits were based on a psychiatrist's evaluation of the college students after two years of study and assigned after some staff discussion. Of the twenty-five assigned, two characteristics, consistent with hardheaded common sense — *pragmatic* and *practical organizing* — were only very modestly correlated with mental health. But these two early traits were far more common among the 75-year-old Republicans than among septuagenarian Democrats. Conversely, five characteristics — quite uncorrelated with mental health but perhaps fitting many people's stereotype of Harvard students — were far more common among 75-year-old Democrats. These five were *introspective, creative and intuitive, cultural, ideational,* and *sensitive affect.*

These clear differences in personality in college correctly predicted voting preferences at age 75 three-quarters of the time, but they did not predict who would be generative or who would become Keepers of the Meaning. And politics had nothing to do with positive aging. Devotees of George W. Bush, Ronald Reagan, and Richard Nixon were as likely to be among the men at 80 who had aged most gracefully as men devoted to Bill Bradley, Gene McCarthy, and Adlai Stevenson. In short, longitudinal study revealed that conservatism is good when it preserves the environment and the past, conservatism is bad when it rigidly opposes healthy change, and political conservatism predicts nothing about the future but one's politics.

In spite of the fact that most of the Study members (like most readers) would have insisted that they were political independents, most were not. Most of the men in the Study clustered at the conservative or liberal poles of the political continuum rather than at the middle, and they had maintained those positions for fifty years. My grandfather was wrong, and Sir William Gilbert was right. In *Iolanthe* Gilbert wrote:

> *I often think it's comical*
> *How Nature always does contrive*
> *That every boy and every gal,*
> *That's born into the world alive,*
> *Is either a little liberal,*
> *Or else a little conservative!*

CHAPTER SIX

INTEGRITY: DEATH BE NOT PROUD

An aged man is but a paltry thing,
A tattered coat upon a stick, unless
Soul clap its hands and sing . . .

William Butler Yeats, *Sailing to Byzantium*

The mastery of Erik Erikson's final life task, Integrity, reflects our final effective reaction to change and to terminal disease, a process over which the elderly have increasingly little control. As already noted in chapter 2, the task of Integrity is the acceptance of one's one and only life cycle as something that had to be and that permits no substitutions. Ultimately, and most bluntly, successful aging means the mastery of decay. Thus, the task of Integrity forces us to reflect upon human dignity in the face of disability. Indeed, to achieve positive aging at the end of life necessitates an almost Buddhist acceptance. At the end of his life the great Swiss psychiatrist Carl Jung was said to have been asked by a journalist how he felt about growing old. "I am old," Jung replied, "so I be's old. I'm not a bloody American!" When I tried to explain Erikson's final life task to my 35-year-old son, he exclaimed, "Oh, I see; Integrity is next best to getting what you want!"

Examining the dynamics of very old age is like the inspection of an old, old tree. One can mourn the branches pruned by time that no longer are or one can admire the craggy simplicity that remains. Always there is the sense of omen, of terror if you will, of imminent mortality. Yet always — as in the case of the blasted oak — each spring new buds sprout; always, aging consists of development *and* decay. At least until death intervenes.

At age 78 a distinguished journalist and survivor of cancer and heart attack and stroke, Marvin Barrett, wrote,

> Old age is a plain, an *alto plano,* with nothing when you come out onto it but horizon; there are few discernible features, at least at first glance, no tracks to follow. Accustomed to limits, to guidelines, to markers, you stand there stunned, amazed. You haven't had such a sense of space since you were twenty — the splendor, the terror of it.[1]

In *The View from Eighty* Malcolm Cowley tried to fill in the landscape. He explains that a man knows he is old:

> When there are more and more little bottles in the medicine cabinet.
> When year by year his feet seem farther from his hands.
> When he falls asleep in the afternoon.
> When his bones ache.
> When he decides not to drive at night anymore.
> When, if you are wearing one brown and one black shoe, quite possibly there is a similar pair in the closet.[2]

Cowley balances this gloomy view with the words of Florida Scott-Maxwell, actress, housewife, author, and consulting psychologist. At 83, in *The Measure of My Days,* she reflected, "We who are old know that age is more than disability. It is an intense and varied experience, almost beyond our capacity at times, but something to be carried high. If it is a long defeat, it is also a victory. My seventies were interesting and purely serene, but my eighties are passionate. I grow more intense with age."[3]

•　　•　　•

A 78-year-old Terman woman, Agnes Eccles, explained to me that in the past three years she had been serially hospitalized for three blocked brachial (arm) arteries. In addition, she had undergone surgery for a broken hip and finally a total hip replacement, "These physical assaults left me disabled but not defeated. My accomplishments since then have been to stay alive and alert and to be thankful for all the blessings that have been mine."

When a recent questionnaire inquired about her aims for the future, instead of checking whether it was important for her to "die peacefully," she wrote beside that box, "Who has a choice? Death comes when it comes." Instead of checking whether it was important for her "to make a contribution to society," she wrote beside the box, "In a minor way I have already done so." Her past retained sufficient meaning for her so that she could accept the indignity of her failing body with equanimity. "Some of us are happy and content to sit and chew our cuds like so many Carnation cows. . . . Our ability to face up to situations and our capabilities of handling emergencies without panic may also be a gift not to be ignored."

Successful mastery of the task of Integrity is not always synonymous with having mastered all prior life tasks, but the study of lives suggests that such prior mastery helps. Positive aging must always reflect vital reaction to change, to disease, and to environmental imbalance. Positive aging is not simply avoidance of physical decay, and it certainly is not about the avoidance of death.

We asked the Harvard sample the following question: "We would be honored if you would share with us wisdom, rules of life, or "pearls" that you have gathered during your lifetime that might be valuable to the next generation." One Study member replied, "I think it is enormously important to the next generation that we be happy into old age — happy and confident — not necessarily that we are right but that it is wonderful to persist in our search for meaning and rectitude. Ultimately, that is our most valuable legacy — the conviction that life is and has been worthwhile right up to the limit."

But it is through their lives, not their words, that the old convey to the young the dignity of the last years of life. Terman woman Ellen Keller had asked that we come to her house at noon because it usually took her all morning to get out of bed and by midafternoon she was exhausted. Terminally ill from emphysema, Keller had been in the hospital at least once a year for the past ten years. In addition to her emphysema, for the last two years she had been chronically afflicted with shingles. Although she also suffered cataracts, the good news, so her doctor said, was she did not have enough time left to live to need to get them fixed. Ellen Keller's house looked more like an old cottage in England, both inside and out, than any California house we had seen. Sited on a very pretty street, it had a white picket fence, a richly blooming garden, and vines covering one wall. Everything within the house was more Victorian than Californian. Each object seemed attached to its own special memory.

Ellen Keller was the widow of a truck driver and the daughter of a small-town itinerant musician. She had a high forehead, a kind smile, and a stylish manner. What was most striking about Keller was her long, almost Bohemian, gray hair. Although her heavily creased face looked old, there was a girlishness about the way she wore her simple jersey, designer blue jeans, and gold jewelry. She was very slender, and had not forgotten how to play.

A monthly Social Security check for eight hundred fifty dollars and a small savings account now financed Keller's life. She had had to take out a second mortgage on her house. When it had become clear twenty years ago that her mentally retarded daughter would have to put her child in foster care, Ellen Keller and her husband had decided, "We would live out our life span to get our granddaughter started." They had carried out that responsibility for twenty years; and now as a reward her granddaughter's son "is the idol of my life." Ellen Keller's own son also telephoned her every night. She remained connected both to the past and to the future, even unto the fourth generation.

Ellen Keller did not get up until ten o'clock in the morning and was back in bed by five o'clock in the afternoon; her granddaughter would bring her supper. She said she was still able to can pears and to make applesauce. If she moved very slowly, she could still shop for herself; but she could not walk to a bus, use public transportation, climb stairs, or make her bed. Taking a shower was pretty difficult and so was getting dressed afterward. The double effort exhausted her breathing capacity. But what was really the hardest was not being in control. Knowing that loss of control was the curse of advanced old age, we asked how she coped. Keller explained that she had had to consciously acknowledge and grieve each loss of function. Then it was easier. To cope you have to connect the prose and the passion.

In the middle of her coffee table was an ashtray — a mute monument to her assassin. Ellen explained that she still could not leave cigarettes alone. She had started smoking in 1937 and had smoked a pack a day for the next half-century. Now, although her lung capacity was severely compromised, she still smoked eight cigarettes a day. She said she had twice tried hypnotherapy to stop smoking, but nothing had been successful.

Besides her girlishness, Keller's outstanding characteristic was her fragility. During the interview she clearly conserved her strength and moved very slowly. Her physical disability was obvious; I felt it would take only a slight breeze to kill her. Yet Ellen Keller still radiated not the brave smile of the martyr but the convincing, if wispy, laughter of a matriarch. If she was reluctantly on her deathbed, her sense of humor remained. She conveyed honesty, but not joy. She had patience, but not vigor. My wife and I were impressed by her likability, her simplicity, and, most of all, by her dignity. Integrity is next best to getting what you want.

Ellen Keller also illustrated acceptance of a late-life task perhaps more difficult for women to master than it is for men. Women must relearn how to be contented with the adolescent's focus upon the self rather than upon others.[4]

Although Ellen Keller alleged that she did not have much going on in her life, only the previous week she had gone with her granddaughter's friends to Candlestick Park to see the San Francisco Giants play baseball. Her granddaughter also had taken her to a street fair in Menlo Park. It was the first time she had been out in her new wheelchair.

Asked about her oldest friend, Keller described a woman with whom she had worked in the Fresno Department of Welfare. The friend now lived in Menlo Park, but her capacity to travel was also limited, so they talked by telephone. When asked whom she would be most willing to inconvenience, Keller said she belonged to a group of four widows "who hang together. We share each other's anniversaries." Keller had depended upon one of the widows to take her to the doctor to get her flu shot.

Reminiscing about death came easily to Ellen Keller. She recalled having been at her mother's bedside as she lay dying. Suddenly, she realized, "I was no longer the daughter, I was the mommy." Her husband's death had been more terrifying. She had protested to her therapist that she could not get over it, but her therapist said, "I could, and when she told me, 'We need you,' that was all the encouragement I needed." As a consequence Keller became involved in hospice work and "helping other people through their recovery from grief." Keller explained that she had spent a great deal of time with people who were dying. She hoped that in dying she would be able to be a role model to her own descendants. She accepted the fact that she was dying, "except sometimes I say, 'Shit, I want to be around a little longer.'" She also believed that somehow she would meet her husband again in heaven. "We don't go through all this to have it just all disappear." Knowing that you are dying does not preclude hope.

Keller regarded being accepted as a hospice counselor as "the high point of my life. . . . The wonderful thing about hospice work is you get so much more back than you give. . . . I've had so much love, there's no place for me to be poor." In her real life her statement was not quite true; for her life was constricted by poverty. But gratitude, like humor, is a wonderful antidote.

As an adolescent, sexual advances from her minister had left Ellen Keller horrified at the hypocrisy of organized religion.

Never again had she set foot in any church. Nevertheless, she asserted, "I know that the universe could not function without someone at the controls." From what wellspring did Ellen Keller's gratitude come? I must confess, I don't know. The origins of gratitude, of hope, and of the mature defenses like Professor Mark Stone's stoicism (suppression) and Keller's humor remain mysterious.

Keller's mood varied, but recently she had become more introspective and anxious. Yet, as we talked about death, she was able ever so gently to laugh at herself. With a smile she explained, "I'm losing ground fast, and there is still so much I want to do." Asked what her greatest legacy would be, Keller at first asserted that she didn't know. Then she mused, "It goes back to my family." Her legacy would be that her family had been loved and supported; she believed that she was leaving them with the feeling that they were cared about. She was able to articulate the burden that she was willing to put on her granddaughter without either seeming guilty or ignoring the fact that her demands were burdensome. She understood and accepted that even if she could no longer be of use to others, she was able to feel contentment. When you are dying, you do place a burden on others.

As Ellen Keller lay dying, six generations filled the room. A year ago her doctor had given her six months to two years to live. As a result, she was trying to get her life together "to make it easy for them when I go." Her room was filled with file boxes and photograph albums. This great-grandmother showed us the albums containing pictures of her mother and her mother's mother. She showed us a chess set that had come from India with her missionary grandparents and a chair that had been made when her mother was born — more than one hundred years ago. As we got ready to leave, Keller told us that she had prepared a living will and that her furniture was all labeled with which child and grandchild was going to get it.

At the end of the interview, my wife and I felt exhausted. Underneath Ellen Keller's great fragility lay very real depression that was contained, defended against, and perhaps even mastered. Her depression was real, but her deep acceptance of death did not allow it to interfere with the warm sunshine that bathed her English cottage. Little in her life had gone as she really would have wanted, but until recently she had given to the world more than she received. And she was not afraid.

•   •   •

When one is near death, the load has been lightened; beloved stamp collections are sold and the voices that once spoke with such authority are now gentled. In winter we let go not just to embrace immortality and to set foot on the other shore of the Styx. We let go to survive all the small deaths that go with aging. Gender is gone, and one is celibate not just because the body ceases to arouse and be aroused, not just from renunciation, but because the self is no longer "sticky." Perhaps this is a necessity to complete the task of Integrity. Thus, the image of the end of life should never be the derelict's hotel, but rather the dignified, if Spartan, cubicle of a monk, or perhaps Henry Emerson's corporate nerve center.

Henry Emerson was a craggy New Englander, born and bred in Concord, Massachusetts. He now lived in the northern California countryside but, "You can see the suburbs creeping in." Emerson began our interview by asking me if I wanted to conduct the interview in "the corporate nerve center." I said that would suit me just fine, and I followed him upstairs to his lair.

When I saw his office, I could not believe that he was not still actively consulting. The computer was on. The printer and the Xerox machine were humming. Postal scales, three kinds of tape, glue pots, sharpened pencils, and paper clips were in readiness. Three attractive file cabinets, two rolling files, and twenty bound loose-leaf notebooks conveyed the complexity of his "corporate" empire. Although Emerson talked with intimate give-and-take, his body language and the way he positioned us on the stage of his office made the interview unlike any other I have conducted. He acted as the president of a large, active company, and I was a visitor. Emerson sat behind his desk, leaned back in his executive chair, and had me sitting kitty-corner in a smaller chair. He was the CEO and I was some out-of-town drummer whom his imaginary secretary had ushered in. At the same time, the office was terribly simple and human. There was nothing pretentious. Indeed, we both knew that it was a stage set, a play office. The executive chair in which he leaned back was a simple, inexpensive model. His computer, so actively used, was ten years old. The carefully bound notebooks — all filled with important, relevant, practical details — concerned his family activities. Emerson was not a show-off. He just knew how to play; and, better yet, he let me join him. Harvard memorabilia, his sailing trophies, and the Napa meadows — all the things that he deeply loved — surrounded him. His face was bright and animated. He was having fun, and it was contagious. He was also dying from leukemia.

Emerson began by explaining why long ago he had stepped down as a senior executive at Hewlett-Packard. He told me that his task had been to supervise making components for NASA, but a company with better political connections beat them out for a business contract, and so he was deemed "redundant." For the next twenty years he had run his own small but successful consulting business. In retirement, however, his chief task at corporate headquarters was to help his wife do her work with the local Sierra Club, of which she was the chairman and he was "the gofer." He did analyses and background work, and he helped his wife out with things like hazardous waste allocation. He was "very proud" of his work with the Sierra Club. I could almost hear his father's New England twang acknowledging approval.

Henry Emerson had spent three days that summer sailing an obscure class of boats in San Francisco Bay. I asked him if he won, and he almost shouted, "George, don't ask that question!" Clearly, I had touched a nerve. The reality was that he had got off the starting line first; he had sped almost a mile ahead of the entire rest of the fleet. Then the wind vanished, and because he had felt weak from his leukemia he had gone below deck to rest. His son and first mate had thought that they could get the tide to take them to the finish line; instead, the tide swept them to one side so that officially "we did not finish." As he explained to me on more than one occasion during the interview, "If I had just tacked earlier, George, we would have won." It still burned him that the local newspaper had noted that they had been a mile ahead but lost. "The tides beat us, George; but I'm still growling at myself." He closed his confession with a contagiously funny "Thank you, Doctor, for relieving my soul." Emerson knew how to laugh at himself.

I could only sit back and marvel at this 76-year-old man. Despite severe asthma, devastating leukemia, and hands so arthritic that he could no longer write, Emerson had been out sailing competitively for a state trophy that he nearly won. Yet on two further occasions he referred to the race as if he could not come to complete peace with his physical limitations. He ranted and raved — albeit with humor — against the dying of the wind.

Henry Emerson still missed his old career, the crucial consultations, the problem solving, and the hurly-burly. He had loved being summoned and told that a company was in trouble. Then, after looking at the problem, he would return to the president and say, "This is what I think we should do." Afterward he loved having the president praise his good ideas. For Emerson loved winning; but always, like the generative coach that he was, he was helping someone else win.

For thirty years Emerson had been complaining to the Study about his work. As with his sailing he was brilliant at his job; but he did not always finish first. His complaining, however, seemed more that of an eternal competitor than true angst. He loved his work, but he hated losing. At 76 he could also look back on his career and say, "Every project I had was enjoyable." He was still hungry, but he was also grateful.

Twenty-five years before, I had written in my notes, "Emerson has an easy laugh, likable. I cannot convince myself that he is as depressed as he says he is. His smile is contagious and his self-criticism seems more like undoing [as in knocking on wood] than despair. But he is concerned with his image." In other words, even when Emerson was 47, he could complain and make his doctor like it.

In my 1997 interview I commented to him, "Henry, it looks to me as though you are having fun." He pounded his fist on the desk. "But the thing I wanted to do was manage people!" He had wanted to be a powerful CEO like his father, not just a caring doctor to sick companies. Nevertheless, he admitted, "In consulting I loved calling the shots. I loved interfacing with others." In other words, Emerson knew more about joy than happiness. In old age such a capacity becomes a valuable talent. When you are racked with arthritic pain and dying of leukemia, it is hard to be happy all the time — but joy, wonder, curiosity, and humor remain.

I asked Emerson what I asked every Harvard man, "What did you do the first six weeks of retirement?" Emerson replied that even though they occurred ten years ago, he could remember those six weeks very clearly. He recalled sitting at the breakfast table saying to his wife, "What do you say we sell the house and move to Napa." He spent the first six weeks of retirement marketing their San Francisco house and planning the wonderful renovations that they were about to make on their Napa Valley vacation home.

I asked him, besides the Sierra Club and sailing, what activities had been important since retirement. He said that he had won a trophy for fund-raising for a major California museum. There had been competition for the job. He had invited two colleagues to join his team because he could not afford to make the leadership gift, but he had done most of the work. "I have to boast. I put my heart and soul into it." He said he had made his final call at 10:00 P.M. on June 30, the last day of the drive. His performance was a landmark for museum fund-raising — not only locally but also for the entire state. It had taken two years of sustained effort — despite his leukemia. Again, he laughed at himself. "Thank you, Doctor, for letting me shoot off my mouth."

Having again knocked on wood, so to speak, Emerson went on to tell me that at the final banquet of the fund drive he had received a standing ovation, and "I thought to myself, 'Hey, Dad!'" (When his CEO father had retired, he, too, had become a trustee of the same museum.) He recalled all the cups his father had won for tennis. But I only had eyes for the top of Emerson's bookcase and the awards that he had won for museum fund-raising and for sailing with his children — even while doing battle with a fatal disease. Emerson always won his victories with and for others.

I asked Emerson what was the best part of retirement. Ignoring what he had just told me about making record-breaking late-night telephone calls, he replied, "Not having the stress on my back of 'Henry, you've got to perform.'" In addition, he had fallen in love with viniculture. His little Napa vineyard had become "my second girlfriend." You can lose at sailing and in business, but you can't lose at gardening. Last year with his vineyard Emerson had even finished $2,000 in the black. He showed me the notebooks where he kept the careful flow sheets that he had created on his aging computer. This was a corporate headquarters of which Bacchus, not Mammon, could approve. For Emerson, old age was simply a joyful way to play. True, he could not resist keeping score, but that was who he was.

I asked Emerson about the worst part of retirement. "Lack of being in charge," he blurted. And then there was his health. "I miss it. It's hard to have your wife so full of life and not be able to keep up." He had to spend 50 percent of every day taking care of his health. He had to undergo a blood transfusion every three weeks; and because his antibody production was impaired, any infection required immediate hospitalization. "It's been tough. I have to sleep twelve hours a night. It chews up the day."

Emerson had always been a gregarious, tennis-playing, skiing-and-sailing man of action. He had never learned to sunbathe, read novels, or listen to music. Suddenly, he was unable to do many of the things that had absorbed him in the past. "George, I have even lost all interest in travel." I asked him how he coped. He explained that he had spent a lot of time looking after his vineyard, playing with his computer in "corporate headquarters," running his modest portfolio, and feeling gratitude that he no longer had the financial pressures that had plagued him as a young man. He said up to this year he had also gotten pleasure out of teaching his children how to race sailboats. Up to last winter, his seventy-sixth year, he was still able to downhill ski. This weekend the Emersons were going up to the high Sierra to visit his oldest friend. The friend had a very primitive cabin on an island in an isolated lake with kerosene lamps and hand-pumped water from the lake.

Emerson also explained that to cope with leukemia he had gotten onto the World Wide Web and found a chat group on chronic lymphocytic leukemia. "Compared to them, my illness is peanuts!" Remember the wise young Edgar's advice to the old and foolish King Lear:

> When we our betters see bearing our woes,
> We scarcely think our miseries our foes . . .
> . . . the mind much sufferance doth o'erskip,
> When grief hath mates, and bearing fellowship.

At 76 Emerson had not only been able to find his way around the Internet — an ability to keep up with a changing world not yet achieved by his much younger interviewer — but he also used his adventurousness to find interpersonal comfort. In short, the seeds of love can be resown — even if you are housebound with leukemia and your Macintosh belongs in the Smithsonian.

The optimist in me argued that Emerson should let go of the future and live in the present, but Emerson insisted that he still wanted to build something to leave behind him. He still raged against the dying of the light. Piously, I asked him if he could not just be proud of the number of companies he had saved and the number of people he had helped grow through his consulting. Did he *have* to leave behind him some corporate equivalent of the pyramids of Egypt? He understood my point, but he gently suggested that I did not understand his. "George, I have this screw inside my head that went in wrong." By this he meant that he was still constantly striving to be like his father, the former CEO. Thirty years ago I had quoted him as agonizing that "my New England conscience is chewing great holes in me." Then, in my notes I had added, "A thoroughly successful, well-adapted guy who, because of his father's great success, saw himself as a failure." But now that his conscience had grown more lenient, Emerson was not just trying to hold on to past conflicts and past struggles as much as to model for me that to live life you have to keep on striving. The future still mattered. Besides, over the past twenty-five years Emerson had also learned how to laugh at himself. That made his screw a lot less painful.

One of the most charming aspects of the interview was watching Emerson with his wife. They were sweet as they played off each other. She was lively, energetic, and protective of him. He was tired, frail, and respectful of her. But they were a team. For our interview at "the corporate nerve center" she became the gofer. She brought us coffee and shortbread on a lovely tray.

I asked Emerson how he and his wife depended on each other — a standard question. "I am completely dependent on her," he replied. "She is superb at taking care of a crotchety husband." I had to remind him to answer how his wife depended on him. He said that he did the finances and that he still did most of the outdoor tasks. When they were younger, they had spent an enormous amount of time with the children; now they had grandchildren in the house three times a week. Two of his children lived nearby in Marin County, so that was easy. To my question about collaboration he replied, "I am her slave and gofer and flunky . . . and quite often her brains." His wife would go to the town meetings, would be the energetic mover and shaker. He would stay home and do the planning and the math. During the years of his consulting business, his wife had been *his* secretary. Always, always they had been a team. But part of aging well is being flexible enough to change positions.

Emerson experienced no difficulty telling me what he had learned from his children. He said he would start with his oldest daughter only to blurt out, "I can't come up with anything. She's a beautiful woman. I'll skip to Bill. I learned to climb El Capitan in Yosemite from that coot. I've learned you have to be sure of your facts. . . . I've learned a great deal from Tom. He lives on the property. He asked me about building a sailboat." He then described how he had given his son the money to build the boat. In the evening his son would come over with his evolving plans and ask his father what he thought. At first, it sounded to me as if Emerson was just telling me what his son had learned *from* him. Again, I had missed his point. What he had learned from Tom was the latter's skill in listening and in giving and taking. Emerson himself had always needed to be in charge and could not listen. Indeed, he suspected that his need to be in control had prevented him from becoming a successful manager. From his youngest daughter, Barbara, he told me, "I've learned what it means to be positive." It was true. Despite the fact that he was dying, our interview was more positive than the one twenty-five years ago when his physical ills were more imaginary than real.

I asked him to tell about his oldest friend. Without pause Emerson described George Davis, the fellow he was going to visit in the high Sierra. They had met after the war and had shared an apartment. Emerson had been the best man in his friend's wedding. Later, they skied together. Their children got on well, and fifty years later they were still close.

Emerson then started to reflect in a very interesting way upon the issues of aging. He had a remarkable skill of creating an engaging dialogue; perhaps a skill that had made him a good consultant. He did not mind growing old, but he told me that every six months he wanted to make "an explosion in the sky." He wanted to go on creating important products; for example, he wanted to write an essay perhaps every six months and have his wife tell him it was wonderful. Suddenly Henry Emerson stopped and exclaimed, "Here's what I'm talking about! I can go down and I can show you my great-great-uncle's clock." His friend, George Davis, it seemed, could do creative things with his hands and "make explosions in the sky. . . . He does it for others," Emerson explained. George Davis had recently refinished Emerson's grandfather clock face and its cabinet; and he had mended the works. After two hundred years the clock still worked, and it was again beautiful. The refinished clock was what Emerson meant by leaving something behind. Finally, I understood that his wish to create explosions in the sky was not an old man fretting about "some nagging unfinished business"; or, as the psychoanalyst in me had suspected, grieving past sexual potency. Rather, his need came from his unquenchable hope in the future — to keep beautiful clocks ticking into their third century. It was the same reason that a dying man's productive vineyard became his "second girlfriend."

At this point in the interview my feelings were mixed. On the one hand, Henry Emerson understood joy and had such a feeling for the creative potential of old age. He so beautifully understood that life was meant to be lived and savored. On the other hand, he had such trouble showing compassion toward himself. He still could not fully accept that he was who he was and shout, "To hell with the screw inside my head!"

I asked Emerson about shifts in his religious beliefs. He revealed that he had told a friend that he believed both in God and the hereafter. "She was surprised that someone as scientific as I would believe in life after death. It led to a good discussion. But I still feel concerned that I can't accept the miracles." Again, what impressed me about Emerson was his capacity to shift the conversation onto profound issues.

Yes, Emerson was a worrier, but he used his worry to get me involved in important existential issues. What was the value of prayer? Should he strive for continual happiness like his son or just for moments of joy? Is the task at the end of life to make explosions happen in the sky or is it a time when you should simply sit in your rocker and watch the grandchildren at play?

Emerson still complained, "My position as the leader of the family has changed. It bothers me." By this he meant that he was no longer the patriarch whom everybody consulted. So I asked him, is there not a time to be comforted by having passed the baton on to your children and letting them be in charge? No, Emerson disagreed. He was a terribly competitive man, but that made him a man with whom it was fun to have discussions. His complaining was not just kvetching; it initiated dialogue.

Henry Emerson ended our interview with "George, this has been a great help. It really has." Would I be willing to see him again in the future, he asked; and I replied, "Yes, gladly!" But we both knew that he would be dead before we could ever meet again.

Six months later I learned that Emerson had died, but he had been a good mentor to me, and he had sure squeezed that lemon.

●　　●　　●

Dr. Eric Carey was a member of the Harvard cohort who spent most of his life paralyzed from the waist down. Although he died young, he began life as a gregarious member of a close-knit and loving family. Both his parents were social workers in the spirit, if not the letter, of the term; and at 13 Eric, too, had made a commitment to a life of service to others. He collected a sense of himself early on, consolidated it, and shared it with discretion throughout his forty-five years in the Study. All life events — and this man faced severe setbacks — were moderated by his relationships with people, on both a personal and a professional level. He was never plagued by King Lear's narcissism and his life reminds us that successful aging means not dying last but living well.

At age 23, when asked about his "fitness for his present work" (medical school), Carey wrote, "Children fascinate me; I enjoy

playing and working with them. . . . I get along well with children, enjoy taking the time to amuse them or to circumvent their
distrust of doctors; . . . I'm patient enough to do with children
what many other people do not have time nor patience to do."
Eric already identified with the world view of a generative pediatrician twice his age.

Later, at age 26, when asked what was stimulating or interesting about his embryonic career, Eric Carey mentioned "the opportunity to provide aid to children through increasing parental
understanding." Even in medical school, he believed that the
meaning of his work was "to make a contribution to the community." He already saw himself living within a widening social
radius. Not only did Carey begin the work of Generativity at an
early age, but he began the work of growing old early as well. At
26, still in medical school, he had already explained to the Study
his philosophy over rough spots: "That no matter what personal
difficulty I struggle with, others have survived worse; and that,
fundamentally, there is a force of events which will carry us
through even though at personal sacrifice." At 26 Carey already
knew what Keller and Emerson discovered only at the end of
their lives.

Just after completing his pediatric residency, Dr. Carey developed poliomyelitis. Thus, he had become ill as well as wise before
his time. For months he was totally helpless. At age 33, newly liberated from six months in an iron lung and knowing he would
never walk again, this scion of social workers responded as follows to a Thematic Apperception Test (TAT) card — the card
that portrays a pensive youth contemplating a violin:

> We start with a young boy, who's been born into a family
> with, perhaps, talented musical parents. Their driving ambition
> from the start was the creation of musical talent in their child.
> We see him as the childhood result of his parents' ambition and
> the driving force that pervaded their life. His face suggests that
> perhaps as a result of illness or accident he has lost his eyesight.

There is a cast to his eyes; the way they are closed reminds you of . . . the classical lithograph of Beethoven after he lost his hearing. The child is still able to produce sounds of beauty from it [the violin]. He uses his fingers to . . . express his feelings and emotions.

To another TAT card, the paralyzed Carey responded:

Here is a young boy who . . . started out in college with brilliant prospects, a bright future but he becomes disillusioned with life, morose, and despondent . . . and decides to end his life. He is apprehended in the process of jumping from a tall building. As he does so, he closes his eyes. Before them flashes a panorama of his past life, hopes, aspirations, sadness, of failure. Realizing, then, the agony of being cornered . . . the despondency [leads him to wish] to end his own life. [Here is no Pollyana, for Dr. Carey was affectively conscious of the indignity and defeat of being confined to a wheelchair. But Carey continues the story.] He'll be examined by a psychiatrist and placed in a hospital for therapy. After months, his goals will be altered. After being in therapy a little longer, he'll get what he wants. He'll be able to be of use to society again, to go on to achieve that which . . . in later years will be satisfying.

By age 35, though crippled by polio, Eric Carey continued to be of use to society both as a pediatrician and as a teacher. For Carey already possessed the wise elder's concept of time: "This too shall pass." Although taken for granted by grandparents, such a concept is usually foreign to young adults. Carey was simply precocious. Dr. Carey wrote that the nurses and the medical students he taught "seem to respond to increased participation and responsibility, in contrast to the passive roles they often play in our clinics." His success as a teacher came from enabling others. His success came from, as it were, giving his self away.

Carey did not use successful teaching as an excuse to withdraw from being a full-time doctor. He shared with his patients the advantages of working as an active clinician from a wheel-chair: "Others can get not only professional help but some measure of comfort from my carrying on as if nothing had hap-pened."

Mentorship and wisdom mean to show and to share, not merely to tell. One of the tasks of a Keeper of the Meaning is to convey to the young that old age is meaningful and dignified.

Twenty years later the progressively more crippled Eric Carey again articulated the challenge and the pain usually felt only in advanced old age: "The frustration of seeing what needs to be done and how to do it but being unable to carry it out because of physical limitations imposed by bedsores on top of paraplegia has been one of the daily pervading problems of my life in the last four years." But three years later, at age 55, he answered his own challenge: "I have coped . . . by limiting my activities (occupa-tional and social) to the essential ones and the ones that are within the scope of my abilities." Eric Carey was *ill* for half of his life; he was *sick* for very little of it — a distinction I shall expand upon in the next chapter.

At 57, although he was slowly dying from pulmonary failure secondary to his twenty-five years of muscular paralysis, Dr. Carey told the Study that the last five years had been the happiest of his life: "I came to a new sense of fruition and peace with self, wife, and children." He spoke of peace, and his actions portrayed it. During this time, like Anthony Pirelli with his stamps in chap-ter 1, Carey had let go of the coin collection that had absorbed him for half a century; he gave it to his son. He understood that, whenever possible, legacies should be bestowed before, not after, death. Besides, please note that Carey, close to death, described his ebbing life as providing "a new sense of fruition," a term pregnant with connotations.

At age 62, a year before his death, in describing to an inter-viewer his risky anesthesia and recent operation, Dr. Carey re-marked, "Every group gives percentages for people who will die: one out of three will get cancer, one out of five will get heart disease, but in reality one out of one will die. Everybody is mortal." Although still only middle-aged, he fully accepted that there is a time to be born and a time to die. As the prematurely wise Edgar counseled King Lear: "Men must endure/Their going hence, even as their coming hither: Ripeness is all."

At age 32 Carey had written of his work motivations: "To add an iota to pediatric knowledge, the sum totals of which may ultimately aid more than the patients I see personally." But it takes a longitudinal study to differentiate between a person's real-life behavior and his facility with pencil-and-paper tests. That Carey's words were not pious good intentions but rather intimations of immortality was confirmed by prospective investigation, by what actually happened after he died. An endowment for a professorship in Carey's name was raised to perpetuate his lifelong contribution to pediatrics. Throughout his life his wife, his children, his colleagues, and his patients had loved him. Now, his professorship lives on. Often the legacy that we leave to the next generation does not rest in the ink of our last testaments but in the strength, sweat, and hope invested in our lives. Carey, too, had sure squeezed that lemon. An independent observer gave Carey 13 out of 14 points for graceful aging. (See Appendix K.) It did not matter that he had died young.

·   ·   ·

Nonetheless, the debate over what it means to age will continue. How shall we regard that last painful year of life? To which middle-aged sage shall we listen? Shall we be lulled by Victor Hugo with his Browningesque optimistic vision of old age? "For the young man is handsome but the old superb. . . . And fire is seen in the eyes of the young, but it is light that we see in the old man's eyes."[5] Or should we trust the usually humane and empathic Charles Dickens when he dismisses old age as but a "horrible and convulsive imitation" of childhood,[6] a sentiment that echoed Shakespeare's view of extreme old age as "mere oblivion, . . . sans everything."

I think to unravel such a conflict we need once more to es-
chew 50-year-old poets and turn to those who in real time have
captured the last months of their lives. Hans Zinsser was such a
poet. Alas, he was not a member of the Study of Adult Development, but he defined the task Integrity better than anyone I
know. The author of *Rats, Lice and History,* Zinsser was also a
pioneer of public health, a warrior against infectious disease,
and a beloved Harvard professor. Like Henry Emerson, Professor
Zinsser found himself dying of leukemia. He looked back; he
reflected about what he had done; and he wrote his autobio-
graphy in the third person, calling himself R. S. He, too, observed that he had "sure squeezed that lemon" and he saw himself
content.

It seemed, he said from that moment, as though all that his
heart felt and his senses perceived were taking on a "deep au-
tumnal tone" and an increased vividness. From now on, instead
of being saddened, he found — to his own delighted astonishment — that his sensitiveness to the simplest experiences, even
for things that in other years he might hardly have noticed,
was infinitely enhanced. . . . "Here am I — essentially unchanged
except for a sort of distillation into a more concentrated me —
held in a damaged body which will extinguish me with it when
it dies . . . my mind and my spirit, my thoughts and my love, all
that I really am, is inseparably tied up with the failing capacities
of these outworn organs.

"Yet," he continued, apostrophizing in a serio-comic mood,
"poor viscera, I can hardly blame you! You have done your best,
and have served me better than could be expected of organs so
abused. When I think of the things that have flowed over and
through you! Innumerable varieties of fermented hops and malt
and of the grapes of all countries and climates: Vouvray, Anjou,
Chablis, Hautes Sauternes, Chambertin, Nuits-Saint-Georges,
Riesling, Lachryma Christi, Johannisthaler, Berncastler, Saint-
Julien, Clos de Mouche, Leibfrauenmilch; endless amounts of
pinard and *vin du pays.* . . . No, no, my organs! I cannot feel that
you have let me down. It is quite the other way round. Only

now it seems so silly that you must take me with you when I am just beginning to get dry behind the ears."

Unlike King Lear, Hans Zinsser did not view himself as sinned against. If there was betrayal in the aging process, he blamed neither God nor his organs. It had been his life, and he took full responsibility, and so he could express gratitude.

As his disease caught up with him, R. S. felt increasingly grateful for the fact that death was coming to him with due warning, and gradually. . . . He set down this feeling in his last sonnet:

> *Nor does he [death] leap upon me unaware*
> *Like some wild beast that hungers for its prey,*
> *But gives me kindly warning to prepare:*
> *Before I go, to kiss your tears away. . . .*
> *How sweet the summer! And the autumn shone*
> *Late warmth within our hearts as in the sky,*
> *Ripening rich harvests that our love had sown.*
> *How good that 'ere the winter comes, I die!*
> *Then, ageless, in your heart I'll come to rest*
> *Serene and proud, as when you loved me best.*[7]

Sophocles, a master of paradox, was another poet who had been there. Even older than Zinsser, he models for us the paradox of successful aging: both in his tragedy *Oedipus at Colonus* and in how he, in the real world, lived out his final days.

Legend has it that the 89-year-old playwright was accused by his son, Iophon, of being too senile for his last will and testament to be regarded valid. In his defense, Sophocles asked to recite a few pages from his work in progress, *Oedipus at Colonus*. Astonished by the brilliance of his great play that captured both the transience and the eternity of human life, the Athenian jury unanimously pronounced him mentally competent.

The more verifiable facts are that Sophocles' brilliant "old man's play" was indeed written at the end of his ninth decade and, more important, that the posthumously produced *Oedipus at Colonus* continues after two and a half millennia to rank with the great tragedies of all time. If nothing else, his play is proof that great poets can continue to create not only after 40 but after 85! And that like winter gardens, after death, we can live on — if only in another's heart as when they loved us best.

In Oedipus Sophocles created an Everyman, an Everyman who sightless and destitute grows and achieves significance before our awestruck seeing eyes. The play challenges our assumption that old age is unredeemed misery and suggests instead that aging has positive value. Perhaps, the unwillingness of Sophocles to conform to that assumption is yet another index of his heroism and his greatness at the end of life.

Sophocles sets his tragedy in a garden — in a sacred grove of vines and olive trees in which nightingales sang. Oedipus, a wretched, exiled beggar without sight, turns to acknowledge to his daughter the fate of a man near death, the fate of a garden prepared for the winter. "I ask for next to nothing and will take less than that as more than enough,"[8] and, later to his daughter directly, "Now that I have and hold what is most dear to me, I am not afraid to die."[9]

But the chorus views old age as do Shakespeare and Dickens; they perceive Oedipus as a miserable specimen of "ruined old age, weak and alone, much despised, with pain as your only friend. This bitter old man is battered down."[10] But already Oedipus has revealed to Theseus, noble king of Athens, his extraordinary offer. "I want to offer you a gift. I offer myself in all my ugliness with a promise of good things to come."[11] Oedipus bids good-bye to his daughters. "This is the day of my death. All things have come to this end and you'll never have to care for me again. It was never an easy task, I know, and now one word, love, will set you free. . . ."[12] After Oedipus has left to seek his final resting place, his daughter Antigone explains to the astonished chorus that her father is "Gone as any of us would wish to go.

Neither the Gods of war nor of the sea took him away, but something else inexplicable, ineffable, wholly mysterious"; and at death Sophocles depicts Oedipus as being "without groans, nor racked with pains, but, if ever mortal was, wonderful."[13]

And so for Doctor Eric Carey, for Professor Hans Zinsser, for King Oedipus, and for the poet Sophocles, death — as is true for winter gardens — was not only an end but a beginning.

CHAPTER SEVEN

HEALTHY AGING:
A SECOND PASS

Adding life to years; not just more years to life.
Motto: American Gerontological Society, 1955

The exercise of our unique human capacity for mindful control is key to vital age versus decline.
Betty Friedan, *The Fountain of Age*

In chapter 1, in my first definition of positive aging, I spoke of joy, of love, and of learning something that we did not know yesterday. I ignored the more mundane but absolutely crucial topic of staying alive. The more recent chapters have addressed some of the developmental steps needed to negotiate the minefield of psychosocial aging. But I must not avoid addressing the minefield of physical survival. True, chapter 6 reminded us that the death rate will always be one per person, but like Sophocles we want to die at our appointed time, not prematurely. In old age death and disability are not just part of "normal" adult development to be valiantly accepted. Often, death and disability are anything but normal and should be avoided like the plague.

Successful aging, then, involves maintaining not just social and emotional health but also physical health. In this chapter I shall use harder data and focus more on what we can do in order to remain physically healthy into our 80s. But to keep both body and psyche in mind is not easy. My discussion is complex and may require patience on the reader's part. Absorbing this chapter may be a bit like rubbing your stomach and patting your head at the same time.

But even to talk about "healthy aging" is precarious. Is not the whole concept of healthy aging merely woolly idealism? Is not trying to define health as foolhardy as trying to define intelligence? Is not successful aging much too complicated, too context dependent, too subjective and value ridden to assess?

I strongly disagree. Good health, both psychological and physical, is a very real and very tangible boon. But the measurement of good health is by no means easy. Two men have colostomies: for one man it is only a minor inconvenience; for the other it is a devastating blow to self-image. Why? Is arthritis more disabling than alcoholism; is depression more disabling than diabetes? If so, why? At age 75 would you rather be able still to play eighteen holes of golf under 90 but have no one to play golf with, or would you rather still have a beloved golfing companion but be able to play only nine holes in chronic pain — and with a handicap the size of the national debt? Old age is rarely getting exactly what you want; and thus, the definition of healthy aging will be by no means simple.

The Definition of Healthy Aging

In this chapter I shall measure successful aging by assessing health — physical health, psychosocial health, death. Death, of course, is the easiest to measure. Physical health is the next easiest but still complex. For sustained activity is very different from longevity but equally desirable. With the passage of time progressively diminished physical reserves are an inevitable part of aging; but, of course, the rate at which these diminished reserves occur is variable.

Biologically, one can be young or old for one's chronological age. Physical health also involves experiencing the biological ravages of age without feeling "sick." Good self-care, high morale, intimate friends, and mental health often make the difference between being "ill" and feeling "sick."

Measuring psychosocial health is a more difficult but equally important task. At age 90 some people are not only active and still climb mountains, but they are able to do so in good cheer and with close friends. That is even more desirable. Healthy aging, then, is being both contented *and* vigorous as well as being not sad or sick or dead.

We need to understand positive health so much better than we do. What a world of difference there is between being ill in the eyes of your doctor and feeling sick when you get out of bed to face the day. In 1948 the founders of the World Health Organization (WHO) defined health as "physical, mental and social well-being, not merely the absence of disease or infirmity."[1] John Kennedy and Dwight Eisenhower both suffered illnesses that would have merited a 100 percent disability from the Veterans Administration; but nobody, including themselves, as they resiliently bore the burden of the presidency, would have called them sick. For thirteen years the crippled President Roosevelt was a vigorous and cheerful president; yet some people half his age and in far better health spend most of their time unhappily in bed. Clearly, subjective health is as important to aging as objective physical health.

First, I shall try to *show* good health and bad health. Only then will I try to *tell* how I measured it. I shall contrast a contented, well man at 75 who epitomized the Happy-Well with a sad, sick, and eventually dead man. As the life stories of Alfred Paine and Richard Lucky unfold, I hope that the concepts of Happy-Well and Sad-Sick become clear in the reader's mind.

Alfred Paine was a model of the Sad-Sick. His greatest strength was that he did not complain. He did not acknowledge either his alcoholism or his depression. Like Pollyanna and Voltaire's Dr. Pangloss and *Mad* magazine's Alfred E. Neuman, Paine was a master of denial. On questionnaires, he described himself as close to his children and in quite good physical health. It was only by interviewing him personally, talking with his wife, examining his medical record, reading the questionnaires from his disappointed children — and then, finally, by reading his obituary — that Alfred Paine's misery could be fully appreciated. The uncomplaining nature of Paine's replies did not alter the fact that his life story had always been terribly sad.

The ancestors of Alfred Paine had been successful New England clipper ship captains. All his grandparents had graduated from high school. One grandfather became a merchant banker and the other a president of the New York Stock Exchange. His father had graduated from Harvard and his mother from a fashionable boarding school. From childhood on, however, Paine was the unlucky owner of a handsome trust fund — unlucky because of how he obtained it. When Alfred Paine was only two weeks old, his mother died of complications of childbirth. When he was only two years old, his father died too.

So it was that the orphaned Paine became an heir. As an only child, Paine was bottle-fed by a variety of surrogates and raised by his grandmother and aunt. They were old and did not enjoy the challenge of dealing with an energetic young boy who was also a head-banger. In adolescence Paine was a "lone wolf."

In college Alfred Paine was often in love. But it appeared to the Study staff that for Paine being in love meant having someone to care for him. His multiple marriages were all unhappy — in part, because of the alcoholism that he maintained that he did not have, and in part because he was frightened of intimacy. At 50 Paine answered "true" to the statements "Sexually most people are animals" and "I would have preferred an asexual marriage." But he did not complain. Thus, of his second marriage he could write, "I have doubts about the real value of marriage. . . . The state of my own marriage, which is excellent, has nothing to do with my philosophizing." But his "excellent" marriage soon ended in divorce.

At 47 Alfred Paine recalled the ages from 1 to 13 as the unhappiest in his life. At age 70 Paine changed his story and believed that the ages from 20 to 30 were the unhappiest. But there had never been a time that Paine was happy. It was only that Paine, as I have suggested, was not a complainer. For example, on a pencil-

and-paper test of depression, Paine had one of the lowest scores in the Study. He had never sought psychotherapy, and none of his doctors ever called him mentally ill.

On pencil-and-paper questionnaires Paine also described his own physical health as "excellent"; but, in fact, by age 68 he was seriously overweight, afflicted by hypertension and gout, and suffering from obstructive pulmonary disease — the result of life-long smoking. Objectively, his health was anything but "excellent." When Paine was 50, his wife called me a "Nazi doctor" over the telephone because I had noted his alcoholism but did not intervene. In contrast, Paine did not complain. Instead, he protested, "How can I be an alcoholic; I never missed a day of work?"

By age 70 gallstones and an ileostomy for diverticulitis of the colon had been added to Paine's objective medical woes. At interview when he was 73, Paine appeared to me like an old man in a nursing home. He had lost all his teeth, both his kidneys and his liver were failing, and he was cursed with a mild dementia, the result of a drunken automobile accident. He was at least thirty pounds overweight and looked ten years older than his age. There was no question that he was physically disabled.

Although he had made a good living in middle management over the years, Paine's handsome trust fund had evaporated and his pension had eroded through multiple divorces and tax troubles. His house looked as though it had been furnished from yard sales. The only exception was the elegant Cantonese porcelain umbrella stand that stood guard by the front door in mute testimony to the fact that his New England ancestors had waxed rich in the China clipper trade. Little other than television now absorbed Paine. He rarely left his sofa. But he did not complain.

Alone of all the men who returned the age-75 questionnaire, Paine refused to answer the part that dealt with life enjoyment. Thus, his subjective lack of joy in life had to be inferred from his behavior. Over the past twenty years there was no area of his life other than his religious activities in which he had expressed satisfaction. Admittedly, in questionnaires he said nice things about his children, but during the interview when I asked him what he had learned from them, he responded irritably, "Nothing. I hardly see my children. They hardly let me see my grandchildren." Turning to questionnaires from his children, one daughter saw him only every three years; one daughter saw him once a year and viewed her father as having "lived an emotionally starved life," and at age 35 Alfred Paine's only son believed that he had never been close to his father.

In terms of social supports Paine, orphaned by 2, had no siblings; and he was close to no relative. Since he had been 50, he had engaged in no pastimes with friends. When I asked him at 73 to describe his oldest friend, he growled, "I don't have any." He rarely talked to anybody on the telephone. His only confidante was, occasionally, his wife. Only Paine's religious affiliation was strong. He was proud that he was a committed Episcopalian, and he went on religious retreats, which brought him real satisfaction. Sadly, although these retreats reflected the only social network he possessed, after age 72 he could no longer afford to go on them. Paine could not care for his teeth, his money, or his soul. But he did not complain.

At age 73 Paine could climb stairs only with effort. He had great difficulty walking even 100 yards, he was unable to drive at night, and he had had to give up golf because of his gout. On his last questionnaire, in a shaky hand, Paine, age 75, referred to his general health as "very good" and reported that he had no difficulty in physical activities. Both his wife and his doctor, however, saw him as seriously impaired. The very next year Paine was placed in a nursing home; a year later he died from his multiple illnesses. For research purposes, Paine was classified with the Sad-Sick rather than with the Prematurely Dead because he survived past his 75th birthday. More about this scheme of classification will follow.

As the lives of the Inner City men brought home again and again, it is poverty in love, not poverty in dollars, that makes all the difference in old age. Access to expensive private dentists was for naught if Alfred Paine did not visit them — if he did not complain. Nor does it help to be loved if you do not take the love inside. In his old age Paine's third wife was protective and loving toward him. In return, he was quite disrespectful and uncaring toward her. Before he died, I had asked how Paine and his wife collaborated; he replied, "We don't. We lead parallel lives."

Similarly, in a study of centenarians a 101-year-old man explained to his interviewer, "The goal, when you're older, is to keep family close . . . to be independent but to have them for help. As you get older, you need people, not dollars and cents."[2]

• • •

Richard Lucky was a different kettle of fish entirely. Richard Lucky was a well-loved child who took excellent care of himself. I am sure that he flossed his teeth. Unlike Alfred Paine, Lucky had come from more modest beginnings. None of his four grandparents had gone beyond grade school. One grandfather had been a police officer and the other a self-made owner of a large baking company. His father graduated from high school and went on to become a successful businessman so that Richard Lucky, like Alfred Paine, had gone to an excellent private prep school. After college Lucky became head of two successful businesses (one of which he created) at the same time. Always careful to take care of himself, Lucky married well. Unlike Paine, he knew how to take care of his money, how to appreciate his wife, and how to make his own luck.

At 70, when looked at through the eyes of their internists, Richard Lucky's objective physical health had seemed actually worse than Alfred Paine's. Lucky had high blood pressure, atrial fibrillation, a cardiac pacemaker, pancreatitis, and was "status post back surgery." He was even more overweight than Paine. On the basis of all this the Study internist classified the 70-year-old Lucky disabled. But if Lucky was ill, he certainly did not feel sick. Truth is revealed through follow-up. Over the next ten years Paine sickened unto death, and Lucky's health got steadily better.

Thus, by 76 Richard Lucky's objective health was no longer classified by the study internist as disabling. He had completely recovered from his pancreatitis. His undated back surgery, which loomed so ominously to the Study internist when Lucky was 70, turned out to have been thirty years in the past; and at age 76 Lucky had just spent two months downhill skiing in Vail. True, he still wore a pacemaker, and, true, his blood pressure remained high. But in his doctor's words — not just his own — "Mr. Lucky continues to enjoy relatively good health. . . . He continues to be active physically and also mentally. He is now writing a book on the Civil War." As Lucky himself expressed it, "I have done less chain sawing, but I still split wood." And I am sure when he needed his wife to do something, he complained.

Another crucial difference between Paine and Lucky was that Lucky had friends with whom he exercised regularly. In addition, he had never smoked, and he used alcohol in moderation. But, of course, it is easier to "button up your overcoat" and "take good care of yourself" if, indeed, you do belong to someone.

At the risk of oversimplification, Richard Lucky's mother had loved him as a child, and a half-century later, "Almost everything we do," he trumpeted, "is family oriented. We have practically no social calendar." His wife amplified. "We rarely go out, but we will have groups for supper such as the church fellowship group or the basketball team for a weekend of skiing, or a vestry meeting at the house." Without a social calendar Lucky was also commodore of his distinguished West Coast yacht club. Actions speak louder than pencil-and-paper questionnaires.

In its efforts to define successful aging, the Study asked each man to describe his relative satisfaction over the past twenty years with eight different facets of living (see Appendix I). Remember, Alfred Paine had chosen to leave that part of his questionnaire blank. In contrast, Richard Lucky described not only his hobbies, his religion, and his income-producing work as "very satisfying," but, more important, he experienced his relationships with his wife and with his children as "very satisfying." His wife and children's questionnaires revealed a similar satisfaction with him. Lucky's daughter had described her parent's marriage as "better than my friends'"; then, for good measure, she had added two pluses. Lucky's wife gave her marriage a "9 out of 9," and clearly, the marriage had worked even better for her husband. Lucky was close to his brother, with whom he skied regularly in the winter and fished regularly in the summer. He stayed in very close touch with and took great pleasure from his children and his grandchildren. His recreational activities included active involvement not only with his brother and children but also with the other sailors of his yacht squadron. Subjectively, Lucky perceived himself with relatively few close friends and would have liked more. Objectively, his friendship network was very rich. Paradoxically, socially isolated men often reported that they were satisfied with their sparse social network. The well loved wished for even more.

At 45 Lucky told the Study, "Tahoe is my retirement plan. I'll just draw a salary [from the resort he had created there] and spend my time skiing." At 55 he wrote, "Death is of course closer, but I don't fear death because I believe in God and afterlife. . . . I believe in physical fitness. I think many emotional problems that I encounter in others would disappear if they took better care of themselves." So easy to say, but so difficult to do if someone has not taken care of you first. Social scientists sometimes express contempt for "muscular Christians" like Lucky; but as I have noted, social scientists are much better at identifying mental illness than mental health.

Perhaps it was not coincidence that both Lucky and his wife were youngest children from very happy families. Lucky saw both his past and his present as rewarding. When he was 60, he wrote the Study of his father, who had died twenty years before, "I have never completely gotten over Dad's death. I will always remember him as the finest man I ever knew." It was so easy for Lucky to take in, to "metabolize," any love that he was offered.

Despite a family income of perhaps $500,000 a year, Lucky's wife at 75 still mowed the family grass and shoveled her horse's manure. Indeed, I met Mrs. Lucky as she was coming out of the barn carrying a stepladder, dressed in blue jeans and work boots. Yet two hours later, at the end of our interview, now elegantly dressed, she brought us coffee on good breakfast china and the best homemade chocolate chip cookies I have ever tasted. Wondering how the Luckys still played together while the Paines led "parallel lives," I asked how his marriage had lasted for forty years. With Churchillian simplicity Lucky replied, "I really love Chrissie and she loves me. I really respect her, highly esteem her, and she is a real person." Enough said.

The demanding Lucky may not have always been easy to live with, but he was a good playmate. At 70 Lucky wrote to the Study, "I am living in the present — enjoying life and good health while it lasts. I think very little about the past or future and don't take myself very seriously." That same year, he and his wife had sailed by themselves from San Francisco to Bali. The trip led to many months of close cooperation and shared physical labor. On the journey Lucky illustrated his sailing journal with his own watercolors. For Lucky creativity and play went hand in hand — a valuable lesson for retirement.

Admittedly, part of Lucky's enjoyment in marriage depended on what he referred to as his wife's "diplomacy . . . she appears to yield to my stubbornness." Yet on her questionnaire Chrissie wrote the Study, "My husband is my best friend; I like looking after him. We have grown closer and fonder every year." Asked about retirement Richard Lucky replied, "I think it is all pretty nice. I don't have a day when I don't have something to do that I want to do. . . . Creativity is absolutely necessary for someone to be healthy." He focused on his watercolors, which were really very good, but he had also built his studio with his own hands. Ten years before, at 67, with no more intelligence than Paine, Lucky told the Study that he had "just finished a screenplay and sent it to a literary agent." No, it was never performed, and to my knowledge his book on the Civil War was never published, but he loved creating. Besides, he had just put on a solo exhibition of his marine watercolors. "With painting," he added dreamily, "you forget everything, and that is why it is so very relaxing." In church Lucky sang both solo and in the choir.

I asked Lucky if he had taken any painting lessons, and he replied gruffly, "You don't learn to paint like this by just hacking around." The reality was that an instructor in Lucky's ski school had become a close friend and had taught his boss painting. (Although Lucky complained that he didn't have many friends, his friends kept cropping up during our interview.)

At the end of life Lucky was not involved just with play and creativity. In addition, at age 75 with an indifferent college scholastic record, he was making a serious effort to master the technology of the Monterey Oceanographic Research Institute, of which he had become a trustee. He was still busy learning new things.

Although one of Lucky's remaining life goals was "to equip myself well and to show my family (as my father showed us) how to die," he had already achieved immortality of sorts. For it was not his music, his writing, or his paintings of which Richard Lucky was most proud. His pride lay in the fact that in the 1960s he had made a lasting contribution by developing skiing in the high Sierra. (Admittedly, Henry Emerson's Sierra Club might beg to differ. But as I have already suggested, successful aging is not about politics.) Long after Lucky is no longer alive, happy skiers will still enjoy skiing down his Tahoe trails — even members of the Sierra Club.

* * *

Some of Lucky's satisfaction and some of Paine's angst came from the fact that in retirement the former had an income twenty times that of the latter. But it was Paine who had had ancestors in the clipper ship trade. It was Paine who came into this world with a handsome trust fund. Rather, the keys to successful aging are in self-care and love, not money. Admittedly, if you know how to build love, sometimes the money will come. And for both the Inner City men and the Harvard men the best predictor of a high income was not their parents' social class but whether their mother had made them feel loved.

Distinguishing the Happy-Well from the Sad-Sick and the Prematurely Dead

Healthy aging is multifaceted, and subject to both the observer's and the culture's distortion. At any single point in time, assessment of healthy aging will be as subjective as the Study internist's wrong deduction about the implications of Richard Lucky's back surgery. In addition, I am as susceptible to halo effects and am as easily conned as the next person. Since all this is true, to assess healthy aging I have depended upon multiple ratings gathered by several independent raters. (Since serial physical exams were not available for the Terman women, I shall focus on the two male cohorts.)

To increase the chances of successful contrast and to minimize value judgment, I shall focus on men at the ends of the health spectrum. I shall contrast the one-fourth of the Harvard men who lived out their eighth decade feeling the healthiest — the Happy-Well, of whom Richard Lucky was a prime example — with the one-half of the men who like Alfred Paine spent most of their eighth decade either feeling sad and sick or were dead. To reduce argument, I shall deliberately exclude the one man in four who fell somewhere in the gray zone of being either healthy or sick depending on the criteria chosen. In short, three-quarters of the men will reflect black-and-white categories of aging — the Happy-Well, the Sad-Sick, and the Prematurely Dead; and one-quarter, the partly healthy and the partly sick, will be excluded.

I followed the same procedure for classifying healthy aging among the Inner City men. Although they were ten years younger than the Harvard men, their objectively rated health (i.e., the proportion physically well, chronically ill, disabled or dead) at 70 was the same as that of the Harvard men and the Terman women at 80.

To differentiate the Happy-Well unambiguously from the Sad-Sick between ages 60 and 80, I have chosen six contrasting dimensions of health.[3]

1. Absence of objective physical disability at age 75 (Harvard cohort) or at age 65 (Inner City cohort):

Every five years, the Study sought from each Harvard and Inner City man a complete physical exam, including chest x-rays, routine blood chemistries, urinalysis, and an electrocardiogram. A Study internist, blind to psychosocial adjustment, then rated all of these physical examinations on a four-point scale. He rated the men as "1" if they were still without any irreversible illness; and "2" if they were afflicted with an irreversible illness that was neither life-shortening nor disabling. Such illnesses might be mild glaucoma, treatable hypertension, or noncrippling arthritis. If in the judgment of the Study internist the College men suffered from an irreversible life-threatening illness, they were called "3," or chronically ill. This category refers to illnesses that could be expected to be progressive and to shorten life or eventually to affect daily living, but which were not in the eyes of the Study internist disabling. Examples of such illnesses are coronary thrombosis, or diabetes or hypertension not fully controlled by medication.

Finally, the internist rated the men "4" if they suffered both irreversible illness and, in his judgment, significant disability. Examples would be multiple sclerosis, chronic congestive heart failure, and disabling arthritis of the hip. Only this category, "4," reflected unhealthy aging. The men, after all, were 75 to 85 years old and could be expected to have some illnesses.

2. Subjective physical health at age 75 (Harvard cohort) or at age 65 (Inner City cohort):

Since human beings are remarkably adaptable and suggestible, physical disability is in part subjective. When asked to rate their health subjectively, a depressed man may whine that his health is bad even when it is quite good; and a happy stoical woman may believe that her health is excellent when in fact it is objectively poor. Still others, like Paine, were rated objectively *disabled* by their physicians and denied subjective disability not from stoicism but by dissociating themselves from reality. The most common ailments of men and women who saw themselves as *disabled* but who were called *not* disabled by the Study physician were arthritis and depression. Health is anything but black or white.

The rating for this second dimension of successful aging was subjective and was based on a 15-point scale of self-reported "Instrumental Activities of Daily Living" (see Appendix F). At 75 some men believed that they could still carry out most daily tasks as before. Such men reported that they still took part in activities like tennis singles, downhill skiing, and chopping wood. They could climb two flights of stairs without resting, carry their suitcases through airports, and walk two miles with their grandchildren, albeit they might perform all of these tasks more slowly than in the past. Finally, they could still drive, care for the yard, travel, and shop without assistance. Other men viewed their daily lives as hampered by physical ills.

Obviously, physical disability also involves areas like mental competence, personal decision making, and balancing checkbooks. These skills are lost to individuals afflicted with strokes and with Alzheimer's disease. However, since such individuals in our Study also felt unable to carry out the physical tasks listed above, mental competence was not included in our assessment of subjective disability. In this Study, the men who remained physically active at age 75, like Richard Lucky, were still in control of their mental faculties.

3. Length of undisabled life:

But what if a man was vigorously active for seventy-nine years and then suffered an incapacitating stroke one week before his 80th birthday? Should he be regarded less healthy than another man, still objectively healthy at 80 but who for the last twenty years has felt unable to play golf, weed his garden, or drive at night? Thus, I have added a third dimension to my definition of healthy physical aging: how many years of living did the men lose by subjective and/or by objective physical disability or from premature death. By definition none of the Happy-Well had spent any time before age 80 disabled — either objectively or subjectively. By way of contrast, before age 80 the Prematurely Dead (those men dying between age 50 and 75) had spent an average of eighteen years either dead or disabled. Before age 80 the Sad-Sick had all spent at least five and an average of nine years irreversibly disabled. (Richard Lucky's brief period when his physicians thought him disabled did not count — because he got over it.) As I have already acknowledged, the measurement of health is not simple.

Because some of the Harvard men are not yet 80, a man needed to survive happily only past his 75th birthday in order to be classified as Happy-Well at 80. But only 1 of the 62 Happy-Well died between 75 and 80; and proportionally ten times as many of the 40 Sad-Sick men died during that period. Alfred Paine was such an example.

4. Objective mental health:

But there is not much fun in living to old age if you are unhappy. So a fourth dimension of healthy aging was objective mental health (see Appendix G for scoring system). At age 65 raters assessed the Harvard and Inner City men's objective global mental health with excellent agreement. By definition none of the Happy-Well and a majority of the Sad-Sick fell in the bottom quarter of mental health. Good mental health reflected late midlife success in four areas: work, love, play, and not needing psychiatric care. A "mentally healthy" man continued both to grow in and to enjoy his career until long after 50. Over the last fifteen years his marriage through both his eyes and those of his wife was clearly happy. He had played games with friends and taken enjoyable vacations. He neither consulted psychotherapists nor took psychiatric medicines. On average he took less than five days of sick leave a year. A low score on any single item was still consistent with excellent mental health, but some men, often those with alcohol abuse or major depression before age 50, fared badly in most or all areas and so fell in the bottom quartile of mental health.

5. Objective social supports:

(See Appendix H.) Social supports are a crucial dimension of healthy aging. Good social supports were defined as being closely connected with wives, with children, with siblings, with play-mates (e.g., bridge and golf), with a religious group, with social networks (e.g., clubs and civic organizations), and with confi-dantes. Richard Lucky's life provided a splendid illustration of good social support. Two independent raters made these judg-ments by reviewing at least ten questionnaires — including those from wives and children — and usually at least one two-hour interview. Again, by definition none of the Happy-Well and a majority of the Sad-Sick, like Alfred Paine, fell in the bottom quartile of social support.

6. Subjective life satisfaction:

What about joy? What about individuals who possessed the "cel-ebrant" sense (quoted in the first chapter) and subjectively said "Wow!" to life when they got out of bed each morning. An ex-ample of such a man would be the 72-year-old Inner City man who wrote, "I'm still married to my darling wife. Physically I feel like 50 years ago." Another example would be the 77-year-old re-tired CEO who wrote: "People constantly ask me what of im-portance am I doing now. Is it okay just to say I'm enjoying a new chapter, the best part of my life? I wake every morning, glad for where I'll be going and what I'll be doing and who I'll be seeing that day. There is so much to do, and who knows how much time. There is so much to love around us. I love the mountains. I love the sea and the shore. I love to sail." And although as a crusty New Englander he did not spell it out, he was also deeply in love with his new wife.

Therefore, the Study developed a scale to quantify joy — a scale to measure still a sixth dimension of healthy aging: subjective life satisfaction. Over the last twenty years had the men enjoyed their:

Marriage
Income-producing work
Children
Friendships and social contacts
Hobbies
Community service activities
Religion
Recreation/sports

To meet criteria for being among the Happy-Well on the last two biennial questionnaires, a Study member needed to regard *two* of the eight activities above as "very satisfying" (see Appendix I). By definition, all of the Happy-Well were satisfied with their lives, and the majority of the Sad-Sick were not. Sometimes evidence of life satisfaction was utterly unambiguous. For example, as a means of describing his life, an Inner City man marked four facets as "very satisfying." He marked three additional facets — friendship, children, and recreation/sports — "very satisfying" with *two* checks. Among the eight facets the only one unchecked was marriage. Here, rather than check an answer, he wrote, "Hard to answer as I have been divorced a long time, but I have a super relationship with my ex-wife." He then ad-libbed, "I just love being with people and family and helping them when needed as well as traveling and having the health and enough money to be satisfied." Joy happens.

The Categorization of Healthy Aging

Each of the six dimensions of aging was significantly associated with each other — roughly, as strongly as height correlates with weight. Of the 237 Harvard men active in the Study, 62 men were categorized as Happy-Well. These were men who like

Richard Lucky had experienced objectively *and* subjectively, biologically *and* psychologically, good health in all six dimensions. Such Happy-Well men could be defined as follows: before age 80 they spent no years physically disabled — either objectively or subjectively. In addition, compared to their peers in the Study their social supports were in the top three-quarters, their mental health was in the top three-quarters, and their life satisfaction was in the top two-thirds.

Forty of the 237 men were classified Sad-Sick. These were men who like Alfred Paine by age 80 had experienced at least five years of subjective or objective physical disability. In addition, all of these 40 Sad-Sick men were classified as unhappy in at least one of the three psychosocial dimensions: mental health, social support, or life satisfaction.

Sixty of the 237 men died after age 50 and before age 75. They were classified as Prematurely Dead. We often think of death, especially premature death, as an act of God; a tumor striking down the innocent in the flower of youth. (This was one reason the twelve deaths before 50 were excluded: 6 men were killed in action in World War II and the others in freak accidents or from rare genetic illnesses.) Among the Prematurely Dead, too, was Eric Carey; surely, he was an example of a death (contracting polio at age 33) that could only be attributed to bad luck. There were other early deaths even more senseless and tragic, but these deaths were the exceptions. By this I mean that before death the 60 Harvard men who died prematurely (i.e., after 50 and before age 75) were almost as psychosocially impaired as the surviving Sad-Sick men. Before death all but 18 of these 60 men had suffered poor social supports or poor mental health or were dissatisfied with their lives. In short, for five or more years prior to death, more than two-thirds of the sixty Prematurely Dead had been enjoying life almost as little as Alfred Paine.

I followed the same procedure for categorizing the health of the 332 participating Inner City men who survived past 45 and for whom the Study had complete records. At age 65 to 70 there were 95 Happy-Well, 114 Intermediate, 48 Sad-Sick, and 75 Prematurely Dead by age 65. Although the proportions of Inner City men in each outcome category were almost identical with the Harvard men, it should be remembered that the Inner City men were 10 years younger.

The Predictors of Healthy Aging

To many it seems as if heart attacks and cancer are visitations from malicious gods and that much of the pain of old age is in the hands of cruel fate — or at least of cruel genes. The whole process of aging sometimes feels completely out of our control. But blessed with prospectively gathered data, I was astonished at how much of a septuagenarian's healthy aging or lack of it is predicted by factors already established before age 50. What seemed even more astonishing was that these factors are more or less controllable.

Ten years ago a leading gerontologist, Paul Baltes, acknowledged that research has not yet reached a stage where there is good causal evidence for predicting healthy aging.[4] True, there have been several distinguished ten- to twenty-year prospective studies of physical aging.[5-9] All have contributed valuable understanding about the course of old age. But none of these studies have followed their subjects for more than twenty-five years, and few knew what their members were like before 50. As illustrated by the lives of Alfred Paine and Richard Lucky, however, the Study of Adult Development reveals many ingredients that allow prediction by 50 of whether a man will be enjoying his 80th year. I shall identify these predictors one by one. But first let me note variables that, surprisingly, did not predict successful aging.

Six Variables That Did Not Predict Healthy Aging

Ancestral longevity: Lacking lifetime studies of humans, scientists have studied aging in fruit flies. You can breed and study many generations of fruit flies in a year, and in the longevity of fruit flies, it appears that genes are very important. Therefore, one of the first variables the Study looked at was ancestral longevity. For the Terman women and Harvard men, ancestral longevity was estimated by computing the age at death of the subjects' parents and their four grandparents. For the Inner City men only the longevity of parents could be computed with accuracy. At age 60 the longevity of the ancestors of Study members who died young was significantly shorter than the ancestral longevity of those who still survived. But to my surprise, by age 75, the average life spans of the ancestors of the Happy-Well and of the Sad-Sick were identical. In a replication study on ninety 75- to 79-year-old women in the Terman Study, ancestral longevity was only weakly correlated with vigorous late-life adaptation. The longevity of the Inner City men's parents contributed not at all to whether they were aging well or poorly at 70. The most likely explanation for the insignificant effect of ancestral longevity is the sheer number of genes involved. Obviously, specific genes are very important in predicting specific illnesses that shorten life; there may be other genes that facilitate longevity. But in a given individual there may be so many good and bad longevity genes that ancestral effects tend to average out.

Cholesterol: Next, everyone worries about cholesterol, especially in popular magazines. But, of course, these magazines would lose valuable advertising revenues if they chose to worry their readers about really significant risks to health — like smoking and alcohol abuse. It is perfectly true that for young men or for those who have already had a heart attack, lowering high cholesterol is beneficial. It was equally true, however, that for both Harvard men and Inner City men cholesterol levels at age 50 did not distinguish the Happy-Well from the Sad-Sick or even from the Prematurely Dead. This finding has been confirmed by much larger more representative studies.[10]

Stress: Under stress many people feel physically sick. They have headaches; they cannot sleep; they suffer ulcers; they get itches or visit the bathroom far more often than they would wish. Consequently, an attractive hypothesis would be that individuals who experience stress psychosomatically in midlife would suffer poor health in old age. In contrast, with stress, some men deny ever experiencing any physical symptoms at all. For the psychologically minded, an attractive hypothesis would be that such men who "hold stress in" might also age poorly. Neither hypothesis was supported by the Study. The number of physical symptoms under stress before age 50 did not correlate with physical health at age 75. The number of illnesses thought by some to be "psychosomatic," such as ulcers, asthma, and colitis that the men had endured between 20 and 65 did not affect physical health at age 75. The reason for this, in part, is that if you wait a few decades people often recover from psychosomatic illnesses.

Parental characteristics: Alas, we cannot choose our families. Without asking permission they endow us with their genes and bathe us in their warmth and riches or parch us with their lack of them. At age 40 the consequences of such arbitrary fate still seemed quite important to the men's physical health.

Surprisingly, by age 70 parental social class, stability of parental marriage, parental death in childhood, family cohesion, and IQ — variables important to young adulthood — were no longer predictive of outcome. This was true for both the Harvard and Inner City Study cohorts.

Childhood temperament: Shy, anxious childhoods predict many facets of young adulthood, including, in this study, poor physical health. But again, after 70 childhood temperament did not distinguish the Happy-Well from the Sad-Sick. I appreciate, however, that this statistical conclusion seems contradicted by the lives of Paine and Lucky.

Vital affect and general ease in social relationships: For the Harvard cohort such personality characteristics correlated highly with good psychosocial adjustment in college and in early adulthood.[11,12] But these variables, too, failed to predict healthy aging.

In short, an important lesson to be learned from this Study is that if you follow lives long enough, the risk factors for healthy life adjustment change. There is an age to watch your cholesterol and an age to ignore it.

Seven Factors That Did Predict Healthy Aging

Six factors assessed prior to age 50 did predict healthy aging for the Harvard cohort. They are epitomized by the lives of Lucky and Paine. They are also graphically illustrated in Figure 1. In addition, a seventh protective factor, education, was important to aging well for both Inner City men and Terman women. Thus, years of education were substituted for exercise in the latter two cohorts. This was because in the Harvard cohort length of education was too homogeneous to be meaningful. Besides, in the other two cohorts we could not quantify exercise as we had for the Harvard cohort.[13]

By age 50 Richard Lucky neither smoked nor abused alcohol, his marriage was stable, and he exercised regularly. His coping skills were exemplary, especially his use of suppression. True, he was a little overweight, but he possessed the other five predictive factors listed below. Alfred Paine enjoyed none of them.

Not being a smoker or stopping young: In both male cohorts not being a heavy smoker before the age of 50 was the most important single predictive factor of healthy physical aging. Among the College men heavy smoking (more than a pack a day for thirty years) was ten times more frequent among the Prematurely Dead than among the Happy-Well. Yet if a man had stopped smoking by about age 45, the effects of smoking (as much as one pack a day for twenty years) could at 70 or 80 no longer be discerned.

Adaptive coping style (mature defenses): In all three samples the second most powerful predictor of being among the Happy-Well was an adaptive coping style. Independent raters — blinded to the men's current physical health and, of course, ignorant of their future — had reviewed each individual's record to rate his or her involuntary coping style. In Figure 1, as in chapter 2, an adaptive coping style is referred to as the use of mature defenses. In everyday life the term *mature defenses* refers to our capacity to turn lemons into lemonade and not to turn molehills into mountains. In both samples mature defenses were common among the Happy-Well and virtually absent among the Sad-Sick. Admittedly, this association was because mature defenses at 50 predicted psychosocial health in older age. Mature defenses did not predict the men's objective physical health. But mature defenses often did keep objectively disabled men from feeling subjectively disabled. Although not shown in Figure 1, a widening social radius at age 50 was just as important to successful psychosocial aging as emotional maturity. Among all three samples generative men and women at 50 were three to six times as likely to be among the Happy-Well in old age as among the Sad-Sick.

Absence of alcohol abuse: The third major protective factor was the absence of alcohol abuse — the only protective factor in this Study that powerfully predicted both psychosocial and physical health. Alcohol abuse was defined by the evidence of multiple alcohol-related problems (with spouse, family, employer, law, or health) and/or evidence of alcohol dependence. Until now, most major longitudinal studies of health, for example, the Framingham Study[14] in Massachusetts and the Alameda County Study[15]

Figure 1

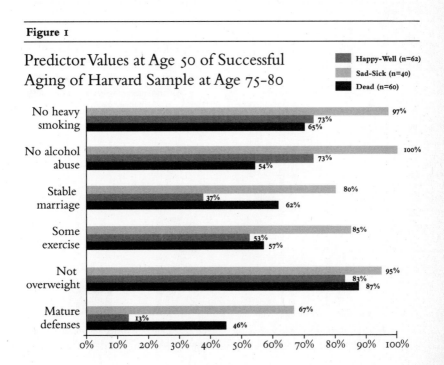

Predictor Values at Age 50 of Successful
Aging of Harvard Sample at Age 75-80

Happy-Well (n=62)
Sad-Sick (n=40)
Dead (n=60)

in California, have only controlled for reported alcohol *consumption,* not abuse. Unfortunately, reported alcohol consumption reflects alcohol abuse (loss of voluntary control and/or adverse consequences from alcohol abuse) almost as poorly as reported food consumption reflects obesity. Neither reported alcohol use nor reported calorie consumption is a useful predictor of poor aging, while obesity and alcohol abuse are. Always, actions speak louder than words.

As mentioned earlier, prospective study reveals that alcohol abuse is a *cause* rather than a result of increased life stress,[16] of depression,[17] and of downward social mobility. In addition, alcohol abuse causes death for many reasons other than liver cirrhosis and motor vehicle accidents. Alcohol abuse causes suicide, homicide, cancer, heart disease, and a depressed immune system. Indeed, as Figure 2 illustrates, alcohol abuse was almost as bad for health in nonsmokers as heavy smoking was bad for health among social

Figure 2

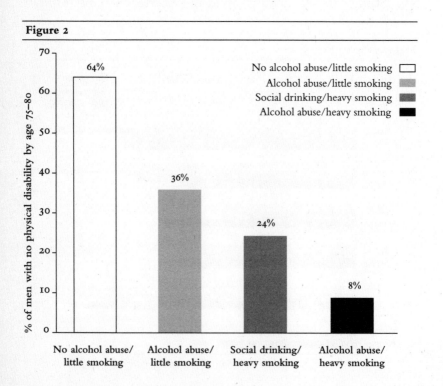

drinkers.[18] Figure 3 illustrates that the first three protective factors were just as valuable to the Inner City men as to the Harvard men.

Healthy weight, stable marriage, and some exercise: Figure 1 and Figure 3 also illustrate that three other protective factors — a healthy weight, a stable marriage, and regular exercise (for the Harvard sample) — were also important to healthy aging. Obesity, like smoking, was bad only for physical health. Good marriages and exercise were good for both physical and psychosocial health.

Years of education: For the Inner City men years of education were an important protective variable. Although length of education is often viewed as merely a manifestation of social class and intelligence, its association with healthy aging depended upon neither of these factors. The components of education that appeared to correlate with physical health in old age were self-care and perseverance — not IQ and parental income. The more ed-

---

Figure 3

Predictor Values at Age 50 of Successful Aging of Inner City Sample at Age 65-70

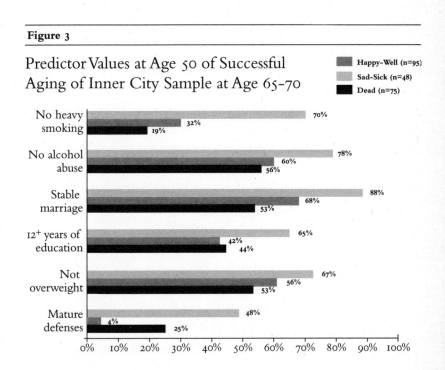

Happy-Well (n=95)
Sad-Sick (n=48)
Dead (n=75)

No heavy smoking — 70% / 32% / 19%

No alcohol abuse — 78% / 60% / 56%

Stable marriage — 88% / 68% / 53%

12⁺ years of education — 65% / 42% / 44%

Not overweight — 67% / 56% / 53%

Mature defenses — 48% / 4% / 25%

0% 10% 20% 30% 40% 50% 60% 70% 80% 90% 100%

ucation that the Inner City men obtained, the more likely they were to stop smoking, eat sensibly, and use alcohol in moderation. Thus, a major reason that the health of the Inner City men declined so much more rapidly than that of the Harvard men and the Terman women was that the Inner City men were not only much less educated than other samples but also, as a result, led far less healthy lives. As is clear from Figure 3, before age 50 the Inner City men were almost twice as likely as the Harvard men to abuse alcohol and cigarettes, and they were more than three times as likely to be overweight.

There is one more piece of evidence that education predicts healthy aging for reasons independent of social class and intelligence. True, the physical health of the 70-year old Inner City men was as poor as that of the Harvard men at 80. But remarkably, the health of the *college-educated* Inner City men at 70 was as good as that of the Harvard men at 70.[19] This was in spite of the fact that their childhood social class, their tested IQ, their income, and the prestige of their colleges and jobs were markedly inferior to those of the Harvard men. Parity of education alone was enough to produce parity in physical health.

The reasons for this surprising finding remain uncertain. But in my own opinion there are two explanations for the link between health and education. First, the capacity to take the long view facilitates both prolonged education and self-care. Second, people seek education because they believe that it is possible to control the course of their lives. And prolonged education probably facilitates appreciation of causal connections between personal behaviors and their consequences.

•   •   •

The protective factors in Figures 1 and 3 — a stable marriage, the ability to make lemonade from lemons, avoiding cigarettes, modest use of alcohol, regular exercise, high education, and maintaining normal weight — allow us to predict health *thirty years* in the future. Like Richard Lucky, 106 Harvard men enjoyed five or six of these protective factors at age 50. At 80, half of these men fell among the Happy-Well. At 80 only 8 of these 106 men were among the Sad-Sick.

Like Alfred Paine, 66 Harvard men possessed fewer than four protective factors at age 50. At age 80, even after excluding the men who at 50 were already disabled, not one — not a single one — of these men was among the Happy-Well; and 21, or almost a third, were among the Sad-Sick. In addition, acts of God notwithstanding, these 66 men — still in adequate physical health at age 50 but with fewer than four protective factors — were three times as likely to be dead thirty years later as men with more protective factors. All 7 men who, like Alfred Paine, had fewer than two protective factors at age 50 were dead by age 80.

Although the average Inner City man at age 50 tended to have fewer protective factors than the Harvard men, the power of these protective factors was just as great. For example, there were 114 Inner City men who at age 50 enjoyed both good health and four or more protective factors. Twenty years later only 5 percent of such men were dead; only 6 percent were among the Sad-Sick; but 58 percent — or proportionally ten times as many — were among the Happy-Well. There were 58 Inner City men who enjoyed good health at age 50 but who possessed fewer than four protective factors. Fully half were among the Sad-Sick or Prematurely Dead and only 1 man in 7 — or proportionally only one-tenth as many — was among the Happy-Well.

Although health data on the Terman women was not collected as systematically, the same six protective factors that helped the Inner City men age well helped the women. Five-sixths of the 23 Terman women who could at 75 to 80 be placed among the Happy-Well had enjoyed four or more protective factors. In contrast, five-sixths of the Terman women who at 75 were classed among the Sad-Sick or Prematurely Dead had enjoyed three or fewer protective factors.

212 • AGING WELL

At Age 50 Does Our Fate Lie in Ourselves or in Our Stars?

A Boston Museum of Science computer, programmed to compute longevity, illustrated the need for caution in identifying risk and protective factors. I had deliberately punched in all of the risk factors that their program offered. Then I queried the computer, "How much longer do I have to live?" Alas, the computer announced that I had died two years before I was born! The experts on individual risks whose advice had been used to program the computer had overestimated the importance of their own favorite health risk factors and underestimated the extent to which the apparent danger of their favorite risk factors was actually a result of competing risk factors.

Thus, it was noteworthy that all the six variables in both Figures 1 and 3 were independent predictors of healthy aging. By *independent* I mean that each variable predicted healthy aging even when the other five predictors were statistically taken into account (see Appendix J).

Figures 1 and 3 contain a hopeful message for the younger generation — destined according to actuarial tables to live past 80. If the six somewhat controllable protective factors in each figure were statistically taken into account, then uncontrollable risk factors (short-lived ancestors, major depressive disorder, and childhoods as bleak as that of Alfred Paine) made no independent statistical contribution to whether an individual fell among the Sad-Sick or the Happy-Well. Of course, there are exceptions. Some people are struck by lightning, are crippled by someone else's stupidity, or die young from hereditary diseases. And I know a chronic smoker and alcoholic whose skid-row lifestyle did not affect his physical health until age 75. But these instances are exceptions.

The good news is that most of us — if we start young and try hard — can voluntarily control our weight, our exercise, and our abuse of cigarettes and alcohol, at least by the time we are fifty. And with hard work and/or therapy we can improve our relationships with our most significant other and use fewer maladaptive defenses. I do not wish to blame the victim, but I do want to accentuate the positive. Whether we live to a vigorous old age lies not so much in our stars or our genes as in ourselves.

What About Inexorable Decay?

As we contemplate surviving past 80, we may still worry about "normal" aging. For men, sexual potency begins to decline at 20. Thus, we may worry that impotence is an inevitable consequence of old age, but Simone de Beauvoir cheers us with the hopeful example of an, admittedly unusual, 88-year-old man. He reported intercourse with his 90-year-old wife one to four times a week.[20] For most of us at 75 to 80 if both we and our partners survive in good health the average is more likely to be once in every 10 weeks. But the spark endures. However, we may have still gloomier fears about survival. We fear that we may "lose" our minds. In the past we may have been told that our brain begins to shrink at age 20 and that by 70, having lost millions of brain cells each year, our brain will have shrunk by a full 10 percent. By 80 we may have lost it entirely. By age 80, of course, dementia is a possibility. But modern studies of healthy octogenarians and nonagenarians — using brain-imaging techniques — suggest that not only is normal brain shrinkage less than we feared, but much of what is lost may be judicious "pruning." True, as we age, our brain does shrink, but bear in mind that the brain is responsive to experience. Thus, much of its cell loss is selective. Remember, too, brain cell loss peaks at age 5. Hopefully, we are much smarter now than we were when we were 5. Finally, more than 90 percent of the Harvard sample who have reached 80 still have all their marbles.

Owning an old brain, you see, is rather like owning an old car. It is as profoundly misleading to look at the "average" old person as it is to look at the "average" twenty-year-old car. Careful driving and maintenance are everything. Old cars become rattletraps, eyesores, and junkers not because of aging but from accidents and misuse. So, too, with humans. Much of what we view as inexorable senility is a result of accident and disease. He may have been a boxer; she may have early Alzheimer's; he may have abused alcohol; she may have had a stroke. But that is pathology, not normal aging.

Eventually, the years take their toll, but the aging brain of a healthy octogenarian can do almost everything a young person's can do; it just takes a little longer and must begin a little earlier. Old people, from age 40 on, can't pull all-nighters, and they have trouble remembering names. Such limitations, however, did not impede Immanuel Kant from writing his first book on philosophy at 57 or Will Durant from winning the Pulitzer Prize for history at 83 or Frank Lloyd Wright from designing the Guggenheim Museum at 90.

Besides, the brain is a master at compensation. Not everything works as well as when you were 21, but crafty 65-year-olds can often beat arrogant 30-year-olds at tennis. At 91 Dr. Michael De-Bakey, the famous Houston heart surgeon, was still a consultant to NASA. While performing his daily routine of cello practice, the 91-year-old Pablo Casals was once asked by one of his students, "Master, why do you continue to practice?" Casals answered, "Because I am making progress."[21]

It is true that the old really do lose the ability to recall names, but this *anomia* begins at 30 and has nothing to do with Alzheimer's disease. Fine. But it is not just forgetting people's names that we worry about. Why can't we remember phone numbers after 70? Why can't we remember jokes anymore? Why do we lose our cars in crowded parking lots? True, the capacity to retain spatial cues and emotionally neutral data does inexorably decline with advancing years. But we remain just as adept at remembering emotionally nuanced events as when we were much younger. Perhaps our brains are like attics. For a decade or two the attic of a new house is filled up carelessly; but over time, as space becomes more precious, we become much more selective about new additions. The sheer number of objects in an attic may change little; but as years pass, the quality and the sentimental value of its contents increase. Over time, much of what is worthless in our attic falls victim to rummage and yard sales. Only what is precious — to us, not to the world at large — remains in our attics and in our minds. Out go the phone numbers and in go the grandchildren's favorite desserts. And as an added bonus, nature usually keeps our brain more tidy than we keep our attics.

What Is the Role of Social Supports in Successful Aging?

Do social supports cause healthy aging? Or does healthy aging enhance social support? Most observers would favor the first answer. But as we have seen, a strong association does not always imply cause. Snow is associated with winter, but snow does not cause winter. Heavy smoking is strongly associated with fatal automobile accidents. But does the accident occur when drivers take their eyes off the road to reach for the cigarette lighter? Of course not. The association is the result of the fact that both heavy smoking and fatal auto accidents are increased by alcoholism. Similarly, exercise is not only good for your heart, but it also reduces obesity. In addition, it is much easier to exercise if you have someone to exercise with. Thus, in part, exercise is important to health because it is a marker of a rich social network.

Certainly, a warm marriage was six times more common among the Happy-Well than among the Sad-Sick. Only 3 of the 34 Sad-Sick Harvard men enjoyed marriages that both they and their wives considered happy. But why? So, did the fact that Alfred Paine suffered poor social supports cause him to take poor care of himself grown old, or did his bad habits drive away those who might have become his friends in adulthood — like his three wives and his children? What is cause? What is effect? Figure 4 suggests that both explanations are correct.

In the Study good habits in the past were if anything more important than good social supports in the present. Good social supports at age 70 have already been defined. Good habits were

Figure 4

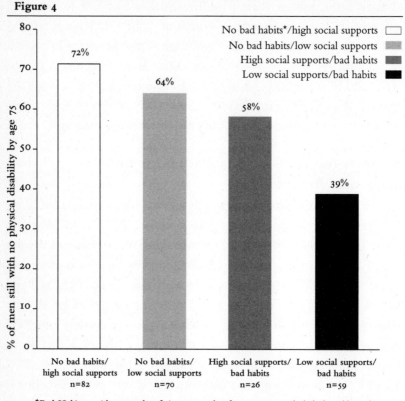

Bad Habits = either 2 packs of cigarettes a day for 15 years or alcohol abuse/dependence prior to age 50.

defined as the absence of cigarette and alcohol abuse before 50. In Figure 4 in the Harvard cohort, three-quarters of 75-year-old men with good social supports and good habits were still healthy. By age 75 most of the men with poor social supports but who prior to 50 abused tobacco and alcohol became disabled or died. But of greater interest, men with *good* current social supports but previous bad habits suffered health somewhat worse than men with *poor* current social supports *and* no prior bad habits. Men with *poor* social supports but good habits enjoyed health almost as good as men with *good* social supports and good habits.

In a similar vein, the same protective factors that predicted good physical health predicted good social supports. Contrasted

to the other 178 Harvard men, by age 70 the 59 most socially isolated men had already by age 50 lacked most of the protective
factors identified in Figure 1. The currently socially isolated were
not only seven times more likely to have been alcohol dependent,
and four times as likely to have smoked heavily, they were also
twice as likely to have engaged in little exercise in the past and to
have already become chronically ill by age 50.

Let me pursue this causal argument one step further still. In
the Harvard sample, for 28 men a happy marriage became unhappy following the onset of alcoholism; in only seven cases did
alcoholism first become obvious following a failing marriage.
Second, divorce does not cause early death; rather alcoholism
causes accidents and divorce and early death. In a large prospective community study divorced men and women were far more
likely to die than the stably married. However, if the divorced
died four times more often from accidents and six times more often from liver cirrhosis, they died only 1.2 times more often from
leukemia as the stably married.[22] In other words, the divorced die
more often only of illnesses made worse by the very factors that
may have led to the divorce.

The question may be asked, however, what causes alcohol
abuse? Cannot cigarette abuse and alcohol serve as effective self-
medication for broken hearts? Most often the answer is no. First,
alcohol, contrary to popular opinion, makes depression worse,
not better. Second, a variety of recent studies have provided evidence that the etiology of alcoholism is more closely tied to
heredity than to stressful environment.[23] Happy childhoods
cursed by alcoholic heredity lead to alcoholism; but unhappy
childhoods scarred by abusive alcoholic stepparents do not lead to
alcoholism.[24] In summary, alcohol abuse is a major and often unrecognized *cause* of unsuccessful aging. And poor social supports.

Well and good. But the reader must remember my experience
with the Boston Museum of Science computer that predicted
that I had died before I was conceived. Investigators of risk variables overemphasize their own favorites at the expense of com-

peting risk factors. Remember, I am a physician interested in alcohol abuse; I am not a sociologist. Thus, take what I say about alcohol abuse being more detrimental to healthy aging than lack of social supports with a grain of salt. Friends are always more fun than good habits! Before and after age 50 cultivate the richest social network you possibly can. Your life will be better for it.

CHAPTER EIGHT

RETIREMENT, PLAY, AND CREATIVITY

Old age is full of enjoyment if you know how to use it.
                                    Seneca, 4 B.C–A.D. 65

The capacity to take a fresh look at things makes a young person out of an old person.
                                    78-year-old Terman woman

There is no question that old age is full of enjoyment if you know how to use it. But, sadly, some men do not. Consider the viewpoint of a businessman whom I never met but who once wrote to me out of the blue:

> I read your article [on learning from our elders] . . . with interest. Since I am in my 76th year . . . I guess what bothers me a bit is — will a true tale of the doings and feeling of the 65-75-year period really be a favor to younger people? Perhaps they should keep all their illusions until they meet the problems themselves.
>
> A number of my friends say that they envy me for my interests and activities. Unfortunately, it is not enough. . . . Until retirement, I loved what I was doing and was much bound up in it. Suddenly I had to stop going at high speed doing things of considerable value. The shock of suddenly stopping and having no way to use the skills I had built over the years was and still is very depressing. I have a 91-year-old sister who has all her mar-

bles. The prospect of those potential years is a bit frightening. I am convinced we were not meant to live this long. I have read about thirty autobiographies and now know why most all are about the first half of their lives. The second half would be dull to write and to read.

In spite of all the foregoing, I shall go sculling tomorrow if the sun is shining, and I shall finish a high chest of cherry wood I am making for one of my children.

If only he could have focused on the glass half full, on his carpentry, on the next generation, and on the light on the water as he rowed, he might have found his life very interesting indeed. Contrast him with a 75-year-old Harvard man, a man of whom Seneca would have approved. He wanted to get out of bed in the morning because "Every day offers a new experience." He regarded the last few years as the happiest of his life, adding:

> Perhaps it is not so important to add up what we are *doing* as what we are being. I am doing nothing that people can admire, that is, I have no consuming "project" or single charity that people can point out to illustrate how focused or "wonderful" I am. I am not accumulating wealth or possessions. I am not producing new knowledge to add to the world's store. What I am doing is probably pretty insignificant. . . . I am a subscriber to a wide variety of local and national charities. I help cook meals for a city soup kitchen and have proctored statewide examination for 3rd and 5th graders in a local school. I care for my house and yard, walk a good deal, and do some swimming.

Like any self-respecting third-grader, he could like his life even if he was not important. Unlike the first man, he understood that not being of "considerable value" at 75 can lead to freedom, not boredom.

* * *

Retirement is highly overrated as a major life problem. For example, in one community survey retirement was placed 28th in severity out of the list of 34 possible stressful life events. Another study found retirement ranked 31st out of 31 possible stressful events.[1] Still a third study showed that retirement leads to lowered stress through exercise and resulted in no increase in depression, smoking, or alcohol use.[2] In the Study of Adult Development, men who liked working the best at 60 liked retirement the best at 75. In sum, those who liked working liked retirement.

There are four circumstances under which retirement is stressful. The first is when it is involuntary and unplanned, and the second is if the individual has no other means of support besides salary. Even among the Inner City men, however, if those with mental illness and alcoholism were excluded, only a small fraction complained that limited finances sabotaged their retirement. Third, retirement also becomes stressful when one's home life is unhappy and work had provided a means of escape, and, finally, when it has been precipitated by preexisting bad health. But in such cases, retirement was not the cause, only the result, of stressful events. Since these caveats affect only a fraction of retirees, my previous statement still holds: Retirement is highly overrated as a major life problem.

There is no good evidence that retirement is bad for one's physical health. Careful review of self-reported health measures and mortality data support the conclusion that retirement does not influence the risk of health deterioration.[3] Indeed, for every person who claims retirement made their health worse, roughly four retirees maintain that retirement has improved their health.[4] Both positions may be illusory, at least in part. A person who feels healthier when he or she retires may actually be feeling relief at the loss of job stress.[5] Conversely, a person who feels worse may actually be experiencing a continuation of the same illness that precipitated retirement; for roughly 25 percent of all retirements occur primarily due to objective illness or disability.[6]

Retirement is made less stressful if giving up one's life work, like any other developmental milestone, is celebrated. In cultures more sensible than ours, retirements are consecrated regularly, as are marriages, christenings, and bar mitzvahs. In the present Study, however, meaningful retirement celebrations were the exception, not the rule. When they did occur, they were always appreciated.

*   *   *

Even if retirement is not a major life problem, in the twentieth century it has become an increasingly important reality. In an age of hard labor Thomas Paine in 1796 believed that workers should receive pensions at 50.[7] However, such pensions did not exist, and until the twentieth century retirement on average began only about three years before death. As recently as 1890, 70 percent of people in the United States over age 70 were still in the work-force. In 1910 only 1 percent of all living Harvard graduates were retired. Greater per person productivity and Social Security have changed all this. By 1970 only 50 percent of 65-year-old men were still in the workforce; and by 1986 this proportion for men had fallen to 31 percent.[8] Today 15 percent of all living Harvard graduates are retired.[9]

One man in 5 from both the Harvard and the Inner City co-horts retired at age 60 or earlier — the most common reason, however, was poor health. After age 65 fewer than 20 percent of the surviving Inner City men are still in the workforce; while after age 65, fully half of the Harvard sample still retained full-time jobs. Thanks to their greater opportunity for advanced training in sedentary skills, by age 70 many of the Harvard men and many of the Terman women, in contrast to the Inner City men, have assumed new unpaid occupations. At age 70 typical job descriptions were: "I have retired from medicine and now pursue wine making"; "new occupations: assistant medical examiner and school bus driver"; "citizen diplomat (with USSR)."

By age 75 one Harvard man in twelve had still not retired. Of the twenty men who were still working for full salary at age 75, most were working for themselves — six lawyers, four doctors, and five CEOs of small businesses. The fact that the Inner City men retired an average five years earlier than the Harvard men was largely because of their much poorer health. Nevertheless, if men with poor health were excluded, early retirement for both the Inner City and the Harvard sample posed no problems to successful aging. By this I mean that to my surprise the Happy-Well were just as likely to retire young as the Sad-Sick. In the last century, the average number of years of retirement prior to death increased from 3 to almost 15 years — a very significant block of time. If these years are not a negative, how shall we turn them into a clear positive? First, retirement should be voluntary. If work is more fun, keep on doing it. Between 75 and 80 the still-working Harvard men gave many reasons why they had not retired:

- "I was bored so started a new business."
- "I like challenges, the people, the money."
- "Nest egg not sufficient after two divorces."
- "The field I am in is in an exciting phase and people want to pay me."
- "I love my work. My forthcoming assignment is one of the most difficult of my career."
- "I am needed by our younger partners."
- "Since I live alone, my job is a sizable piece of my social life."
- "A writer writes, a painter paints. I enjoy teaching; this is what I do."

A 78-year-old member of the Harvard Study conveyed his joy in assuming a full-time job as the editor of a major arts magazine:

> After eight years of enforced "retirement" I have gone back to work, and this is making me very happy. . . . I had never wanted to retire in the first place, and had accordingly over-programmed myself with an assortment of eleemosynary activities — tutoring English as a second language at a tough neighborhood high school, participating in the English Speaking Union's English-in-Action program of conversations with educated visiting foreigners, chairing a distinctly not-for-profit record company specializing in contemporary classical American music. . . . Two weeks ago today, I had a cataract removed from my left eye and

for the first time in my life I have 20-20 vision in that eye. This is another reason for my good morale, although I'm disappointed to report that the significantly improved vision doesn't significantly improve my tennis game!

When this happy Study member was only 28, a Study psychiatrist had been skeptical of his insistence on always looking on the bright side: "His whole philosophy would seem to be that of one who speaks of basic optimism and talks of fabulous luck as if he is quite content to be guided by some divine or happy Providence which looks after him and shapes his future." There are worse ways to adapt to life, however, than to be afflicted with half a century of sustained optimism.

* * *

There are four basic activities that make retirement rewarding. First, retirees should replace their work mates with another social network just as they should replace their dead parents and deceased companions with new friends. In meeting such needs grandchildren often work spectacularly well.

Second, and essential to happy retirement, retirees must rediscover, as did Henry Emerson in his corporate nerve center, how to play. Competitive play — social bridge, cribbage, shuffleboard — lets one make new friends. Play provides a wonderful magic that is especially suited to retirement, for play permits a person to maintain self-esteem while giving up self-importance. For example, a hole in one at 75, like success in fourth-grade art class, provides pride without recourse to the need to be club champion. Besides, play makes retirement fun.

The third basic activity is creativity. Creativity requires protected time — even solitude; and thus, while raising a family and earning a living, creativity is not always possible. In retirement, however, creativity, like play, should be a primary goal.

Fourth, retirees should continue lifelong learning. The challenge in retirement is to combine the fruits of maturity with the recovery of childlike wonder.

In their answers to the 1999 questionnaire, two men perfectly illustrated what these four retirement activities mean. The questionnaire asked the men to list up to five people "now close to you that you were not close to in 1990." One man replied:

> In the last ten years we have made a great many (40-60) new friends, about 30-40 of whom we feel very close to. We have been welcomed into a play reading group, a bowling group and into the local yacht and beach club. These folks brought food and flowers etc. during my recent illness. Several came over voluntarily to perform tasks that I could not do such as getting stuff put away when the hurricane threatened and getting our vegetable garden ready for winter. We have felt extremely close to these folks for four to five years. I also think that I am closer to my brother and sister-in-law, and to my wife's brother than I was in 1990.

What made him want to get out of bed in the morning was: "Greeting another day. A wonderful gift that so many friends and relatives no longer enjoy." Not surprisingly, he regarded the present decade as the happiest in his life. In contrast, unsuccessful retirement was illustrated by a man who answered "None" to the question about new friends he had made in the past decade. The only thing that made him get out of bed was "breakfast." The present was not a happy time for him. Nor did he play, create, or feel good about himself.

A third illuminating 1999 questionnaire came from an octogenarian who illustrated play, creativity, and new learning. What made *him* get out of bed in the morning was: "To make breakfast for my wife, piano practice, and my bladder! I am beginning to read the *Odyssey* in Greek. My sister is a Greek scholar, and she is helping me. In the next decade I want to complete learning Mozart sonata *KV 545 in C major.* I have done all of it hands apart and am using the metronome to pick up the pace hands together." This was the same man who at age 75 had written that "SEX!" was the most enjoyable collaboration between him and his wife.

Creating a New Social Network

Let us look at the four basic tasks of retirement in greater detail. As in the rest of life, the first retirement activity should be to create new relationships as fast as the old ones are lost. Mary Elder was a master at that. All her life Elder had used activity to defend against grief and depression. Thus, the challenge posed to Elder by retirement was potential inactivity. When young she had been able to out-ride and out-swim all of her friends. Now, like Henry Emerson, owing to poor health resulting from fifty years of heavy smoking, Elder had had to give up even golf. Asked how she dealt with the loss of golf, she replied with infectious humor, "It's awfully easy — I never did like walking." But, in fact, retirement posed a problem.

Mary Elder lived in a scruffy Pasadena "professor's house" that had a huge double lot and garden. It had once been owned by a botanist and therefore its garden boasted very exotic plantings. But cultivating her garden was not Elder's idea of fun, and she had let the yard turn into a jungle. Indeed, housekeeping inside or out was not Mary Elder's forte. Her living room was made up of rather shabby, dusty furniture. The sole exception was a single bright, multicolored cushion that looked as if she might have sewn it herself.

Asked what she now enjoyed most, Mary Elder replied, "Being lazy." Pressed further, she initially conceded little ground. "I travel, and, frankly, I am lazy." Elder explained that she had no pressures, no problems. Pressed still harder, she admitted to us with great enthusiasm that she had just returned from an Elderhostel class that had traveled to England. Traveling with one of her oldest friends, she had seen plays, explored the countryside, and had a perfectly splendid time. She also regularly played competitive Scrabble with another friend; they creatively made up their own rules. In fact, Mary Elder remained very active in many Pasadena community activities. True, one of her bridge-playing companions had recently committed suicide, but she hastened to reassure us, "It was not because of my bridge!"

As a young woman Mary Elder had been a rising news correspondent. She had interviewed Greta Garbo and had been in Berlin when Hitler invaded Poland. However, gender discrimination, World War II, and her family had cut short what might have been a brilliant journalistic career. Decades later, widowed and with her children out in the world, Elder joined the Gray Panthers. Beginning as a proofreader, she worked up to editorial assistant and, finally, at the time of our interview had become responsible for putting together their newsletter. She proudly explained how they had influenced legislators; and she admitted that she had placed the plaque thanking her for her work on the coffee table "just for you to see." Her Gray Panther chapter specialized in helping older women to build self-confidence and to offer their talents to the community. Altruism works best when it copes ingeniously with our own needs as well as transmitting the goodness in our hearts to others.

Indeed, twenty-five years ago, Mary Elder had become involved in a project that created activity programs for senior citizens; "Little did I know that these programs would be useful to me." She was now taking classes at the imaginative senior center that she had helped to create. She had just completed a course in art history, in which her class visited a different museum each week. Asked how she felt about modern art, Elder acknowledged that she initially knew very little about it, but she reminded us that it was easier to learn something new with others than alone. She was taking another class, *Masterworks in Literature,* in which the group discussed a different author each week. She attended a third group in which people discussed their problems of living. Finally, she was taking both a current events class in which the class discussed world issues in depth and an exercise class that she found very relaxing. As Elder warmed up, we began increasingly to doubt the veracity of her self-designation as "lazy." Instead, she conveyed a contagious enthusiasm that made her rapt interviewers feel that it might be fun to grow old.

At the start of the interview, Mary Elder had also alleged that being with people was not important to her. But in reality she was as ingenious in surrounding herself with people as she was with activities. Behavior speaks louder than words. As can happen in old age, Mary Elder had recently lost her lover, a man her intellectual equal, to cancer. The affair had lasted from age 70 to 75. He had been a friend from long ago whom she had run into in Paris. Not every "lazy" septuagenarian woman of limited means travels from California to Paris and finds a very intelligent lover. Since his death Elder had sublimated with the "crowd" at the senior citizen center's pool table. Since she was the only woman there who played pool, she had the field to herself; but she wryly acknowledged, "The various gentlemen with whom I play pool are hardly the answer to anyone's dreams." But Mary Elder remained a contender.

Recently, she had taken in a boarder who had moved away from an unhappy family situation. This young woman, just the age of Elder's daughter, paid rent, did the necessary gardening, and desultorily cleaned Elder's house. More important, she made Elder feel needed.

Mary Elder remained close to her own daughter, but she explained that geography made it difficult for her to see her grandchildren as often as she wished. Then, suddenly, Elder remembered that the previous summer, in order that her daughter could have a vacation at a Mexican resort, her grandchildren had come to live with her for two weeks. That spring Elder had also gone to her first Seder in thirty years. Retirement allowed her to become connected to both her future and her past.

Finally, Mary Elder had bonded with her physician. "We love each other. He is the most caring person imaginable. I bring him my one documented accomplishment, plum jam." So when she was not going to museums with groups, playing pool with her men friends or cutthroat Scrabble with her women friends, or caring for grandchildren, or taking separate trips in the last six months to Paris, England, and San Diego, or editing her newsletter, she made plum jam. Mary Elder's notion of being "lazy" in retirement was clearly not in *Webster's Dictionary*. Elder's definition of "lazy" was learning, playing, creating, and making new friends!

Play

The second task of retirement is learning how to maintain self-respect while letting go of self-importance. In contrast to creativity, which it resembles, play is less goal oriented. After 65, being world class should no longer be the issue. What is helpful to old age is being able to play — not to be able to paint as well as Pablo Picasso, but to be able to play as well as Pablo Picasso — to play as well as any red-blooded kitten. Unfortunately, adults consider play to be different from work. Thus, in the eyes of others what old people do is often undervalued. But we should all be allowed to change over time, and society should help us feel good about ourselves at every age. "As people grow up, they cease to play," wrote Freud, "and they seem to give up the yield of pleasure which they gain from playing."[10] Indeed, sober commitment to career is a proper role for the fully employed mature adult. But joyful play is a proper role for both child and retiree. A career must be of value to society as well as to oneself. Play need be of value only to oneself and maybe to a few close friends.

One of the misfortunes of growing older is not being able to take a cut in salary. That is one reason why men and women at 65 are forced to retire. It is not that the old are necessarily less competent, but they are less interested than the young in seeking approval. They only do what they want to do. Fine, but this makes them less valuable to their employer. As older employees "play" more and more, they should be paid less and less.

If they wish to keep their jobs, they should accept that in old age the task is not to be first or best or to beat one's own past record. Mindless bowling on the green, atrocious golf, and amateurish watercolors can provide great pleasure and, equally important, freedom and meaning. In retirement what is important is to live life fully, and that in many ways is achieved through play and through minimally paid creativity. In retirement you can finally quit your daytime job and follow your bliss.

Play and creativity lie along a continuum. I shall try to separate them, but my efforts to tease them apart will seem arbitrary.

Creativity puts into the world what was not there before — and creativity in the eyes of the beholder is meaningful. The products of play are not. In other words, in art there is not only novelty but communication — usually purposeful communication. In addition to his talent and his playfulness, Picasso worked tirelessly to be sure that the whole world was watching. In contrast, a kitten performs acrobatics never exactly performed before; and a grandmother lovingly shapes her garden, a garden not quite like any garden ever seen before. But we, the audience, are not impressed by the kitten's inspired acrobatics or the grandmother's tenderly crafted garden because we believe that we have seen it all before. Thus, retirement play, like the kitten's gambols, is less inhibited, more confident, freer from convention, less approval seeking, and with less performance anxiety than publicly recognized creativity.

Only in the most intelligent mammals is play obvious, yet ethologists have been hard pressed to understand the survival advantage of play. As anthropologist and poet Melvin Konner points out, "Play is an expenditure of energy that is both pleasurable and impractical."[11] Play produces joy, and joy requires neither reinforcement nor reward. The creative novel that is written against a deadline and becomes a minor motion picture is highly rewarded; but its creation may have felt like an onerous burden. The playful novel that rests unpublished in a bottom desk drawer may have provided its elderly author only joy, but only the author can appreciate its creativity.

A psychologist of creativity, the creative author of *Flow*, Mihaly Csikszentmihalyi, underscores the similarity of play to technical rock climbing.[12] Both "are voluntary, satisfying in and of themselves, and offer the player a highly structured setting in which to control external forces." The same can be said of solitaire, raising orchids, and playing monster with your granddaughter.

How deep-seated is the power of play can be illustrated by a story told by the father of a four-year-old to a great scholar of play, Johan Huizinga. The friend had found his son sitting in front of a row of chairs playing "trains." The son was the locomotive.

As the father bent over to greet his little son, the boy reproved him, "Don't kiss the engine, Daddy, or the carriages won't think it is real."[13] Just so, play becomes central to retirement. Bocce playing in a public park or playing pool like Mary Elder and Susan Wellcome can become as absorbing as a hostile takeover and a great deal more graceful.

*   *   *

Sammy Grimm and Francis Player, two Inner City men, stood in stark contrast in their ability to play. Neither man had enjoyed an easy childhood; but, if anything, the childhood of Player had been even more troubled. The tested native intelligence of both men was low average. Both men were raised in blue-collar homes without great parental warmth, but there was a marked difference both in their boyhood and then in their later capacity for play.

At age 14 Francis Player was in the top 2 percent of Inner City men in coping skills, and he rose from his blue-collar tenement origins to the upper middle class. He found his way to college and continued to manifest very mature defenses in midlife. He enjoyed an excellent thirty-four-year marriage, and three out of four of his children graduated from college. Although he earned up to $75,000 a year, Player was also careful to take five weeks of vacation and retired, as planned, at age 56. Photography was his principal hobby, but he also engaged in active community service. He was president of several nonprofit agencies serving the poor, including one that ran a clothing center for the homeless. He also became a Keeper of the Meaning in his capacity as president of his town's historical society and as an officer of the Association of Town Monuments. Subjectively, he found retirement "exciting and rewarding. . . . I like it." Besides his photography, his play activities included fishing, baby-sitting grandchildren, and cultivating his garden. As he summed up ten years of retirement, "I don't know where I got the time to work." His health was splendid; and, not surprisingly, he was among the Happy-Well.

In contrast, Sammy Grimm had not only manifested poor

coping skills when young, but he hated retirement. Prior to retirement he had "worked all the time." Grimm didn't socialize off
the job, developed no hobbies, and had never vacationed. So in
retirement he was "bored." He did not have the foggiest notion
of how to play. When asked for the best part of retirement,
Grimm exclaimed, "There is none!" Asked what was the worst
part of retirement he complained, "There is nothing to do."
Asked how he coped with not working, Grimm grumbled, "I
haven't. . . . I don't like retirement. I was never sick until I retired. . . . If I didn't feel well, I would go to work and forget all
about it." Not surprisingly, Grimm's health — his main retirement preoccupation — was subjectively "poor," and he was objectively disabled. Like Alfred Paine in the last chapter, he was
among the Sad-Sick.

. . .

Frank Wright, a Harvard man, also knew how to play. When I
met him he was 74; he was quite thin and dressed in slacks and
a polo shirt. In appearance he looked rather like an elderly Danny
Kaye. His facial expressions were wonderfully alive and conveyed
fascination. Everything interested him, but he was particularly
enthusiastic about people. Wright lived on the sixth floor of a
gentrified Manhattan warehouse. The heart of his apartment was
a beautifully decorated sixty- by fifteen-foot living room filled
with light and with a large floor-to-ceiling bookcase. A beautiful
scroll from China and good modern art completed the forty-foot
panorama that a collection of a thousand well-used books began.

Wright took me up a wrought-iron circular staircase to show
me his roof garden that overlooked the busy Hudson River. Unlike Fifth Avenue penthouses, his roof garden had no fancy lawn
furniture and no exotic plants. Instead, there were tomato plants,
ready to bear fruit, and birch trees. Wright had done all the carpentry to make the deck himself. It wasn't a penthouse garden in
which to entertain his business contacts. It was a backyard in
which Wright could garden.

Although his sister died when he was 7 and his mother when he was 8, Wright's most salient trait had always been turning lemons into lemonade. From his days on the *Harvard Lampoon,* the college humor magazine that nurtured the talents of William Randolph Hearst, Robert Benchley, George Plympton, and John Updike, Frank Wright had known how to temper work with play. Along with his roof garden he continued to cultivate a wonderful ability to see everybody in positive terms and every personality as a glass half-full. As a writer he had always supported himself through his creativity, and his chief defenses were mature sublimation and humor. At 74 Frank Wright was very comfortable not being important. He was still working 25 to 30 hours a week because he liked it, but he was earning only three to ten thousand dollars a year. "I don't feel retired. . . . I think it is just wonderful to still have a check in the mail." Any self-respecting, ambitious New York City wordsmith would have dismissed Wright's wages as "chump change"; he was wise enough to regard them as Christmas.

Frank Wright had once thought of becoming an architect except that he could not draw. So instead he became a writer. Asked what his most important retirement activity was, Wright replied, "Writing articles . . . that is what I do . . . the rest is fun and games." But so was writing articles. At age 55 when asked about his retirement plans Wright had replied, "I have already sort of retired and it is fine." But two years later when asked his anticipated age of retirement, he wrote, "age 95. . . . The name of the game is to keep being alive and actively interested in a number of things, keep meeting new people — especially younger people." Now he was quite happy to know that every now and then a check was in the mail. If I had not come to interview him, Wright would have spent the afternoon at the public library. When I asked him the topic he was researching, he admitted, "I'm fishing." He had fully mastered the New York Public Library computer system, which was, like his roof garden and his writing desk, another playground. He had started out writing an article on plywood only to find out that plywood had been around since the Egyptians. Then he became interested in two-by-fours and went from understanding them to studying Sheetrock and then to researching the mass production of nails. I asked Wright what he most disliked about retirement; he replied, "I don't dislike anything, I am doing something all the time." He then told me that he loved taking photographs and that he wished that he could also pursue photography and study Beethoven quartets, but he just didn't have the time.

When I asked Frank Wright how his marriage had lasted for four decades, he replied, "We have a good sense of humor, and we don't disagree on anything big." If he had it to do over again, he would marry the same person, and he regarded his current feelings toward his wife as much deeper than they had been. Better yet, the last five years were the best in the whole marriage, "We keep learning new ways to get along together and have fun." It was not that Wright had one of the very best marriages in the Study; it was just that as he had done with retirement, he transmuted their life together into play. Recently a wealthy in-law had died, and the Wrights found themselves very well off. Now they could spend three or four weeks in Italy and France every year. His wife's rule was "A year should not pass without going to Paris."

I asked him to describe a shared experience between him and his wife, "You mean what has been fun to do?" He described their last trip to Rome, during which "We decided to focus on Renaissance architecture." Together they picked out four architects, studied their buildings in Rome, and contrasted these with their buildings in Florence. Yes, retirement is more fun if you are rich; but Frank Wright had enjoyed retirement when he was still relatively poor.

As with many men in the Study, over time Wright and his wife remained a team, but they had changed roles. "For the first twenty years she was a housewife, and I took the commuter train into New York City. For the last twenty years she has gone to work, and I stayed home. I do the laundry." Growing old was easy for Wright because knowing how to play he did not have to take himself seriously.

Frank Wright's physical health was as good as that of any man in the Study. Since early childhood, he had always enjoyed an unusual absence of disease. At 79 he still took no medicines except for the aspirin that he consumed daily because his father had died of a stroke. He acknowledged, "I can't run up the subway stairs . . . if I exert myself I will get shortness of breath"; but there was "no mental diminution." I asked him what he had had to give up; he replied, "I can't think of anything. . . . I haven't given up sex!" I asked Wright what he did when he got a cold. He laughed. "I have the biggest goddamn martini that ever lived. If that does not work, I take a Contac." He turned even the common cold into play.

Creativity

Creativity, like play, can turn an old person into a young person. One way creativity can be differentiated from play is by considering the close relationship of creativity to sublimation. Sublimation is the ego mechanism that underlies much creativity and only some play. Sublimation is magic. Sublimation transmutes raw instinct into religion; sublimation transforms Freudian id into art; sublimation, as it were, creates pearls from irritating conflictual sand and spins the grimiest straw into the purest gold. In short, creativity contains more passion than play.

Sublimation and creativity are visceral — they come from the heart and the gut. Play can exist only in the mind. Play is more frivolous than creativity. The mental mechanism of sublimation is very different from less adaptive mental mechanisms of fantasy and dissociation that can underlie play. Fantasy lets us escape pain by walking happily with Judy Garland along the yellow brick road to Oz or, as in the popular song, having a paper doll that I can call my own. We can dissociate ourselves from pain when we bungee jump, do technical rock climbing, lose ourselves at a

Mardi Gras masked ball, or gamble during a gin-soaked bender. In contrast, creativity allows us not just to wish upon a star, but to throw ourselves into life. Fantasy and dissociation — and some play — are only head games in which we escape and lose ourselves. They lack the nourishment and the direct deep participation of sublimation. For in becoming lost in creativity, we are found — not only by ourselves but also by others. Just so, the artist is found in her studio and the prize-winning rose maven found in his garden. When Frank Wright sells an article, when the weekend painter sells a painting, of course, play crosses my imaginary line into creativity.

Creativity differs from play in another way, in that the artist takes herself or himself seriously, for unlike play, creativity produces awe. In short, creativity provides a means of containing wonder as well as a means of resolving conflict. Painful childhoods may allow the psychobiographer to illustrate the alchemy of sublimation, but inner torment is by no means a sufficient nor even a necessary impetus to creativity.

The sources of creativity are many, but its expression requires one thing — committed talent. There must be talent enough to produce both pleasure in the observer and joy in the creator. True, creativity and talent are not essential to positive aging. But if you have a talent, use it.

In judging creativity, however, we should always remember to keep perspective. For example, we set the bar at a very different height for our children and friends than we do for artists in the outside world. We may pronounce a cousin brilliantly creative who does no more than write witty birthday poems and collect rejection slips from *The New Yorker*. At the same time, we may scoff at the "undeserved" Nobel Prizes earned by novelists Sinclair Lewis and Pearl Buck.

But creativity should never be a contest. Creativity only need harness enough talent to elicit an "Ahhh!" from someone in the audience. Talent is just as important to 78-year-old Mary Elder creating plum jam for the admiration of her doctor as it was to

80-year-old Georgia O'Keeffe in her studio eliciting admiration from thousands.

. . .

Debate continues as to whether creativity is diminished in old age. The debate is fueled by two artifacts of aging. On the one hand, the reputations and the creative products of the elderly can be burnished from the halo of past achievement. On the other hand, in old age brain disease is more likely to occur. Let me label these two issues as "halo effect" and "corkage." First, reputation is important. Any wine will taste better if poured from a bottle labeled Château Latour (1970). So it is with creativity in the elderly. Many of Picasso's late-life ceramics and paintings might seem crude or, more charitably, like child's play if they were not signed "Picasso." In contrast, the brilliantly creative products of young Einstein and young Picasso, in retrospect their most innovative contributions, seemed quite unimpressive to many in 1905. Thus, before the old can be deemed more creative than the young, their halos must be removed. So, too, the original contents of a bottle of Château Latour (1970) will taste dreadful if its cork has deteriorated, for great Bordeaux wines improve with age but only if carefully cellared. Similarly, Eugene O'Neill did not lack creativity after age 55 because the elderly cannot write plays; witness Sophocles. O'Neill's career came to a halt because he suffered from a still imperfectly diagnosed brain disease.[14] Van Gogh was one of the very few artists who created better with brain pathology than without.

Some individuals with intact brains give up creating as they mature. They give up creativity as they take up Generativity. The once creative scientist may move out of the laboratory to look after other scientists who are younger. Medical school deans and university presidents were often promising innovators when young. Robert Sears, one of the gifted boys originally selected by Lewis Terman, was the editor of his Stanford literary magazine in college; he was a brilliant professor and innovative contributor to the psychological literature in middle life. Then he spent his retirement years "gardening" in the Terman archives and Keeping the Meaning. By this I mean that Robert Sears devoted his brilliant research mind to the orderly sorting and computerizing of the six decades of data in the Terman Study, of which he had been a member. He performed this task so that a host of young working adults, like me and my wife, could use the data, so that we, too, could put into the world what was not there before.

In addition, facets of the process of creativity change with age. The ability to respond quickly, to memorize quickly, to compute quickly without error, and to draw rapid inferences from visual relationships — those skills peak between 20 and 30 and diminish significantly after 70. Psychologists call such skills fluid intelligence. Fluid intelligence is crucial to creativity in mathematics.

Then there is what psychologists call crystallized intelligence: the capacity to recognize similarities, to use inductive and logical reasoning, and to retain vocabulary. These abilities are characterized by the capacity to reflect and recognize rather than to recall and remember. These abilities actually increase until 60; they can often be the same at age 80 as age 30. I am reminded of the roofer who "measured twice and hammered once" and, thus, created a better roof more quickly than his nimbler, younger colleague who measured only once and thus had to hammer twice.

Finally, like the rest of us, some artists give up their highly creative daytime jobs in order to retire and play. Winston Churchill had never painted oils to win the wars, the votes, the Nobel Prize, and the awe that he had won with his prose. Thus, when Churchill retired, he put his pen aside, and continued to paint for himself. In old age Churchill played.

* * *

But thus far I have evaded answering the question "Can the elderly be creative?" I shall now stop my waffling and reply, "Damned straight!" Monet did not begin his water lily panels until 76; Benjamin Franklin invented bifocal spectacles at 78. Houston heart surgeon Michael DeBakey obtained a patent for a surgical innovation at age 90. Titian painted what many regard as his most original, beautiful, and profound works after age 76. Leopold Stokowski signed a six-year recording contract at 94, and Grandma Moses was still painting at 100.

A generation apart, H. C. Lehman[15] and Dean Keith Simonton have each undertaken exhaustive studies of creativity over the life span. Both found the age period from 35 to 55 to be the most fecund for most fields. Simonton, however, summed up the most recent evidence by noting that "usually creators in their sixties and even seventies are at least as productive as they were in their twenties. . . . An octogenarian can still hope to make important contributions, albeit at a slower rate."[16]

What does decline with time, of course, is energy. Our energy, our ability to exercise without oxygen debt does down in linear fashion from age 20 on. If at 90 Pablo Casals could still play his piano and cello brilliantly in the morning, by the late afternoon he was often too tired. Some octogenarians can still run marathons, but they do so slowly and not often. And "measuring twice" involves a caution that the young may call rigidity. But such caution is essential to all those who pilot unwieldy craft, be they ocean liners, the government of China, or an octogenarian's shaky legs. Caution, as it is often practiced by the old, creates the virtues of thoughtful planning and care.

Finally, all life is a journey. Thus, at the end of the day, even if we are traveling more slowly, we are often closer to where we wanted to go than we were at the beginning. William Osler's brilliant textbook of medicine was better, if less innovative, in its eighth edition than in its first. Thomas Edison's lightbulbs got better, if less awe inspiring, with each iteration.

•   •   •

If I am to assert that creativity is unimpaired after 70, however, I must offer the reader more than pious platitude and dramatic anecdote. I need to provide real evidence. Let me begin with the work of psychologist Mihaly Csikszentmihalyi, who interviewed a large number of people in their 70s who had been highly creative in their youth. He demonstrated a clear relationship between continued creativity and successful aging. Just as Erikson's model of adult development as a widening social radius would have predicted, Csikszentmihalyi noted that "often their interest had broadened to include larger issues: politics, human welfare, the environment, and occasionally transcendent concerns with the future of the universe."[17] In his 30s pediatrician Benjamin Spock wrote bestselling guides to help mothers with their children. In his 70s Spock worked for world peace and in his 90s he wrote on spirituality.

As Csikszentmihalyi would have predicted, the creative men and women in the Harvard and Terman studies aged more successfully than their less creative colleagues. Counterintuitively, high creativity in middle life predicted sustained physical vigor in old age better than it predicted good psychosocial adjustment. Nevertheless, the most creative Harvard men were twice as likely and the creative Terman women were four times as likely to be among the Happy-Well. In both cohorts, the least creative were two to four times as likely to be among the Sad-Sick.

Most creative men and women met criteria for Generativity, but the acts of creating the "new" and the acts of caring for the next generation are not identical. Some individuals are gifted at one but not the other task. For example, Fred Chipp was more generative than creative; while Picasso was highly creative but often outrageously self-centered.

In addition, there were many ways in which creative Terman women and Harvard men could not be distinguished from the less creative members of their respective cohorts.[18] For example, there were no differences at all in intelligence between the creative and less creative individuals. Nor were differences in creativity correlated with years of mothers' or fathers' education nor with the number of books in the childhood home nor, in the case of the Terman women, with parental support for a career.

In late life the Terman women had an easier time being creative and feeling good about it than the Harvard men. Rightly or wrongly, after age 70 the Grant Study men saw their creative stars in decline and the women perceived their creative stars in ascent. Csikszentmihalyi noted the same phenomenon in his highly creative men and women. In their teens a majority of the Terman women dreamed of becoming artists, poets, or novelists. Virtually all of the Terman women were active in high school dramatics and/or editors of high school publications. After 18 for most women these dreams evaporated. Their parents sent their bright daughters out to support the family during the Depression. The separations and divorces associated with World War II made the Terman women into single mothers without alimony. Unlike Frank Wright none of them could afford to quit their daytime job.

After 65 the Terman women had finally achieved Virginia Woolf's wish for the brightest women of her generation — "five hundred pounds a year and a room of one's own." Thus, the empty nest, extra room, pensions, and Social Security set septuagenarian women like Mary Elder free to be creative once more. Sometimes they even had retired house-husbands for assistants. In addition, as mentioned earlier, their androgens were increasing, not decreasing, like those of men;[19] this, too, I suspect, gave them a sense of fresh power. Lastly, often the Terman women had never seen themselves produce anything as good before 60 as after 60. This, too, was reinforcing and encouraged them to go forward. In contrast, many of the most creative men in the Grant Study by age 65 had diminished energy, and repeating their past successes no longer brought great pleasure. The golf course and the historical society beckoned.

Thus, after the age of 65 fully a quarter of the Terman women continued to "put things in the world that were not there before." For example, there was Mary Elder, a previously inhibited writer, who after 75 became the editor of a small newspaper; and another woman, Martha Meade from chapter 3, who published her first serious book at 65. The public literary achievements of a third woman peaked at 75, and two more women became more successful painters after 60 than they had ever been before. Two women, after 60 (remember Matilda Lyre from chapter 1), gave their first public musical recitals. Still another woman won her first sculpture prize after 70. This upsurge reflects more than simply escape from prior societal inhibition. Rather, it is concrete evidence that creativity remains a possibility in late life for those of us less gifted than Benjamin Franklin and Claude Monet.

The other thirty Terman women included many who engaged in creative play such as sewing, gardening, pottery throwing, or flower arranging. Or they were active in pastimes like dog shows, stamp collecting, or ornithology, and in taking courses in art or folk dancing. Retirement should be at least as much fun as fourth grade.

* * *

If social disadvantage did not impair the Study's recognition of Generativity, it did impair recognition of creativity. Thus, the Study failed woefully to capture creativity in the lives of the Inner City men. True, one Inner City man wrote the national anthem for an emerging nation, but for most of his life he had to stick to his daytime job. Owing to stigma when young and observer bias when old, the Inner City men were less often labeled creative. Poets who write in our own language always seem so much more gifted to us than those who write in other tongues. The creativity of men with tenth-grade educations could not always be judged accurately by interviewers with the blinders of graduate degrees.

* * *

In addition, as Virginia Woolf's plea for a room of one's own and an independent income suggests, social advantage facilitates creativity. Although he was eventually blessed with a Harvard Ph.D., it took John Boatwright decades to overcome his burden of disadvantage. In his undergraduate years, he was forced to make Harvard a trade school. Professor Boatwright began his college career as an engineering science major. Like many a scholarship mathematician before him, Boatwright had been seen in college as asocial and uncreative, bland, and without a special interest of any kind. He had come to Harvard having read *The Adventures of Huckleberry Finn* over the summer and finding himself excited by English literature. Nevertheless, although all of his college science grades were A's, and he was admitted to Phi Beta Kappa in his junior year, in the one literature course he took, in the Victorian novel, he received a C. Besides, since his father made only $1,000 a year and he was on scholarship, Boatwright could not afford to continue the college music course which he loved and in which he was receiving A's.

Eventually, Boatwright became a professor of mathematics at a small, well-regarded liberal arts college in Maine. At 47 he was already interested in early retirement from his teaching job. Although he had made no actual plans for retirement, he told me that he "had heard that you should plan for retirement," and he dreamed of becoming a carpenter so that he could continue to work. Nevertheless, he had stodgily dismissed his son's wish to build a forty-foot sailboat as an impractical expense. Yachts, like music courses, were only for the rich.

I intolerantly summarized John Boatwright, aged 47, as "a man who had the passivity and the complete lack of aggressiveness consistent with a schizoid character. There was a lack of energy about him that made it very hard for him to come across as a vivid person." What did I know? My way through Harvard had been paid for; financially secure, I had taken courses only because they excited me.

When I reinterviewed John Boatwright in 1975, he was now 64, retired, and living on about $10,000 a year. When he reached 65, his pension would increase to $25,000, but already he felt secure. His decision for early retirement had arisen for a variety of reasons. His college had fallen on hard financial times and that brought out the worst in its administrators. In addition, Boatwright had been getting less satisfaction out of his teaching because of the decline in quality of the students. He saw the most recent crop of college students as disrespectful and uninterested in learning.

But that was not all. John Boatwright was a man whose adaptational skills and defenses had steadily matured. From 20 to 45 his overintellectualized defenses had placed him in the bottom quartile of the Study. From age 50 to 75 the maturity of his defenses advanced him to the top third. Now he used not only sublimation but also altruism. In retirement he was surprised to find himself working actively for the Community Chest.

Twenty years before, John Boatwright had been one of the most forgettable of the Grant Study men. Now, at 64, he became for me one of the most memorable. What had changed was his access to his creativity. He was dignified, controlled, well-mannered, and certainly cultivated. The scholarship boy and geek-engineer had vanished. Now he brought to mind an aesthete or a painter with an independent income. He wore a turtleneck covered by an expensive brocaded sport shirt. He displayed a beard and a whimsical sense of humor. Direct and animated in his expression, Boatwright related easily. Although I was to leave Boatwright's house feeling that I had just spent time with a professional artist, when I arrived, fortunately for me, Professor John Boatwright also remained an engineer. He managed to figure out why I, who at Harvard had majored in the humanities, could not get the key to my rental car out of the ignition!

In college John Boatwright had been forced to give up music; now he compensated for not teaching mathematics by reveling in music and by working for his distinguished college literary review, for which he was the book review editor. Boatwright reviewed about fifty books a year and read about a hundred. But he assured me, "I don't review anything I don't like." He proudly showed me the review he had just written of Richardson's pioneering eighteenth-century novel *Clarissa*.

There was a lively, almost relentless quality in him that radiated the feel of a much younger man. Creativity was everywhere.

John Boatwright's enormous animation and enthusiasm made it clear that his writing was play, not work. He had begun by reviewing books on science, but then "I spread," and for the last twenty years his own reading had been largely novels and short stories.

Asked about the roots of his literary interests, he recalled "My literary career at Harvard was a bad one." Most devastating had been the fiction-writing course in which the teacher had dismissed his dialogue about football players as not realistic. I could imagine his naive enthusiasm being squashed by a teacher — as intolerant as I was when I had interviewed him fifteen years before — who mocked the efforts of this mathematically inclined engineering major to write about football players. As a young parent Boatwright had written some short stories, but he never dared submit them for publication. Instead, he told them to his children. His chief character, Sir Mugger Muggeridge, was a little bit like Inspector Clouseau in the Pink Panther movies, "someone who just bumbled around." Thirty years later his children still remember those stories with pleasure. Creativity is putting into the world something that was not there before. And Sir Mugger Muggeridge was one of a kind. But in Boatwright's age-47 interview, I had not thought to ask about bedtime stories. What did I know!

Even at age 64, however, words did not come easily to John Boatwright. Direct questions from me about his marriage provided little but monosyllables. At the end of the interview I asked Boatwright, as I did all my interviewees, what his dominant mood had been in the last six months. "About usual," he replied, "even keel, no highs or lows." The word "keel" reminded me to ask him about the yacht — no longer dismissed as impractical — that he and his son had been building. Boatwright's eyes lit up. It was to be ocean-going, and they planned to cruise it along the Maine coast. Yet in planning my visit, not having met the retiree, I thought of the boat almost as a figment of his imagination. Adult development is filled with surprises.

John Boatwright offered to show me his creation. We walked across his large, carefully tended yard of perhaps an acre. We walked past the snow fort that he and his grandson had constructed after the last snowstorm. Finally, we arrived at a good-sized barn, which to my utter astonishment was filled with a perfectly enormous ocean-going yacht. It measured perhaps 16 feet in height from its three thousand-pound lead keel, which Boatwright and his son had hoisted into place themselves, to the top of the deck. The boat was thirty-two feet long and mounted with steel braces on the chassis of a school bus. Eventually, by opening the barn the way one might open a dirigible hangar, they could roll the boat outside, down the highway, and into the Atlantic. Fifteen years later as I recall my wonder, his yacht has grown in my mind to the size of a zeppelin; so to tell the story without exaggeration I have to depend on my original notes.

Boatwright had described the yacht to me with the same kind of excitement and pride with which he told me about his work on the college literary review. When he and his son had finished the hull, they invited a hundred friends over. Energized by a keg of beer, the friends had carried the boat, which weighed several tons, out into the Maine sunshine. Floating on the arms of a hundred people, Boatwright marveled, "was like seeing it ride on an ocean." Leonardo da Vinci, eat your heart out.

Lifelong Learning

Finally, in order to have a full old age and an enjoyable retirement, you must keep on learning. Gusto for education in late life is highly correlated with psychological health. The capacity to take a fresh look at things makes a young person out of an old person. Indeed, in ancient Greece the word scholar meant leisure, underscoring that what you did with free time in Athens was to learn new things. Although lifelong learning was a characteristic of most of the best examples of successful aging in this book, Frank Wright, the retired writer, was an exceptionally ardent lifelong learner. For several years Wright had been taking music courses at the Juilliard School. Currently, he was taking a course in string quartets, which required him to develop fluency in reading music. The year of our interview he was taking a course on contemporary music, in which Debussy and Bartók were only the beginning. "It has made a tremendous difference to me," he explained. "It has helped me understand why people want to push the envelope."

Mary Elder, at the beginning of this chapter, and John Boatwright also provided examples. But perhaps the most memorable illustration of lifelong learning was provided by Mary Fasano — who, alas, was not a member of the Study of Adult Development. However, in terms of her initial social disadvantage, her vibrant intelligence, and her Harvard diploma, she could have qualified for all three cohorts. At age 89, Mary Fasano, not a pseudonym, entered the history books as the oldest person ever to earn an undergraduate degree from Harvard. On June 12, 1997, the *Harvard University Gazette* reprinted her graduation address:

> I remember one night a few years ago when my daughter was frantic with worry. I usually arrived at the bus station near my home by 11:00 P.M., but on that night I was nowhere to be found. . . . My daughter checked the bus station, drove around the streets, and contacted some friends. But she couldn't find me — until she called my astronomy professor, who told her that I was on top of the Science Center using the telescope to gaze at the stars. Unaware of the time, I had gotten lost in the heavens and was only thinking about the new things I had learned that night in class. This story illustrates a habit I have developed over the years: I lose track of the time when it comes to learning.
>
> My studies were interrupted when I was in the 7th grade, back sometime around World War I. I loved school but I was forced to leave it to care for my family. I was consigned to work in a Rhode Island cotton mill, where I labored for many years. I eventually married and raised 5 children, 20 grandchildren. But all the while I felt inferior to those around me. I knew I was as smart as a college graduate. I knew I was capable of doing a job

well — I had proved it by running a successful family business for decades that still exists. But I wanted more. I wanted to feel confident when I spoke, and I wanted people to respect my opinions.

But I am here today — like you are — to prove that it can be done; that the power gained by understanding and appreciating the world around us can be obtained by anyone regardless of social status, personal challenges, or age. That belief is what has motivated me for the last 75 years to get this degree.

Play, create, learn new things and, most especially, make new friends. Do that and getting out of bed in the morning will seem a joy — even if you are no longer "important," even if your joints ache, and even if you no longer enjoy free access to the office Xerox machine.

CHAPTER NINE

DOES WISDOM INCREASE WITH AGE?

> The compensation of growing old, Peter Walsh thought, coming out of Regent's Park, and holding his hat in hand, was simply this: that the passions remain as strong as ever, but one had gained — at last! — the power which adds the supreme flavour to existence — the power of taking hold of experience, of turning it round, slowly, in the light.
>
> Virginia Woolf, *Mrs. Dalloway*

> I am a very foolish fond old man.
>
> William Shakespeare, *King Lear*

Aging is not a simple concept, nor is wisdom. At age fifty — seventeen years ago — when I applied for a grant from the National Institute of Aging to undertake the Study on which this book is based, my initial application was turned down. How, the 70-year-old chairman of my review committee fumed, could I plan to study *aging* if I defined aging in terms of decay. The chairman viewed aging as a vital life process, not as senescence to be postponed as long as possible.

When I received my pink rejection slip, I groused that he was just a pedantic curmudgeon who rigidly dismissed a splendid grant request written by a fifty-year-old-height-of-my-powers-still-fitting-into-suits-of-twenty-years-earlier me. But of course, he was right; I was still a mere stripling of fifty. What did I know about aging? Fearing my own future, I had proposed studying aging as merely the relative rate at which physical deterioration took place. Up to then, it had rarely occurred to me that old people could be interesting.

So in writing this book I must acknowledge a great debt to the wisdom and experience of my 70-year-old grant review chairman, James Birren, éminence grise of the science of gerontology. Thanks to him I paused, reflected, and rewrote the grant. I would study aging as a process. My grant request was not only approved, but subsequently received an NIH Merit Award — ten years of continuous funding. Why? Because the vision of a 70-year-old could be wiser than that of a 50-year-old.

It is true that cream and eggs have a limited shelf life, and that twenty-year-old Chevrolets rarely excite envy. But it is also true that cheese, wine, and stately oaks often grow more complex with age because of, rather than in spite of, their "decay." And Homer made Nestor, the oldest of the Greek chieftains at the siege of Troy, also the wisest.

But one swallow does not make a summer. Anecdotes do not answer whether wisdom really increases with age. Perhaps the association of wisdom with old age is merely an old wives' tale? Do we endow the elderly with wisdom only as a good-hearted effort to jolly them along — like telling the obese that they have sweet dispositions? Or is wisdom a special boon that life bestows upon the elderly? Or were the wise always that way and in old age we finally noticed it? Or perhaps the reason that we associate wisdom with age is simply that, unlike motor skills, sexual prowess, and memory, wisdom does not usually decline with the passing years.

Which epigraph shall we believe? Woolf's or Shakespeare's? The very wise William Shakespeare, in the last tragedy that he ever wrote, had the wisdom to make Lear's young fool wise and the 80-year-old king foolish. Lear's fool had to admonish his king, "Thou shouldst not have been old before thou hadst been wise." Wisdom is the opposite of being self-absorbed, and yet Lear epitomizes the narcissism of a foolish old age when he screams at his child, "Better thou hadst not been born than not to have pleas'd me better." Young Edgar and Cordelia, too, are wiser by far.

Two of the very best definitions of wisdom that I have encountered came from young relatives. My wise young niece, Marian Wrobel, provided one definition: "Wisdom consists of many rich experiences that have been reflected upon until they can be empathically communicated to others." My wise young son-in-law, Michael Buehler, noted that what all definitions of wisdom "have in common is the capacity and the willingness to step back from the immediacy of the moment — whether it is an affect, a judgement, or a conflict — in order to attain perspective."

When the question was posed to them at age 75, "Wisdom is often associated with advanced age; what qualities would you look for in a wise man?" several of the Harvard Study members replied that they had been wiser when they were younger. Others answered the question:

"Empathy, through which one must synthesize both care and justice."

"Tolerance and a capacity to appreciate paradox and irony even as one learns to manage uncertainty."

"A seamless integration of affect and cognition."

"Self-awareness combined with an absence of self-absorption."

"The capacity to 'hear' what others say."

"Perspective, sense of the larger context of life, realization that there are two sides to everything, nothing is black or white. Patience. Sense of the irony of life."

"You gotta remain inquisitive about your surroundings."

"A sense of the connectedness of all things; or as the wise old guru said to the Coney Island hot-dog seller, 'Make me one with everything.'"

But what is the most salient characteristic of wisdom? Everybody has a different definition. Paul Baltes, of the Max Planck Institute in Berlin and perhaps the leading scholar in the world of wisdom development, has wisely pointed out, "There are exactly as many distinct solutions to the structure of wisdom as there are investigative teams at work on the problem."[1] Everybody's definition of wisdom will be different in the words; but the melody, I suspect, will be the same. Wisdom consists of multiple facets. Among the more important facets are maturity, knowledge, experience, and intelligence — both cognitive and emotional.[2]

•   •   •

We all regard the acquisition of wisdom as an essential part of successful aging, but there is scant evidence that the old are any wiser than other people over 30. First, consider King Solomon, who, if we believe the Old Testament, was far wiser as a young man than he was grown old. After the very young King Solomon cried, "O Lord . . . I am but a little child: I know not how to go out or come in,"[3] the Lord replied, "Lo, I have given thee a wise and an understanding heart."[4] Then the young King Solomon made his famous judgment that identified the true mother among two women each claiming to be the real parent of an infant. But in his old age King Solomon was as big a fool as King Lear and an increasingly poor king.

Next, consider wise men who are better documented: Jefferson, Gandhi, Martin Luther King, Jr., Muhammed, Lincoln, Tolstoy, Shakespeare. They all reached the pinnacle of their wisdom between age 30 and 50.

Third, consider a true story told me by a young grandmother who could have been, but was not, a Terman Study member. As a brilliant young woman in her twenties she had emigrated from Louisiana to Cody, Wyoming, during World War II. There she encountered one of the notorious internment camps for Japanese-Americans evacuated from the West Coast by our government. In Cody the Japanese-Americans were relegated by the xenophobia of Anglo-Wyomingites to second-class citizenship. There, to her indignation, they were excluded from many of the stores and denied any role in town affairs. As a solution this young Caucasian woman pointed out to the city fathers that the Japanese-

Americans still had the vote and that they outnumbered the Anglo citizens of Cody. How would the city fathers respond to the
challenge of having a Japanese mayor, a Japanese superintendent
of schools, and a Japanese police chief after the next election?
She thought she could arrange it. She got the city fathers' attention. Overt intolerance vanished, and the internees were treated
more empathically. But prematurely wise, this young political ac-
tivist understood context, past and future. She made an exception
for the town pharmacist, whose daughter had been an army
nurse captured on Corregidor and subjected to the cruelty of the
Bataan death march and Japanese imprisonment. In his drugstore,
he alone was permitted to discriminate.

In terms of the multiple facets of wisdom, first this young
woman was *mature* enough to empathize with two cultural
groups other than her own. Second, she had displayed *common
sense* and *sound moral discernment*. Third, because she *appreciated
context,* all the Cody villagers trusted her. Fourth, she was *intelligent* — already a published *New Yorker* author in her teens — she
saw through to the heart of the matter. As a result, peace, not
violence, resulted from her meddling. Fifth, she showed *emotional
intelligence.* She integrated care and justice and had the chutzpah
to get away with it. But like King Solomon, in the days when he
was wise, she was very young.

• • •

And yet, it is hard to believe that wisdom does not increase with
time. The longer one lives, the more of the world one has visited
and the less parochial one's vision. Once we have learned, we
never forget how to ride a bicycle; once we have walked in another's moccasins or traveled a painful road on our own, we never
completely forget. Anecdotally, presidential advisers Clark Clif-
ford, Bernard Baruch, Henry Kissinger, and General George
Marshall were more useful at solving the world's problems after
age 55 than before. If only we could measure it properly, wisdom
ought, like experience and gray hair, to increase steadily with age.

Experimental evidence, however, suggests that this belief is not true. For example, one research study, using a test called the "Mature Reflective Judgment Interview," found a clear increase in wisdom up until age 35.[5] After that the investigators found no good evidence for further wisdom growth. In another study middle-level managers could solve complex social relationship problems as well from 28 to 35 as they could from 45 to 55; the only difference was that the younger managers had to gather more and sometimes quite extraneous data. From 65 to 75, however, the manager's performance was clearly inferior.[6] Others have obtained experimental results that confirm these findings.[7,8]

Paul Baltes sums up a lifetime of research on wisdom as follows: "The current evidence is not that the majority of older adults, in areas such as professional expertise and wisdom, demonstrate superior performances when compared to the young."[9]

In our imagination the old are always wiser than ourselves; for you cannot be wise about what you have not lived through. Thus, in one study people of differing ages were asked to nominate wise individuals. If the nominators were in their 20s, the average age of the people nominated as wise was 50. If the nominators were in their 40s, the average age of those they nominated was 55. But the age of those nominated as wise became 70 if the nominators themselves were over 60.[10]

So why do we regard the old as wiser than we are whatever age we may be? One reason is that experience really does increase with age. Until we are over 40 most of us don't have the experience to be put in a position of a wise person. Judges, baseball managers, high-level diplomats, directors of international organizations, need decades of seasoning. Indeed, only the old have the experience to view the life span in its fullest context.

Another reason is that consensual recognition of wisdom often occurs only after the passage of time. Cassandra was very wise as a young woman, but it took the villagers a long time to come around. Was not Tolstoy far wiser when he wrote *War and Peace* in his late thirties than when he ran away from his wife, Sonya, to die in a railroad station as a possibly demented and certainly foolish old man? Yet our memory of Tolstoy is as an old man. Gandhi, Thomas Jefferson, and, arguably, Einstein were as wise when young as they were in old age. Yet, in our mind's eye Gandhi, Jefferson, and Einstein are portrayed as old men.

· · ·

In the Study of Adult Development our best pencil-and-paper measure of wisdom was Jane Loevinger's Washington University of St. Louis Sentence Completion Test (WSCT).[11] In the WSCT the respondent is asked to complete sentence stems. For example, the sentence stem "When people are helpless . . ." could be answered, "I move away" (low maturity score) or "I try to show them how to help themselves" (high maturity score). Adults score higher than adolescents, and achieving 16-year-old adolescents score higher than 18-year-old delinquent adolescents. The test is thought to measure interpersonal sensitivity, discrimination of emotional states, moral maturity, and tolerance of ambiguity. But even though the Harvard men's WSCTs were scored by Loevinger's group, their WSCTs failed to correlate with maturity of defenses. Of greater significance, for both the Harvard and the Inner City cohorts, high WSCT scores — reflecting in theory several facets of wisdom — failed to predict successful aging. This negative finding reaffirmed a basic finding of the Study: it is what people do, not what they say or write, that predicts the future.

In one of the few existing prospective studies of wisdom development, Ravenna Helson and Paul Wink came to the same conclusion. They measured "wisdom" through a pencil-and-paper measure. They noted that what they were calling wisdom increased between age 27 and age 52. But they also noted that what they measured on paper failed to correlate with success at working and loving.[12]

In trying to identify the wisest men in the Grant Study, the deployment of mature defenses and wisdom appeared rather congruent. I suspect this was because defenses reflected the behavior of these individuals and not their words. The distinguished Harvard philosopher Robert Nozick has suggested that what all conceptions of wisdom have in common is "what you need to know in order to live well and cope."[13] A Harvard man echoed this same point when he defined wisdom as "Humanism, sense of history [anticipation], patience [suppression], tolerance and compassion [altruism] and a sense of humor. . . ." (The bracketed words noting the parallel between his words and mature defenses are mine.) In other words, wisdom and mature coping have much in common, and the evidence from the Study of Adult Development suggests that coping strategies improve with age.

Put differently, over time the mature person evolves the ability to tolerate and to hold strong emotion in consciousness. He or she learns to differentiate, to modulate, but never to ignore, the passions. Most readers might agree that such evidence of wisdom abounds in most of the successful lives in this book. But then, as Paul Baltes reminds us, there are as many definitions of wisdom as people trying to measure it.

·   ·   ·

Let me close this ambiguous chapter with the admonition that wisdom involves the toleration of ambiguity and paradox. To be wise about wisdom we need to accept that wisdom does — and wisdom does not — increase with age. Age facilitates a widening social radius and more balanced ways of coping with adversity, but thus far no one can prove that wisdom is greater in old age. Perhaps we are wisest when we keep our discussion of wisdom simple and when we confine ourselves to words of one and two syllables. Winston Churchill, that master of wise simplicity and simple wisdom, reminds us, "We are all happier in many ways when we are old than when we are young. The young sow wild oats. The old grow sage."

CHAPTER TEN

SPIRITUALITY, RELIGION, AND OLD AGE

Think of the inner life — where the music exists.

Yo-Yo Ma

A beautiful wave was rushing toward the shore. "Alas," he cried, for he saw the rocks, "I shall crash and be destroyed forever." A voice behind him advised, "Relax, son. You won't be destroyed. For you are not a wave; you are the ocean."

Anonymous

The centrality of hope and love to life span development goes unchallenged. Chapter 3 linked what Conrad called hope and Erikson labeled "basic trust" to healthy maturation and successful aging. Saint Paul called love "charity," and Erikson renamed love "Intimacy" and "Generativity." In chapter 4 love was clearly linked to maturation and successful aging. But whatever the words, the melody is the same; the last years of life without hope and love become a mere sounding brass or tinkling cymbal.

But what about faith? Certainly, it would provide symmetry if life also ended with a deepening of faith and spirituality. It is true that if basic trust and hope depend upon faith in the future, then mastering the task of Integrity depends upon faith in the past. But alas, as with wisdom, the jury is still out as to whether religious faith and spirituality really deepen in old age.

Spirituality, like wisdom, is supposed to increase with age. It did for Adam Carson in chapter 2. But in the Study he was an exception. For every Adam Carson, there were many men and women whose lives moved away from, not toward, religion and spirituality. One such Harvard man wrote, "Before I was married I used to pray every evening as I went to bed. Now my spiritual activities consist mainly of trying to go to Sunday services once a month at St. John's Church in Cleveland where I have been Treasurer for 30 years."

* * *

With increasing age the Happy-Well Judge Oliver Holmes acknowledged that with time his satisfaction with religion had declined. As his personal life became ever more filled with love, his evaluation of his religious participation had gone from "generally satisfying" at age 40 to "not very satisfying" at age 68 to "it does not apply to my life" at age 80. Yet, responding to the Study statement "My spiritual beliefs are what really lie behind my whole approach to life," he checked "Definitely true of me." But he then added a lawyerly caveat: "I try to live by a personal set of principles, but I'd describe them as 'moral' rather than 'spiritual.'" At 75 Holmes substituted poetry for legal prose. To a Meeting of his fellow summer residents on his beloved Block Island he gave a sermon that conveyed his faith as follows:

> An old Quaker expression has it that when attending Meeting for Worship, one should try to 'center down.' We are to sit quietly and listen and reflect, in the hope that what is important to life will emerge. Block Island helps me center down. . . . To have spent a little time on this magic island of health and dunes, of birdsong and surging surf; to have been warmed by its sun and refreshed by its fogs; to have renewed and deepened friendships made here; to have watched our children, and their children, grow, in strength, and courage, and delight — to have done all these things before our own little life is rounded with a sleep, is to have been blessed, blessed many times indeed.

In short, he acknowledged that his magic island was a power greater than himself. Should we perhaps acknowledge that his sermon provided evidence of deepened spirituality rather than just or simply the secular reverence for life that comes with being a Keeper of the Meaning? Perhaps the difficulty is semantic. The poet Edwin Arlington Robinson suggested that humanity, analogous to kindergarten children, was endlessly trying to spell "God" with the wrong blocks. As I say, the jury is still out.

The Difference between Spirituality and Religion

The comforting certainty of specific religion or faith tradition is epitomized by the wonderful bumper sticker that I once saw in Idaho, "My God is alive and well. Sorry to hear about yours." Adolescents need such certainty in order to affirm their identity. For Identity is the first task of adult development, and religion is often part and parcel of adolescent identity. You can't have an identity if it is not your only identity. Thus, Erikson observes that adolescents must "artificially appoint perfectly well-meaning people to play the roles of enemies; and they are ever-ready to install lasting idols and ideals as guardians of a final identity."[1]

Cotton Mather and Torquemada would understand. Without such commitment we might never grow up. But with maturity adults become increasingly tolerant of paradox and ambiguity. Maturation permits nationalism (my country right or wrong) to evolve into pan-nationalism and religious observance to evolve into spirituality. A surprise of the Study of Adult Development, however, was that the presence or absence of either spirituality or religious adherence had little association with successful aging. It was hope and love rather than faith that seemed most clearly associated with maturity of defenses, with successful aging, and with Generativity. It did not matter whether the Study labeled faith as strength of religious affiliation or as the depth of one's spirituality. Neither religion nor spirituality was any more salient in old age than it had been in midlife.

I shall begin by noting some differences between religion and spirituality, but the reader must forgive me for rendering the differences more black and white than they really are. To some, the term *religion* conveys an exclusive faith — one that draws a circle that keeps others out. Thus, in college I had a history professor who insisted, "If you don't believe your religion is the only religion, then you have no religion." In contrast, spirituality involves a faith of inclusion — one that draws its circle so as to draw the whole world in. If you do not believe that we are all children of God, your spirituality might need development. The table below tries to caricature some of the differences. Admittedly, the table ignores the fact that it is possible to be deeply religious and very mature and to be "spiritual" and utterly self-absorbed.

It was the certainty of religion, of that "ol' time religion," of a child's religion, that allowed the deeply religious Puritan clergy to slowly crush to death imaginary witches and innocent agnostics. It was precisely because he "had" religion that the devout Torquemada could burn imaginary heretics and innocent Jews at the stake.

Religion involves creeds and catechisms. Spirituality involves feelings and experiences that transcend mere words. Religion is imitative and comes from without; religion is "so I've been taught." Spirituality comes from within; spirituality comes from "my strength, hope and experience." Religion is "left-brain" — it is rooted in words, sacred texts, and culture. Spirituality is "right-brain"; it transcends the boundaries of body, language, reason, and culture. However, just as both sides of the brain are inseparable, just so for most people religion and spirituality are inseparable. The oversimplifications in the table are there to illustrate that with maturation we move from the left-hand to the right-hand side of the table. But both sides of the table reflect faith.

Most religious beliefs involve dogma. Spiritual trust involves metaphor. So what is the difference between dogma and metaphor? Metaphors are open-ended and playful; dogma is rigid and serious. Metaphors mean "analogous to" and "as if"; dogma conveys "so I've been told" and "it's right there in the Bible (or in the Freud *Standard Edition*)." Metaphors allow the truth of our dreams to become clearer with every retelling. In contrast,

Adolescent Religious Belief	Mature Spiritual Trust
Erikson's task of Identity	Erikson's task of Integrity
Dogma	Metaphor
"They drew a circle that drew me out"	"I drew a circle that drew them in"
Omnipotent and closed	Vulnerable and open
"The Lord is my shepherd; I shall not want"(parent-child)	"I dress the wound, God heals it" (partnership)
Shaming, obligation, judgment	Affirmation, gratitude, forgiveness
A wish to stay out of Hell	The result of having been there

dogma may insist that heretics be executed. Metaphors add leaven to theory and to poetry, but dogma adds dead weight to Thomistic and Talmudic prose. Metaphors conceptualize; dogma enshrines. Dogma retards science; metaphors advance science.

Developmental psychologists have long appreciated that the cognitions of children evolve from concrete, literal operations into more complex, more metaphysical views of the universe. Jean Piaget, the great child psychologist, pointed out that children's morality matures — and matures quite independently of religious instruction.[2] Piaget used a child's rules for playing marbles to illustrate how children's rules of morality evolved first from self-centered rules (e.g., might makes right and God is on the side of the big battalions) into black-and-white Old Testament laws of retaliation (e.g., an eye for an eye and a tooth for a tooth and it is worse to break ten cups by mistake than one cup on purpose.) Then Piaget observed that older children's rules for games evolved into the more merciful and more relativistic morality of the Golden Rule. Motivation became important. Breaking one cup on purpose deserved more severe punishment than breaking ten cups by mistake.

James Fowler,[3] a developmental psychologist and theologian at Emory University, and Jane Loevinger,[4] a Washington University psychologist, have devoted their lives to carrying Piaget's ideas further into adult development. As children mature, "Christian" insistence on shame, obligation, and judgment evolve into "Christ-like" affirmation, forgiveness, and gratitude. Adolescents enjoy intellectual certainty and youth; supreme court justices endure old age and doubt. There are many religious martyrs; there are very few spiritual ones.

Identity, if we are lucky, is acquired in adolescence; it provides the first stage of our adult development. Religion, too, provides a secure base on which to build. But with time, a reassuring personal god evolves into a Higher Power that is intangible, universal, and well beyond easy comprehension. Just as in the last chapter empathy and the appreciation of context — a result of brain maturation and experience — led to wisdom, just so, the same ingredients *plus* dialogue with others lead to spirituality. Thou and I possess separate identities; we may possess quite separate religions; but if we talk to one another, we may find that we honor the same Higher Power. Put differently, a spiritual vision is far more than humane sentiments, useful virtues, and civilized values. Surely, spiritual maturity requires a dialectic of science, ethics, psychology, religion, and generations. Truth may be unitary from God's perspective, but it is many faceted from ours. Hopefully, as people grow older they learn to communicate with individuals from a variety of faith traditions. And to age well, remember to have dialogues, not monologues. To the question "Taboos on obscenity, nudity, pre-marital sex, homosexuality, pornography seem to be dead or dying. Is this good or bad?" a 75-year-old Harvard minister responded: "NEITHER. What human beings need are limits to their behavior and freedom to realize their true selves — we really need a societal consensus on limits balanced with freedoms. I think these limits & freedoms and the balance changes with the culture." He had developed the skill to imagine the world from eyes other than his own.

Hearing other people's stories about their religious and spiritual experiences may contribute to the evolvement of spirituality. Spirituality, like mutuality, involves identification not comparison. We can't help trusting Lincoln when he says, "with malice toward none, with charity for all." Put differently, we mistrust another person's religious beliefs more often than their spirituality. In short, I am not suggesting that to have a personal faith tradition — in other words to derive comfort from a specific religion — is immature. I am only suggesting that with maturity come understanding and reverence for what all religions share. To age gracefully the old must learn to part with all that is nonessential — and most religious differences arise from nonessentials.

*   *   *

Having said all this, I must acknowledge that my interviews over decades with both the Grant Study men and the Terman women were based on my firm belief that with age their spirituality would deepen. Over time my own certainly has. Cross-sectional Gallup polls agreed with me. Since at the end of life a mastery of Integrity necessitates faith, I had believed that mastery of the task of Integrity would be associated with heightened spirituality. Thus, at first I clung to the few cases, like Adam Carson, whose religious and spiritual commitment did indeed deepen in old age. Finally, however, I realized (at least for the members of the Study of Adult Development) I was backing the wrong hypothesis. Neither spirituality nor religiosity appeared associated with successful aging. Asked at age 75 if their spiritual life had deepened, the majority of the Harvard men and Terman women answered, "No." (If you wish to maintain pet theories intact, refrain from longitudinal study.)

It is true that in many churches there are more old people than young people but that does not prove that people go to church more as they grow older. It may simply reflect that as the younger generation gets more science, anthropology, and history in school than their grandparents — and less religious instruction — they may also attend church and temple less than their grandparents ever did. In old age they may continue to do so.

Again, as with wisdom, our linking of deepening spirituality to old age may be an artifact not only of cross-sectional study, but also of memory. Our last memories of great spiritual leaders are often as old men and women, but in fact spiritual leaders usually achieve prominence when young. Was the spirituality of the elderly Gandhi, Billy Graham, Tolstoy, or Mother Teresa any deeper toward the end of life than it was when they were 40 or 50? I suspect not. Albert Schweitzer's guiding moral principle, "reverence for life," began to rule his own life at 40. He realized that such a principle was necessary to establish a spiritual and humane relationship with both people "and all creatures." But in our mind's eye the deeply spiritual physician who would not kill even a mosquito wears a crown of white hair.

•   •   •

An interesting finding from both the Terman and the Harvard studies was the positive association of depression with religious affiliation. I contrasted the 30 Harvard men with the strongest religious affiliation and participation to the 127 Harvard men who over the past 20 years had little or no involvement. To my astonishment, the men with extensive spiritual or religious involvement were no more likely to age successfully, but they were four times as likely to have experienced depression. A hundred years ago William James had already linked severe depression to deepened spirituality and to being "twice born." Deep interest in both spirituality and major depressive disorder had afflicted multiple generations of the James family. The men in the Study, too, with the strongest religious affiliation were two and a half times as likely to have multiple relatives with depression.

A history of past depression — whether measured as a present/absent variable or assessed as a continuum (i.e., the number of indicators of depression before age 50 or the number of depressed relatives or lifetime use of psychotropic drugs) were *positively* and significantly associated with strength of religious affiliation.[5] But the same three variables were *negatively* associated with richness of overall social supports and with being among the Happy-Well. I do not mean to convey that religion is bad for you;

doctors and hospitals are not bad for your health either. It is simply that people who are in pain use both doctors and religion more often. To the lonely, religion, like psychiatry, is always a source of empathic friendship.

The good news, however, is that religion works. The influential Duke Longitudinal Study of Aging followed 252 older men for 25 years or until death intervened. They found that religious involvement in men was *negatively associated* with mortality.[6] Religious affiliation and psychiatrists both serve as an effective balm for depression and lack of love. For example, strong religious affiliation — although positively correlated with a history of depression — was not associated with psychiatric visits or with *currently self-reported* symptoms of depression. In other words, at least in the Harvard sample, religious affiliation may have been used in lieu of psychiatrists to relieve rather than prevent major depressive disorder. General population studies have also noted that high religious affiliation is correlated with low self-report of *current* depressive symptoms.[7,8] In addition, religious adherence prior to hospitalization for depression is the most powerful premorbid predictor of rapid remission.[9,10]

Let me offer a paradox. Erikson suggests that basic trust and hope evolve out of the matrix of a loving mother and a receptive infant. However, spirituality often develops in the absence of a loving mother. It's no accident that the hymn *Amazing Grace* was written by a once unloved convict. Nor was it accident that the orphaned Leo Tolstoy's spirituality was sufficiently profound to inspire both Mahatma Gandhi and Martin Luther King, Jr.

A close friend of mine stopped going to church when his fourth child was born. His rationale was that there were too many snowsuits to put on. The reality was that with four children he did not need any more social supports. Thirty years later he returned to church — his children were grown and his wife had left him. Anna Love was introduced in chapter 4 as a model of a woman with strong social supports. Nevertheless, when I asked how her religious beliefs had deepened with age, she replied,

"They remained very much the same all the way through until my husband died. After he died, I needed more from God and from prayer and from my church fellows. I have asked for it and received it. I think my faith is much stronger now because I needed it so badly." Perhaps it is no accident that in many religions, lonely celibacy is considered a powerful means of maintaining and deepening spiritual commitment. Only the lonely can overcome God's apparent distance. Within each Study cohort there were examples of deepening religious affiliation and spirituality in men and women who when young had been denied hope and love.

Although almost blind from cataracts, Terman woman Martha Jobe was still working at age 77 — not from desire but from necessity. She did not feel sorry for herself, and she retained great dignity. Nevertheless, she was profoundly weary of life. Unlike most of the severely depressed individuals in the Study, Martha's difficulties did not seem due to mental illness. She did not make mountains out of molehills. She had never seen a psychiatrist nor taken a tranquilizer. Rather, it was life, and not her brain, that had treated her shabbily.

Recently, Martha Jobe had developed a very painful disorder, temporal arteritis. The only effective treatment, prednisone, had accelerated her cataracts. Because of the cataracts, Martha Jobe explained, "I can no longer paint watercolors. I can no longer see beauty anymore. Nothing is left . . . at a certain age everything goes out of life . . . that's where I am." In addition, prednisone had compromised her immune system, leading to repeated episodes of shingles (one of the most painful illnesses extant). As she explained to us, "Four episodes this year, four episodes last year. You are only supposed to get [it] once." Her repetitive bouts of shingles led to increasing lameness; "I am sort of a cripple." But she hastened to assure us that unlike painting, "walking has never been a hobby." Despite her illness, she retained a sense of humor. Indeed, what was most striking about Martha Jobe was her wonderful smile. She made us feel instantly included in her world. Even as an unhappy teenager, she had loved reading joke books. Unlike individuals with clinical depression, during the interview she did not leave her audience feeling depressed, only admiring of her stoicism and her humor.

Like many individuals who become deeply spiritual, Martha Jobe had had a terrible mother. When as a highly intelligent child young Martha would contradict her mother, her mother would spank her. At age 30 she had written to the Study, "Mother is constantly causing trouble and unhappiness"; and when she was 77, Martha Jobe confessed, "I never really liked her." But at the very moment that Jobe graduated brilliantly from college, her mother had had a stroke. "That clobbered the whole thing." Having hated her mother as a child, Martha Jobe was fated to become a "nurse companion to [her] ailing mother." But Jobe blamed herself. "I wasn't strong enough to go the whole way. . . . I became a caretaker of people. I was cowardly. I did not assert myself against my mother. . . . She was a selfish character."

No sooner had her mother died than Martha Jobe was saddled with a dependent, chauvinistic husband. After ten years and two children, she left him. "It was a mistake" that they had married. Asked what the best times were with her husband, she said that she at first had been very much in love with him. She thought she was marrying an artist and would be able to work with other artists. But her husband started a pottery business. "That was his independence, but it was hard work for me." She almost shouted. "I was the bookkeeper, and I got pretty sick of it. . . . A man should be able to take care of his own money."

Whereas Jobe was stoical about the destruction of her life by her mother, she spoke with force and anger about her husband. Making his pottery glazes became her artistic career. "I did the hard work and he created. . . ." He would go off to have coffee with his Greek friends, and she would stay home glazing his pottery. Then she softened and tried to explain it. She could not speak Greek, and so, "He forgot me. It wasn't malicious." After their separation, "I stopped talking to him. It was a cruel thing for me to do." When the interviewer sympathetically said, "It must have been miserable," she mistook the remark as meaning that the interviewer was sympathizing with her husband. Yes, she tried to agree, deciding to leave him had been a terrible thing for *her* to do.

From age 25 to age 40 Martha Jobe had watched her older son inexorably die from cystic fibrosis. She had been helpless to save him. Then one day she found herself in the public library reading a book on yoga. "A great golden light appeared. A pale glow flooded everything." There were no words, but the glow had permeated her and everything around her. Shortly afterward she was led to the Unity Church by this experience of inner illumination. She found the Unity Church and their upbeat advice comforting. "They send you prayers," she explained. "Those prayers would pull me out of depression, when I was in the depths of despair over my son."

After her son died, despite her summa cum laude degree in art, Jobe took a job as a nurse's aide because "it seemed logical." Her wage in 1960 was $1.35 an hour. One day she saw an ad indicating that the physics department at Cal Tech needed a high school graduate with a flair for art. She told her nursing supervisor she was going to leave. The supervisor replied that there was no way Martha Jobe could work at Cal Tech because "I was just a nurse's aide." The supervisor was wrong. For Martha Jobe "Cal Tech was an exciting and beautiful experience. My ability to fill a place in the highly scientific world of nuclear physics came as a shock and a delight . . . the privilege of working with truly great minds and to see the works of the universe so closely."

Before computers existed that could register atomic scintillation, Martha Jobe would study the films of the atomic particle collisions and then create an artistic rendering of the theoretical physicists' films. She described the work in which she originally participated as "absolutely magical . . . I still take a great interest in understanding their physics. They had theories that nothing was real, and everything depended on probabilities." She also read articles on astrophysics. The fact that the two disciplines, of tiny particle physics and of enormous cosmic galaxies, had come together fascinated her. Martha Jobe was sustained by a deep spiritual communion with the unity of the universe. She was no longer an unhappy wave; she was the ocean.

Asked how she would live her life over, Martha Jobe said, "I would pick art. . . . I was going to be an artist . . . but so what? It did not work out. I was an artist from birth — I've always been an artist." But it was not in Jobe's nature to blame anyone else for her pain. Asked if society had given her a fair chance, she replied with dead earnestness, "It was my fault. All this talk of equality of women . . . a great deal of it is their own fault." She thought that women were "full of hormones" and that this led to "flighty ideas." Women were simply "unable to overcome the physical aspects of being a female." She said that there was a weakness and ambivalence in women. In short, like Maria, the poor Latina in chapter 5, Jobe reflected the hobbling internalized self-criticism that comes from social stigma.

If Martha Jobe made any contribution to her own pain, it was that, like many artists and physicists, she had not maintained an adequate social network. Jobe was lonely. She derived comforting prayers from the Unity Church, but not from the community. She spoke with real warmth of her granddaughter, whom she took pains to visit; but her pension from Cal Tech was $140 a month and her granddaughter lived in North Dakota. Asked how she stayed in touch with her other grandchildren, Jobe sighed. "I write them letters." She took out a carefully maintained scrapbook to show us their pictures. Her oldest friend was a woman who had been her invalid son's homeroom teacher. "She invites me to Thanksgiving." But there was no one else.

Asked what she did with other people, she said, "I don't do a thing. My legs hurt." Asked again what took the place of friends, she laughed and she parried us with humor. "I make enemies." At this point she became very, very sad. She admitted that her chief companions were the counter staff at Denny's Restaurant. Every morning Martha Jobe went to Denny's for breakfast. The waiters and waitresses would greet her cheerily, and she always tried to say something nice in return. "Except for their happy faces, nobody cares." It was a terrible thing, she explained, when in order to have someone say something nice to you, you had to get it in a public place, and "even then you don't get it for free." With the exception of the Unity Church and its loving prayers, Jobe's social supports were almost nil.

Asked what she saw as the attributes of successful aging, Martha Jobe replied, "I don't think there is anything good . . . let's face it — you're on the downhill." She explained that every time she tried to pass on information, "Someone tells you you're out of date." When asked who was her model for growing older, she said, "The men are all ugly and bald, and the women dye their hair. There is no way to age gracefully."

As we were leaving, we asked if we could see any of Martha Jobe's watercolors. She showed us a beautiful painting relegated to her back storeroom. It was of the Napa Valley countryside and looked rather like a Van Gogh — another deeply spiritual painter with poor social supports.

*   *   *

Ted Merton first appeared in chapter 1 as my "testy" friend and again in chapter 3 as having the "mother who has not exactly made up for Dad's shortcomings." He wrote at age 72:

> Before there were dysfunctional families, I came from one. Others may list accomplishments in the wider world, but it's the internal journey I savor and celebrate. My professional life hasn't been disappointing — far from it — but the truly gratifying unfolding has been into the person I've slowly become: comfortable, joyful, connected and effective. A year in bed with pulmonary tuberculosis, decades of psychotherapy and nine months of hospitalization for major depression are parts of the story. . . . Since it wasn't widely available then, I hadn't read that children's classic, *The Velveteen Rabbit* [a stuffed rabbit who came to life through a child's love], which tells how connectedness is something we must let happen to us, and then we become solid and whole.

As that tale recounts tenderly, only love can make us real. Denied this in boyhood for reasons I now understand, it took me years to tap substitute sources. What seems marvelous is how many there are and how restorative they prove. What durable and pliable creatures we are, and what a storehouse of goodwill lurks in the social fabric. . . . I never dreamed my later years would be so stimulating and rewarding.

Ted Merton suggested that like the Velveteen Rabbit he became healed through love; but two marriages, two psychoanalyses, and even two children had not fully healed him — only his return to St. Luke's Episcopal Church.

Ted Merton had attended a church-affiliated private school, and in college he had briefly flirted with the ministry before deciding on medicine. At 19 he had gone with his closest friend to work at the Anglican Grenfell Mission in Labrador. Much later he recalled, "Being in nature has always been a spiritual experience for me — a way to rest in God — never more so than the summer I spent with Bob in Labrador. . . . We'd lie on the dock at night looking up at the aurora borealis in all its glory." For the next fifteen years religion played only a minor role in his life, until he was stricken with tuberculosis.

One evening shortly after supper, I lay abed when something amazing happened. In the stillness of twilight, there was suddenly a blinding light in the corner of the room, an indoor supernova. Instinctively, I climbed out of bed and onto my knees, sensing I was in the presence of the Holy, like some Old Testament character. I heard no voice, yet the injunction was plain: Follow Me. Limp and in tears, I slowly climbed back into bed. Though for years I discounted this event as paranormal, I have to admit my life has gone much better since I hearkened to it. In retrospect, it seems a message from Jesus, an experience of grace.

But even after that experience, Merton's religion for the next twenty years was psychoanalysis, not Christianity. Indeed, after his first divorce, at age 55, Dr. Merton wrote to the Study, "Since divorce I'm learning how to be comfortably intimate for the first time and how to be sensibly parental in the face of an unspent youth. . . . I don't go to church at all. I hate organized religions." This was to change very soon.

Five years later, Merton's second divorce was accompanied by a very severe depression during which he lost not only his wife, his savings, and his job, but even his network of professional colleagues. "It was as if blue-black ink had been spilled on my mind." It was at this point that he returned to the Episcopal Church for the first time since college. "Something got put into me that was never really there before." He described his process of involvement. "It was like sleepwalking at first, but bit-by-bit I've gotten involved." People have described falling in love or recovering from alcoholism through AA in similar fashion. I would guess the same recovery process — being loved and internalizing the love — takes place in the lives of velveteen rabbits.

It was not until Merton was in his 70s that I asked him about his shift in religious belief and his return to the Episcopal Church. He felt sure that the reason had been his depression. "I did hit bottom. I was almost on the street; that's how I felt." He explained that his hospitalization for depression at age 55 brought to mind his hospitalization for tuberculosis twenty years before, when suddenly a corner of his room seemed "filled with nearly blinding white light." Later Merton confessed to me, "I have become a bit of a contemplative." But perhaps our spirituality changes less than it sometimes seems. At 19 Ted Merton was already a contemplative; he was already finding in the aurora borealis a power greater than himself.

At 77 Ted Merton viewed the past five years as the happiest in his life. He is very active at his church, working to bring it into an awareness as a center for community life — scheduling events on family life and the environment. "I do a lot of stuff for the church." He helps with pastoral care and as a lay Eucharistic minister, which means going to shut-ins to give them Communion. As he aged, Dr. Merton understood the underpinnings of Integrity and confided to me, "I know there is a God who nudges me in subtle ways and by whom I feel loved incomparably. When my time comes to die I'll be ready. That's an experience so many have had that I don't want to miss it."

Increasingly, he appreciated a widened social radius. "I've relearned that all life is connected biologically, ecologically and spiritually. All life has power and deserves respect and understanding. . . . I find myself getting more mystical as time passes. Thomas Merton [the author of *The Seven Storey Mountain*] speaks to me clearly as wouldn't have been so decades ago." He did not need to go to Denny's for companionship.

* * *

Bill Graham's life had been no happier than Jobe's or Merton's. Asked at age 68 about his childhood, Bill Graham had acknowledged, "I don't have any pleasant memories of childhood." His early years were full of "abuse, starvation, lack of love and aloneness." Review of his record compiled fifty years earlier revealed that he had not been exaggerating. He had not seen his mother since she gave him up to foster care when he was three and a half years old. At 12 he could not even recall what she looked like. Indeed, Graham did not even know where he had lived before age 6 — his age when his father was committed to a state hospital for psychosis. From age 6 to 11 he lived with a family in South Boston who regularly beat him. These foster parents, he believed, were more interested in the state aid support money than in having Graham around. "I always knew someone was coming to visit because I got fed and cleaned. I was young enough to mess my pants and to be thrown down the stairs because of it," he recalled. "I remember being beaten and not having food." But he explained that by far "the most abusive thing was nobody caring. . . . Having no one to care for me, no one responsible."

Asked how these experiences of abuse affected him as an adult, he replied, "I learned to be more compassionate. . . . Shit happens and you get over it."

His actions spoke louder than his words. Even though his

father never cared for him, as an adult Bill Graham took the older man out of "the inhumane conditions of the state hospital" to live with him. In the last years of her life when she was lonely and isolated, he regularly visited the mother who had placed him in foster care. In 1976, when Graham was 47, his interviewer had written, "He has [had] the worst childhood of the men I have seen." Indeed, by our scoring system, only 16 out of the 456 Inner City men in the Study had suffered a worse childhood. "Yet," the interviewer continued, "I was struck that with a background of such deprivation he has gone on to mold a rich and full life for himself. I have seen few other subjects who seemed as enthusiastic about their activities as Graham."

At age 47 the secular reasons for Graham's resilience seemed not hard to find. Although he had been a lad from a no-hope background, with all of the risk factors that resilience researchers believe damn children to poor adult outcome, Graham had married well. Through the alchemy of a strong marriage — in Graham's case a woman ten years older than himself who spoiled him — Graham eventually attained Generativity. It was obvious to the interviewer, even when Graham was 25, that he was very proud of his wife, and she in turn informed the investigator that she thought Graham was wonderful — and that her parents thought so too. For the first time Graham felt he had a real home.

It was noteworthy that at age 25 Graham was not at all religious. He attended services only occasionally. By age 45 he had stopped all together. As with Judge Holmes, he found his Higher Power within his family matrix. At age 45 Bill Graham described his wife as "devoted to me and the family." She was "unselfish, kind, loving and generous." He was deeply touched by her understanding and reassured by the fact that she was dependable, considerate, and kept an immaculate home.

Then, when Bill Graham was 53, his wife of thirty-three years died tragically of cancer. For the next five years his life was in disarray. Two years after his wife's death he explained to an interviewer:

I lost my wife, okay? It's very simple to say I lost my wife, but that's not true. That's not true of anyone. In no significant sequence, in no particular order of importance, I say I lost a friend, I lost a lover, I lost a mother, I lost a sister, I lost a doctor, a nurse, a teacher, a finance expert, a fighter, I lost many, many people when I lost this one person. That's a lot. A lot of people think it's just . . . a wife, just a person, just one person. But unless you've walked that path, it's hard to imagine all the things you have to do for yourself all of a sudden.

At 58, five years after his wife's death, Bill Graham was hospitalized for major depression. At 59 he was still subjectively severely physically disabled, and there was no joy in his life. Then, while attending a spiritual healing center, he was relieved of a long-standing stomach problem. Later, he was healed by a Catholic priest of a back problem that had been at the root of his physical disability. Wanting to learn more about healing, he began his spiritual mission. He obtained a Doctorate of Metaphysical Science (Msc.D.) from the International Metaphysical Ministry. His thesis was titled "Metaphysical Healing: A Natural and Divine Process." After he undertook his healing mission at 60, he entered into the "happiest 10 years of my life."

The interviewer found Bill Graham at 68 to be a very spiritually committed man. He is now retired and lives with his second wife on Cape Cod. He is a short, thin man with glasses, a thin white mustache, and thinning gray hair. Although raised a Catholic, he said that as an adolescent "I had found that it didn't serve me." More recently Graham had broadened his perspective on organized religion, attending services and learning to live and think nondenominationally.

But his spiritual life is centered in his current work, a healing mission that he describes as a "ministry of hope." After starting to work as a healer, Graham finally found real purpose in life. Given the problems he had with anxiety and depression earlier in his life, Graham now considers that achieving inner peace has been one of his major life accomplishments. He understands that he ministers to people's psyches as much or more than to their bodies. He teaches them about inner peace, and he tries to help them feel safe and comfortable. The laying on of hands, he explained, awakens a natural healing process in the body. He is convinced that such healing is effective, but he acknowledged that he did not understand how. He believes that everyone is here for a reason and discovering this purpose would lead to a feeling of richness and gratitude.

Graham does not accept money for his healing work or for his inspirational lectures. He enjoys helping people, but he does not want to take or feel that he deserves credit for the healing process. Rather, "It is important that people know I don't do it. I say to them, 'Don't thank me . . . go and praise God.'" He has concluded that the basis of healing is found in love and in spirituality and not in religion. Between age 54 and age 68 the changes wrought in his life by his spiritual involvement were extraordinary. Bill Graham's spiritual life deepened and his psychiatric symptoms vanished. By 69, despite being clearly objectively disabled (by bladder cancer, kidney failure, and triple bypass heart surgery), subjectively he saw himself as just barely disabled. His life satisfaction score now qualified him for the Happy-Well. He found both spirituality and his second wife "very satisfying." In addition, his first wife of thirty-three years still lived on inside of him. As Graham explained to the interviewer, Rachel, his first wife, "supported me in everything I did, including music."

The interviewer asked Graham to tell him a little more about his music.

Graham brought out his songbook and was excited and impassioned as he explained the creative process of his songs. He sang parts of several of them to me in his soft and lovely voice. He felt that the meaning of many of his songs came from people who have died speaking through him. He believes this because the songs just come to him and he writes about things that he knows nothing about. His songs were pretty and moving. He sang parts of songs entitled The Power of Prayer, and another about a mother trying to comfort a child frightened by thunder. . . .

I liked Bill Graham very much and had a terrific time with him over the four hours of our interview. I found his sense of inner peace to be deep and sincere, and I was impressed by his current contentment given his illness and his terribly difficult history of abandonment and abuse in childhood, and the cancer and death of his first wife.

Graham's kidney failure required chronic renal dialysis. His response to dialysis was sufficiently courageous that one of his dialysis nurses asked him to speak with a particularly irritable and complaining patient who was having difficulty with the procedure. In short, in Graham's world not only his interviewers and his clients but also his caregivers were impressed by his inner peace and his ability to raise hope.

"I just love retirement," he wrote to the Study the year after the above interview. What got him out of bed in the morning was "opening the gift of a new day." His enjoyable retirement activities consist of "theater, helping others, gardening, travel, reading for the joy of it, spending time with his wife and just 'being.'" Although he was a tenth-grade dropout, Graham made no mention of depending upon television, which some Harvard men, in far better physical health than Graham, watched for twenty hours a week.

Successful aging, Graham explained, was to "learn to live in thankfulness, looking back at what you have had, and at what you didn't have [then] but that you do have now." Not a bad definition of Integrity. It is next best to getting what you want.

There is an almost miraculous addendum to Graham's narrative. Kidney function is a physiological function that declines inexorably with increasing age. After this book was written, however, Graham revealed to the Study that for more than a year, he had not required dialysis.

Does Spirituality Deepen with Age?

In theory, spirituality *should* deepen in old age for all of us. For if growing older does not inevitably lead toward spiritual development, growing older does alter the conditions of life in ways that are conducive to spirituality. Aging slows us down and provides us time and peace to smell life's flowers. Aging simplifies our daily routine and facilitates the acceptance of the things we cannot change. Aging banks our instinctual fires and increases our capacity to be internally quiet. Aging compels us to contemplate death and to familiarize ourselves with ceasing to be a special and "terminally unique" wave. Aging focuses us toward becoming one with the ultimate ground of all being. Aging allows us to feel part of the ocean. The Hindu concept of life stages suggests that when we become grandparents, we should turn away from the world and take up spiritual interests.[11] When devout Brahmins become grandfathers, they turn their worldly belongings over to their sons.

One of the best cross-sectional studies of late-life spiritual development is by Lars Tornstam,[12] who found that a majority of his representative sample of 912 Danes over the age of 75 perceived an increase in spirituality. Compared to when they were 50, they responded with statements such as: "I have more delight in my inner world"; "The border between life and death is less striking"; "How unimportant individual life is, compared to the continuation of life as such." But Tornstam's study was cross-sectional and could have been explained by "cohort effects."

In the Study of Adult Development, at least, strength of religious affiliation, openness to new ideas, and generous political views did not predict successful aging. Nor did the three deeply spiritual exemplars in this chapter — Jobe, Merton, and Graham — score particularly high in successful aging. Their social relationships remained more limited than those of most of the Happy-Well. Rather, the keys to successful aging seemed often to lie more in the realm of secular relationships.

But then, spirituality does not exist in a secular vacuum. Spirituality is often manifested where two or more are gathered together in recognition of a power greater than themselves, to listen to the inner life — where the music lives. The debate whether faith in God is merely the shadow of love or whether our love for each other is created by the shadow of God is, I think, similar to the physicist's debate over whether light is made up of particles or waves. It all depends on how you choose to view light — or to view love.

CHAPTER ELEVEN

DO PEOPLE REALLY CHANGE OVER TIME?

My intention is to tell
of bodies changed
to different forms . . .
The heavens and all below them,
Earth and her creatures,
All change,
And we, part of creation,
Also must suffer change.

Ovid, *Metamorphoses*
(translated by Rolfe Humphries)

Thus far, everything I have written has been predicated upon my belief in adult development. I have stressed that growing older is not just a matter of decay. Rather, I have marshaled evidence that with aging there is a widening social radius, a greater tolerance, and a maturation of involuntary coping mechanisms. In fact, successful living, not just successful aging, involves learning to take others inside and to grow in the process. As Carl Jung suggests, "Many — far too many — aspects of life, which should also have been experienced, lie in the lumber-room among dusty memories; but sometimes, too, they are glowing coals under gray ashes."[1] Watching such coals burst into flame has made pursuit of the lives of the Study members infinitely exciting.

.   .   .

But such a premise depends upon my assumption that human character and behavior are not set in plaster at 30 and essentially immutable thereafter. Such a premise depends on my assumption that adults, like children, continue to develop. Such an assumption is by no means universally accepted.[2]

Let me put the alternative view — "folks don't change" — into historical perspective. The 1970s were an exciting time for those who believed that personality evolved over time. Beginning with Erikson's earlier *Childhood and Society,* based in part on data from the Institute of Human Development at Berkeley, many of the great longitudinal studies begun in the 1930s — especially those from Berkeley[3-5] — had finally begun to bear adult fruit. Carl Jung's and Dante Alighieri's romantic ideas about the importance of the midlife crisis and Gail Sheehy's popularization of the concept of life stages in her phenomenally bestselling *Passages*[6] seemed irresistible. In the 1970s, too, Daniel Levinson, a brilliant Yale social psychologist, fascinated by his own perception of how he had changed between 30 and 60, wrote his wise and influential *Seasons of a Man's Life.*[7] All these forces gave authority to the idea of personality change and of a midlife crisis.

Besides, there were stunning examples of personality change in the news. In the 1960s as a left-leaning "Yippie" and one of the notorious Chicago Seven, Jerry Rubin had established a national reputation as an antiestablishment caterpillar. Then, ten years later, from his chrysalis he had emerged as a Wall Street butterfly resplendent in conventional suits and expensive neckties. And in the 1970s Richard Alpert, son of a conventional railroad president and once an ambitious Harvard academic, reemerged as Baba Ram Dass, an India-trained guru sporting a long beard and white robes.[8] Conservatives could become hippies and hippies conservatives.

In the 1970s, I, too, climbed on the bandwagon with *Adaptation to Life.* Long fascinated by recovery from mental illness, I had previously written articles in respectable academic journals demonstrating that defenses and personality "matured" over time. Projection could evolve into altruism and empathy. Perversions could evolve into sublimation. Passive-aggressive jerks could evolve into mature humanists. Character was not set in plaster!

In the 1980s, however, a reaction set in. Belief in genetic predestination became no longer solely the province of right-wing bigots. Even liberals admitted the importance of heredity. Personality psychologists administered personality tests to the same people six, ten, even thirty years later, and found remarkable stability.[9] Extroverts remained extroverts, and introverts remained introverts. Young adults high in neurotic traits did not abandon them in middle life; individuals low in neurotic traits remained that way decades later. Indeed, I have already admitted in chapter 5 that little liberal caterpillars do not usually evolve into Wall Street conservatives, nor do conventionally ambitious and successful conservative caterpillars often exchange the title of Ivy League professor for guru. The Richard Alperts and Jerry Rubins are exceptions.

Soon after Levinson published his ideas, careful objective research showed that his concept of midlife crisis was honored more often in the breach than in the observance.[10,11] After harvesting the best prospective study in the world of adolescents maturing into parents of adolescents, Berkeley professor Jack Block came to the same conclusion. "Amidst change and transformation, there is an essential coherence to personality development."[12]

In spite of this sea change, I continued to believe that character is not set in plaster. In the year 2000 I was sure that given the passage of time many of the Happy-Well would have been men dismissed as "C's" by the Study staff in 1945. I felt equally confident that many of the Sad-Sick would be found among men once classified in college as "A's."

To my consternation, one of the very best indicators of how the Harvard men adapted to old age was whether they had been classified an A or a C in college! Of the 85 A's — those men seen as the best adjusted in college — 28 were among the Happy-Well and only 9 were among the Sad-Sick. In a majority of cases those

A's who aged badly had developed the personality-distorting illnesses of alcohol abuse or major depressive disorder. Among the 40 worst-adjusted college men — the C's — only 3 men at 80 were among the Happy-Well. The findings in chapter 3 that the past affects the future seem true.

Again, as I have followed the lives of the Inner City men, one of the best indicators of successful aging was how well they had adapted in junior high school. Of the 150 Inner City men with the best scores for coping in junior high school, 56 were among the Happy-Well and only 13 were among the Sad-Sick. Of the 19 Inner City men with the lowest scores for adolescent adaptation, only a single man was among the Happy-Well, and 11 men, three-fifths, were among the Sad-Sick or Prematurely Dead. Successful adolescence predicted successful old age.

• • •

But, of course, life is not that black and white. The paradox remains. My polarized representation of the argument does not capture the fact that both change and continuity are true. Personality is the sum of temperament and character. Temperament is what provides continuity to our personalities, and temperament to a large extent is set in plaster. Our temperament, which is largely hereditary and which comprises such personality elements as extroversion or introversion, our tested IQ, and the genetic component of our social intelligence, does not change very much. With the passage of decades, identical twins separated at birth became more, not less, alike.[13] Thus, if one defines personality by traits measured with pencil and paper — intelligence, extroversion, even self-esteem, for example — then over time little changes.

Character, however, does change. If one defines personality by an individual's adaptive style (e.g., at 40 does an abused daughter marry yet a fourth abusive husband or does she run a shelter for abused women?), then over time personality changes profoundly. For character, in contrast to temperament, is profoundly affected by environment and maturation. In addition, although our genes are set in plaster, many of these very genes are programmed to promote plasticity.[14] Folks do mature. They outgrow and recover from restrictive environments. In the absence of illness, mental health improves into the seventh decade.[15]

With age we all become more experienced and less frightened of other people and more comfortable in expressing our own opinions. When we were adolescent, it was the other way around. Our self-assurance, our tendency to criticize our children, our satisfaction with our lot, are highly inconsistent between ages 30 and 70.[16] By 60, many of us cease to admire the noisy music that we once loved as adolescents, and we become convinced that we always loved Mozart. Our signatures are theoretically set in plaster. But in actual fact, our adolescent signatures often bear little resemblance to our signatures in old age. Even if temperament stays the same, character evolves.

• • •

Resilience, of the sort epitomized by Anthony Pirelli in chapter 1, can also lead to change. Resilience reflects individuals who metaphorically resemble a twig with a fresh, green living core. When twisted out of shape, such a twig bends, but it does not break; instead, it springs back and continues growing. In resilience both genes and environment play crucial roles. On the one hand, our ability to feel safe enough to deploy adaptive defenses like humor and altruism is facilitated by our being among loving friends. On the other hand, our ability to appear so attractive to others that they will love us is very much dependent upon the genetic capacity that made some of us "easy" attractive babies. In tracing how vulnerable, poor children on the Hawaiian island of Kauai became effective adults, psychologist Emmy Werner has stressed the importance of being a "cuddly" child and of being a child who elicits predominantly positive responses from the environment and who manifests great skill at recruiting substitute parents.[17] But being an attractive adult is very much dependent on our social intelligence and our mature defenses. In other words, the factors promoting resilience are catalyzed in part by resilience. Put differently, in understanding the sources of resilience simple cart-and-horse causal sequences are rarely identified.

Besides, love is never enough. Social support must not only be present; it must be recognized, taken in, and then "metabolized." Just as part of the skill of a good football running back is his ability to find existing blockers, just so part of resilience is the ability to find the loving and health-giving individuals within one's social matrix wherever they may be. This is why extended families are one of the great boons to mental health. Extended families provide more chances for healthy identification and provide the chances in a greater variety of "flavors."

Among the Inner City men there were 41 who came from spectacularly dysfunctional families. Such families received *ten* points or more on a scale of troubles so stringent that a family's being known to five social agencies was worth only half a point. Having a mentally retarded mother or an alcoholic father or being separated from both parents for more than six months while still a child each contributed only one point.[18] Thus, in order for a man to receive ten points or more, a lot needed to have gone wrong when he was a child.

Nevertheless, at age 47, the 41 men from families who received ten points or more were not more likely to be chronically unemployed or below the poverty line than men from more functional families. At age 70, only 9 such environmentally disadvantaged men were among the Sad-Sick and 13 were among the Happy-Well; this was the same proportion as for men who came from happier families. There were 99 Inner City men whose fathers belonged to social class V — that is, their fathers were either unskilled laborers or on welfare, had less than ten grades of education, and lived in rundown tenements.[19] Of these 99 sons of "underclass" fathers, only 13 remained in social class V when adult, and only 16 were among the Sad-Sick. At 47 only 16 of the

99 were themselves below the poverty line, and only 13 were un-employed for ten years.[20] Admittedly, these men had white skin, had enjoyed the benefits of the GI bill, and had come of age in the boom times of the 1950s. In addition, their fathers' destitu-tion was in part a product of the Great Depression and in part a product of belonging to Irish and Italian minorities, despised in their fathers' generation but not in their sons'. Over generations not only can folks change but so, too, can stigma.

Resilient Lives

Lives change, and so the course of life is filled with disconti-nuities. What at one point in time appears to be mental illness at another can appear quite adaptive. For example, at age 67 a Har-vard man, David Goodheart, remembered his childhood.

> The Depression for me, as a boy in the pre-teens, was a kind of early exposure to survival training. My father's income as a salesman on commission wasn't enough to sustain our family in Birmingham, Alabama where both my older brother and I had been born and thus far raised. So in the summer of 1931 my mother, my brother, and I packed up and headed for a "visit" with my mother's bachelor uncle at the old home place in rural Mississippi. My father remained in Birmingham for his catch-as-catch-can sales efforts. The visit stretched out to two-and-a-half years.
>
> Life on the farm was spartan. There was no electricity, central heating, or plumbing; just a wood burning stove and fireplace, a well with windlass in the backyard, kerosene lamps, and an out-door privy. My brother and I walked every day five miles to and from the crossroads where the school bus stopped; and after the consolidated school burned down, classes were held in unheated attics or in the old ramshackle Odd Fellows hall.
>
> As a city kid I was looked on by my rural contemporaries as an alien intruder, fair game for taunts, crude practical jokes, and school yard "whuppings." Although my level of educational achievement was no great shakes by national standards, it was

high enough to affront farm boys who considered intellectual activity pretentious and unmanly. As most children do, I struggled hard to find some tolerable adjustment to this dilemma.

Finally, I hit on a solution: I became the outstanding behavior problem in my class. I broke all the rules, uttering crude sotto voce jokes, engaging in spitball duels, and otherwise provoking my formerly doting teachers to fury. The customary punishment for serious offenses was a flogging in front of the class with a sapling freshly cut by the culprit himself. This became an almost daily occurrence for me; it was administered with double intensity when I notched the switch so that it would fall apart in the teacher's hand, to the uproarious amusement of my classmates. This routine was physically painful, but it was also spiritually liberating. Before long, I was accepted by my country cousins as a city kid who was, after all, a good ol' boy. I never could explain to my mother, however, why my otherwise all A report cards were invariably marred by a big "F" for deportment. A school psychologist, if there had been one, would probably have found me "maladjusted." It makes you think about definitions.

But Goodheart's troubles did not rest only in the schoolyard. As an adolescent Goodheart had grown up in a family where he was often caught between his embattled and racially prejudiced strict Southern Baptist parents. For most of his childhood he was terrorized by his father's alcoholic violence. In college, he had encountered great difficulty in sharing his earlier fears with college interviewers. Thus, the psychiatrist who interviewed him dismissed Goodheart with the following adjectives: "self conscious, gloomy, pessimistic, avoids social contacts, colorless, frequent diffuse anxiety, ineffectual, unattractive in a dish-rag way, self deprecating." Another staff member saw Goodheart as a thin, pale passive boy with excellent manners, but one who was "rather nervous and self-conscious, with cold, wet hands." Admittedly, these adjectives were offset by the adjectives "goodhearted, likable, sympathetic and agreeable," but on balance, in college Goodheart was still receiving low marks for "social deportment" and was labeled a "neurotic" to boot.

At 19 Goodheart himself was already consciously curious about where his feelings were hidden. He recognized that he "wore a mask" to hide them. "You could turn aside many a shaft if you could be clever," he explained. For humor also lets one loose blunted arrows against others; and Goodheart had already discovered that writing for the college humor magazine provided an acceptable vent for his angry feelings.

During World War II, the "neurotic" David Goodheart soon mastered his struggle with family conflict not through witty displacement but in the real world. The United States Army was still segregated, and as a white officer in a largely black division, Goodheart found himself facing "a very ticklish business to keep both superior officers and the men placated." But he succeeded, and his superiors awarded him high marks as an officer. No longer did anyone view Goodheart as "unattractive in a dish-rag way."

Then, having succeeded brilliantly in war, Goodheart set about mastering the fear-provoking situation of being caught between embattled forces in civilian life. By age 25 Goodheart wrote, "I used to think I am not my brother's keeper, but I've now developed a social conscience." Goodheart spent the next decade in the urban ghettos of Detroit and Chicago, devising ways to mediate between city officials and foundation executives and the Southern migrant workers, both white and black, whom they served. It was a replay of his family and grammar school experiences. In a very real sense he was protecting white men like his bigoted father from attack, even as he was openly and professionally combating his father's prejudices and defending the disenfranchised.

As in the schoolyard, Goodheart's solution was to induce others to laugh *with* him. However, as a child his "humor" had been passive-aggressive and perceived as misbehavior. At age 40, as he mediated between angry urban factions, Goodheart's humor made him a civic hero. *Life* magazine recognized Goodheart as a courageous civil rights leader and a leader in the battle to achieve urban minorities' civil rights. Along with other 40-year-olds such as Murray Gell-Mann and Burke Marshall, future senator Daniel Inouye, and New York mayor John Lindsay, Goodheart was placed among 100 young leaders destined to shape the future of the nation. His "passive aggression" (like Gandhi's) now won him an A for altruism. Nobody would have called the middle-aged Goodheart a neurotic with cold, wet hands.

In contrast to the college psychiatrist who interviewed Goodheart at 19, I described Goodheart when he was 47 as follows: "He was easy, open, relaxed and warm. He looked the very model of a Harvard professor educated in excellent schools. . . . I felt completely at ease with him. Although he had a sense of humor, it was wry. . . . There was a kindliness and a gentleness about him that was extremely winning. . . . He sums up his life with 'Everything I do depends upon a personal relationship.'"

The rest of Goodheart's life was an exciting search to gain for others what he had not received for himself. At age 67 Goodheart wrote, "It's impossible to say what effects that Depression experience had on my life that wouldn't have occurred without it. But I doubt that I would otherwise have acquired quite the same empathy for society's underdogs and victims of needless cruelty." His own past mattered — and yet it did not matter.

But as he grew older David Goodheart was definitely unlike Professor Mark Stone. Despite abject promises, Goodheart seemed incapable of returning his Study questionnaires on time. Some of his old passive aggression remained. He ate too much, he drank too much, he smoked too much, and so he died young. Part of me wished, again, to give him an F for social deportment. Folks don't change.

True, David Goodheart did die at age 70; but as with Dr. Eric Carey, his legacy, an urban civil rights organization, lives on. In his obituary the *New York Times* described Goodheart as having "joined the civil-rights cause well before it became fashionable. And long after others had lost their fervor, he continued to work for that cause . . . a brilliant, effective, indefatigable worker for an integrated America in which blacks and whites could prosper alongside one another."

At Goodheart's funeral his eulogist referred to him as the "Wizard of Wit. It was his empathy, his warmth and humor, his wit and wisdom, that made me and hundreds of others feel enriched by his friendship. In a vacuous age of shameless hype and celebrity, he was an anonymous saint, a tarnished angel passing out little bon mots of humor and affection and hope."

Once again, the real world had awarded Goodheart an A for social deportment. Folks do change.

•   •   •

After following disadvantaged Hawaiian youth for almost half a century, Emmy Werner explained that "the most salient turning points . . . for most of these troubled individuals, however, were meeting a caring friend and marrying an accepting spouse."[21]

Jim Hart's life was an example of such a "salient turning point." If Fred Chipp had enjoyed one of the best childhoods in the Harvard Study, Jim Hart had endured one of the worst. For all his childhood his mother suffered a serious mental illness, and in his words at 47, "By age ten I emotionally wrote off my parents. . . . I did not respect my father for the abuse he took, and I did not like my mother for handing it to him." At 49, when a questionnaire asked him when he was best friends with his parents, Hart replied, "Not since I can remember. Certainly not since I was eight or nine." As a child, Hart had compensated by bonding with boys his own age in his Brooklyn neighborhood and by hanging out with his maternal grandfather, whom he regarded as the only normal member of his family. "He was always an inspiration to me and was always my best friend in the family."

Years later Jim Hart found another best friend, his wife, Julia; and Julia agreed that Hart's maternal grandfather was the finest man she had ever known. Marrying Julia was to change Jim Hart's life forever.

For marriage is not only important to healthy aging, it is often the cornerstone of adult resilience. As a young man Hart wrote to the Study of his wife, "She is my type of person. We are a lot alike. Same values, interests, family background. I expected a wonderful marriage with Julia — who is perfect for me — and it's been just that — a wonderful marriage." By age 47 his view had not changed. "My wife has been the best thing that ever happened to me." At 56, when the Study inquired about significant changes in his marriage, he wrote, "No change, only better." At 58 on a nine-point scale Hart circled his marriage as a 9, "perfectly happy." At 56 Julia Hart, always less effusive than her husband, rated her marriage as a mere 8 out of 9. She then explained what made her marriage last so long. "1. My husband is my best friend. 2. We've grown closer and fonder every year. 3. We have such fun together." Both of the Hart children saw their parents' marriage as better than that of their friends.

But before marriage, Jim Hart had been too much of a diamond-in-the-rough for the Harvard Study to appreciate. A staff member called him "hypomanic," "aggressive," "hard," "insensitive," and "emotionally cold." One of the less competent Study psychiatrists had sputtered, "His philosophy of life just doesn't jibe with ours." Hart's tough carapace and Brooklyn manners, as necessary for surviving his adolescence as Goodheart's passive aggression had been for surviving his childhood, violated some of the staff's quaint Cambridge folkways. In addition, they complained, "One gets the impression of one better adjusted to interpersonal relations than intellectual pursuits." God forbid that someone at Harvard should put friendship ahead of studies. Again, long-term follow-up showed clearly who was right. For if Jim Hart's pencil-and-paper intelligence scores were below average for the Study, he still finished in the top 2 percent of his class at Harvard Business School. And at age 75 his emotional life had become far richer than that of most of his critics. Even the Study staff admitted that if at age 25 Hart was "shrewd, selfish, and naive," he was also "very energetic, invulnerable, no neurotic traits. One would predict good success both materially and for personal and family happiness."

Hart had frequently talked tough about wanting to make a pile of money. But always he had seen money as merely a means and a happy family as the end. At 50 Hart confided, "I still wonder about the prestige and recognition of being a corporation chairman; and, then, I say, 'That's bull shit!' One part of me wants power, prestige and success. . . . I look at business school classmates who are presidents of major companies, and I find myself envying them." Then he admitted, "But I have come to the conclusion that all is vanity and chasing after the wind. Deep down, all I've wanted out of life is a good family relationship and to give my children adequate tools for life. The problem is that a lot of people who take an active part in civic activities have lousy family lives and people who had good family lives have lousy civic participation. I love to be home." And so Hart's old age was happier than that of some of the clinicians who when Hart was in college had criticized him for being insufficiently civic minded.

Nevertheless, when I first interviewed Jim Hart in 1970, I, too, did not imagine that by the end of life he was to become a Study role model. I simply noted that Hart was "a tough scrapper who is every inch an 'A' Study member even if he could not convince the staff he was a graceful one. . . . He is as honest as his mother was dishonest, and as tough as his father was passive." But I was still emphasizing his rough exterior and minimizing the diamond within. Social scientists, like me, are sometimes blind to the creativity and maturity that it takes to build four successful companies and one successful family.

In 1998 I interviewed Jim Hart again. When I arrived at his house in Lake Forest, Illinois, both my hosts radiated care. Jim Hart asked me if I wanted something to drink, and Julia brought me some fruit. Their home contained much attractive art and sculpture collected from their many travels, but more important, there was a wonderfully human, cozy quality that enveloped the visitor. The living room fire was going; the chairs were overstuffed and comfortable. The guest bathroom was beautifully wallpapered and there were three rows of initialed hand towels for guests. It was hard not to feel welcome.

Jim Hart had graying, grizzled hair and a heavily lined face. Having just come from a brunch, he wore a fancy designer sweater, slacks, and good shoes. He was kind, but very tough. His manner was to the point and direct. He didn't waste words. Yet, in spite of his outward, almost abrasive, veneer of no nonsense, there was a simplicity to him that made him really quite endearing.

I asked the Harts what originally drew them together. Hart answered, "Julie looked good. She had a good sense of humor. She was feisty and she had a sense of herself. She was smart and she had a really good figure." I asked how they depended upon each other. Jim replied, "A great deal. I depend on her. She is the best thing I ever did. I enjoy her company. I'd be lost without her. . . . Of course, if I lost her, I'd marry a twenty-two-year-old." He needed to lighten the possibility that such a loss could occur. They would be married fifty years that June, and Julia was in mortal danger from recently diagnosed cancer.

Late in the interview I asked Hart what his mood had been in the last six months. "I'm not real moody," he revealed. "My mood is fine, but I got very disturbed about Julia's cancer." When it was first diagnosed, he had felt, "This is the end of everything." Julia added, "He even said he would build me a new kitchen." Hart quickly assured me that as soon as Julia's cancer surgery had been successful "the deal was off," but he closed more somberly. "It has made the summer pretty difficult."

Julia Hart then addressed the issue of how they depended on each other. "Jim is my best friend. We laugh together. We discuss things. We share things." Whereas her husband was funny, Julia was philosophical; "It's as in The Prophet. We're two separate pillars and there is space between us. We're a very close family." Her husband interrupted and exclaimed, "It's really been a wonderful marriage!" Julia responded with more reserve, "But you have to hold loosely."

One of the most stunning things about the interview was how well they collaborated. Julia was a dance therapist. She loved to dance, and her husband did not. But the interview was a dance.

They were gracefully in step. Their sense of timing with each other was perfect. Hart would hide his sentimentality by teasing her, and she would accept the covert affection with wisdom and grace. As they talked with me and with each other, they did not compete nor did they disagree. They approached each question together; looking at different sides of it, each very accepting of the other — and using their differences to provide light and not heat. Julia thought in terms of collaborating; Hart was more dominant. But Julia explained to me she was by nature manipulative, so "I often notice that Jim manages to come up with my ideas."

I asked how they fought. Hart replied, "We don't." Julia added, "I have a temper. I get upset, but I get over it almost immediately." He said, "I don't have a temper. It's not worth it." When they fought over whether they should have a friend over that he didn't like, Julia would say, "Well, I won't do it." Then Hart interjected, "I find myself begging her to do the very thing I had asked her not to do." The resolution did not come across as a passive-aggressive struggle as much as a harmonious dance step that they had worked out in order to temper Hart's forcefulness. Julia was perhaps the only person in Hart's entire life whom he had tried to conciliate rather than confront.

One of the remarkable characteristics of this tough, cocky man was his psychological insight. Jim Hart was a top sergeant who knew how people ticked. He manifested a sensitive awareness for emotional nuance even though that was not what most concerned him. He explained that he enjoyed "close, stable friendships marked by intimacy." Asked at 47 to describe his oldest friend, he retorted, "Let's not say oldest, let's say best," and proceeded to tell me about *two* friends — one a friend for thirty years and the second a friend for twenty-five. Asked the same question at 74 Hart revealed that his oldest friend, with whom he had gone to high school, had just died. He then described four other close friends. There was Mark, whom he had known since freshman year in college; Mark was rich and an aesthete, but "I like him very much." There was Bennett, who was a friend from college with whom he had just recently again become close. There was Morris, with whom he had been friends for thirty years; they skied together. And there was Reg; "I have lunch with him every Tuesday." No Harvard man whom I interviewed acknowledged intimate friendships more readily.

At his twenty-fifth reunion, when I had asked Jim Hart about what he would do his first week of retirement, he exclaimed, "Jesus! I don't have the faintest idea. . . . I'd probably visit my grandchildren." He might travel, ski, play doubles; and he would like to read. He could see himself tutoring minority students, for he had long nurtured a dream of giving up business and teaching high school.

At his thirtieth Harvard reunion he acknowledged having abandoned his former retirement dream of teaching high school. He spoke now of mentoring young businessmen instead. His wife interrupted, "You're a dean in your field." During the reunion he had attended a seminar given by Erik Erikson. Afterward he explained that he had been thinking about Generativity, and wondered if he had been generative enough. "We all want some meaning in life, and I'm supposed to be in that decade." He was still competing but no longer with his fists on the Brooklyn streets or for money among Tokyo skyscrapers. At 50 Hart now wanted to succeed in life by excelling at Erikson's life tasks.

At 55, when asked about retirement, Hart wrote, "Formed a new company in July. Actually, I now have more responsibilities." His anticipated age of retirement was "probably never. I have too much fun working." Two years later he wrote, "I'm in partial retirement at 56," but that lasted less than a year. Thus, at 62 when asked what he looked forward to most in retirement, Hart wrote, "Haven't really thought about it." He was still working sixty hours a week at his job. At 66 he had "moved from being a CEO to Chairman of the Board," and he was still working fifty hours a week. He had not retired because "I like the job and find it stimulating." At 70 he wrote, "The fellow who was scheduled to be my successor died several months ago; so reluctantly I am still fully in harness." Hart, like Chipp, enjoyed Generativity too much to tolerate the emotional distance necessary to become a Keeper of the Meaning.

Hart was 74 when in Lake Forest I interviewed him for the third time and had been retired for about two years. His wife explained, "Jim enjoys every day. Besides, his retirement permits us to do more things together. We play golf. We rake leaves. We go shopping. We go to early movies. . . . Being together is a plus." She then closed with, "We've got more time to get in touch with old friends."

Since 1970 Hart had spent no days in the hospital. He still had only two fillings, and he was in the best objective physical health of any man in the Harvard Study. He said the most annoying aspect of aging was arthritis. His hands, his knee, and his shoulder were all affected; but he still played squash with people twenty-five years his junior. At 76 the only medicines that Jim Hart took were vitamins and a prescription for arthritis. As a result of aging he said he had had to "give up nothing. Not one damn thing!"

Asked what was the best part of retirement, Jim Hart replied, "It's all good. I enjoy my life, but I always did. I feel kind of blessed." This from a man who had never been friends with either parent. The wisdom he offered others was, "Each moment should be appreciated and fully lived. Dwelling on the past or anticipating the future at the expense of the 'Now' cheats a person of life's wondrousness."

After a perfectly miserable childhood Jim Hart had achieved one of the best retirements in the Study. Instead of being an object of the Study staff's criticism, he had become an icon of admiration. A tough kid became a gentle grandfather. But it did not happen overnight. And as was true for the most resilient Inner City men, a key factor in his resilience was a wonderful marriage.

•   •   •

The major factors involved in negative personality change at midlife were the same factors that caused negative aging at 70; bad habits, bad marriage, maladaptive defenses, and disease.

Ninety percent of the Inner City men who at midlife were chronically unemployed or below the poverty line were mentally ill or alcoholic or intellectually challenged (IQ < 80). Of the 48 Inner City men classified in old age as Sad-Sick twenty years later, all but 8 had been mentally ill or alcoholic before age 50. Once more let me underscore that it is disease — or sustained social bigotry, a societal disease — not economic poverty *per se* that led most often to unsuccessful aging.

For example, interviewing Study members who had once endured psychotic depression was like seeing someone long after injury by a severe fire. The burns were healed; medical intervention was no longer needed; but they were scarred. The scars, in turn, interfered with return to a completely normal life. When Humpty Dumpty falls off the wall, his benign past may no longer matter. None of the 21 Harvard men who were diagnosed with definite depressive disorder before age 50 (i.e., meeting clinical criteria for a major depressive disorder) fell in the top quartile of psychosocial adjustment at age 65; at age 80 none fell among the Happy-Well. But on admission to the Study, few had seemed in any danger.

Nor did Zelda Maus seem in danger. Maus's childhood had been of average happiness for the Terman sample. Her family solidarity and warmth had been in the top half and, unlike Jim Hart, she had been close to her mother. She had no nervous symptoms. Bill Loman, the alcoholic lawyer in chapter 2, had been captain of his high school football team; Maus had been captain of her high school basketball team *and* editor of its yearbook. Unlike many adolescent women of her era, she looked forward to sexual activity. Had she been in the Harvard cohort, she would have been classified an "A."

Zelda Maus married at 21. But then her life ended. By 25 she was divorced; and prior to our interview at age 78, she had suffered five episodes of depression, each of which was severe enough to require electric shock therapy. Although her last course of therapy had been fifteen years ago, several months before our interview her physician had again put her on antidepressants.

Maus lived as far out on the outskirts of Sacramento as a person possibly could. Driving to her house was like leaving the California suburbs and entering Appalachia. A winding road took me over a single-lane bridge, past small houses with their front yards filled with junk, and signs warning intruders Beware of the Dog. Her house had no number and no yard to speak of. It consisted of a single large room that served as kitchen, living room, and dining room and off that I imagined a bedroom and a bathroom. The plate-glass windows were filthy and looked out on a garden of weeds. As she explained, the man who used to clean the windows had died.

When I had first called her to request an interview, Maus had growled, "What are you selling?" When I explained I was from the Terman Study, she agreed to see me; but almost as soon as I began the interview, she grumbled, "I never should have let you come here." Her long suit was not making new friends.

Maus was a small woman. Her brown hair was cut very short, and her flat, sad face, with huge eyes and large-frame glasses gave her the appearance of a panda. As I entered her house, I saw that it was clean but unbelievably gloomy. Everything was brown. Despite the dirty windows and despite the rainy day, Zelda Maus did not turn on a light when I arrived. Most of the interview was filled with a sense of Maus's own aloneness and her perception that everybody had died or moved away. She looked continuously sad except for the rare occasions when something made her laugh; indeed, it was her occasionally engaging use of humor that kept the interview from becoming a disaster.

In the living room there were no books, only her precious collection of 78 r.p.m. record albums that dated back to the 1930s. They had once represented her entire savings. No new mementos or even 33 r.p.m. LPs had really replaced them. On the wall were a large photograph of her pet cat, a small photograph of her only son, and a tiny picture of her only grandson. There was an elaborate pipe organ that she had not played in two years and an elaborate VCR that her son had given her so that she could record late-night television shows. The only problem was that despite her IQ of almost 150, Maus could never learn how to operate a VCR. In contrast, with an IQ nowhere near 150 Henry Emerson got on the Internet to chat with other people with leukemia. Positive aging is learning the rules of the new world, and treasuring what they bring you.

Early in the interview Maus interrupted the conversation to let in a very damp, asocial black-and-white cat, Thomas. She turned her back to me; and as she started to dry off the cat, she explained to Thomas that he had company: "If he doesn't like cats, we'll throw him out." Then she turned back to me and boasted, "He's afraid of everyone but me." She told me that the only reason she had to go on living was to take care of Thomas. She proudly explained that Thomas did not need a litter box like other cats; he scratched to go outdoors.

When I asked Zelda Maus what she enjoyed most, she sighed and replied, "Right now it is resting." In the last ten years, she explained, she had gone downhill and "It is time I did a lot of nothing." Then she querulously asked, was she supposed to be achieving things? She alleged that she did quite a bit of reading; but when I asked for examples, she admitted giving up the daily paper and only reading the newspaper on Sunday. She was going to cancel her subscription to *Audubon* magazine because she did not read it. She had not read a book in five years. "All I do is nothing. When you get to be seventy-seven you're allowed to do nothing. As long as I'm happy, what does it matter?" Had she been even remotely happy, her rebuke would have been quite justified.

When I asked for her most important activity, Maus became silent. Then she volunteered that so very many of her friends had died; but her statement appeared to have more to do with inner misery than with the number of close friends that she had actually lost by death. Again I asked her for her most important current activity; once more Maus grumbled, "I don't know why I let you come down here."

All three of Maus's marriages had been unhappy. Unlike Jim Hart, Anna Love, and Susan Wellcome, Maus had not found her spouse an ally. Before being widowed, Maus had been married to her third husband for almost ten years; four of her hospitalizations for depression had occurred during his watch. His chronic alcoholism had not helped. After her husband had died fifteen years ago, Maus had had no further hospitalizations. But she still had had to look after her hated mother-in-law in a convalescent home. Actually, she had not seen her mother-in-law for three months — not since she had visited her on her hundredth birthday. As Maus explained, if her husband had lived and his mother had died, her life would now be fine. At this point she became tearful. Later, I commented that all her husband had really left her was his mother. Maus laughed. "I don't understand her," she mused. "Everyone is dead but her."

I asked Zelda Maus how she had dealt with her husband's death. She shrugged, "Well, life isn't fair." She got up again to let out the cat. I asked what were some of her good memories about her husband; all Maus could say was that they did *not* like having friends in. "We liked to be quiet together. . . . I can't recall too much." Repeatedly, on emotionally pregnant subjects, Maus seemed to have trouble remembering. She had no difficulty remembering inanimate detail, but with emotionally tinged issues her mind went blank. For those experiencing healthy aging the inanimate is forgotten and the emotionally valenced is remembered. She ended our discussion of grief with "It didn't seem possible that things would go the way they did." She suddenly switched to regret that she had never met Dr. Terman. He had died, too, she noted pensively; and added that she thought his son was dead too. Like her window washer, all the people in her life had died, and no one new had entered.

There was nothing for which Maus felt grateful. All the psychiatrists she had known, she believed, had just wanted to see her for the dollars; she had never known a psychiatrist whom she had trusted. I asked her if her IQ had been a blessing or a burden. She said without hesitation, "It's been a burden. If I were half stupid, I'd have had a lot more friends." In addition, Maus pronounced, "Church doesn't do me any good. I don't need any religion to tell me how to treat people." Maus allowed herself no source of comfort, not even God — only her damp, motheaten-looking cat. I asked Maus how her life was financed, and she said she had her husband's IBM pension. She also got a Social Security check. "I didn't ask for it," she grumbled and added querulously that she did not see how the government was going to keep going if it kept sending checks to everybody who was over 65. She could not even be grateful for federal largesse.

The real tragedy of Zelda Maus's life was not that she had lost loves by death, but that so few loves had entered in. The photographs on Maus's wall told the story. In her life her cat was larger than her still-living son and grandson combined. A still-living brother, a deceased sister, and her deceased, and allegedly still mourned, third husband were not even represented.

Maus talked to her son once a week. But although Thanksgiving was only five days away, there had been no discussion of whether they would spend the holiday together. Asked what she had learned from her son, she sighed, "I'm glad I only had one — I'm not the mothering type." Zelda Maus remained quite interested in her grandson — the child in the small picture — but she acknowledged that she had not seen him for six months. Every now and then her son, Gene, would bring him by and they would go out for dinner. Nor did Maus keep in touch with her three nieces and nephews, although at least one nephew lived nearby.

She revealed that her brother was able to be wonderfully funny in a way that "just breaks me up." He had a special kind of humor and funny bone that reminded her of her grandmother. Having gotten the sense that she talked about her brother with far more warmth and tenderness than she did her son, I wondered if she had thought of visiting her brother for Thanksgiving. "I've never been asked," she grunted. What would happen, I persisted, if she invited herself? She burst out laughing and said, "Why? My brother would think I'd lost the other half of my mind. . . . Besides, Thanksgiving is just another day."

Maus could not hold on to the good in people. Well, perhaps there was one exception. I asked Maus when was the sunniest period of her family life. She misheard me. "The saddest?" she inquired. At this point she looked very sad indeed. I explained that I had asked for "the sunniest." She relaxed a little. It was when she was in love with a married man, she said. She had been 37, and he was 35. At the time she was living in Phoenix. He would not get a divorce, and besides, she would not trust as a husband a man who divorced his wife. Later, when she was living in a mobile home with her second husband, her former lover rang her up "and it started all over again." He was the one person who had touched her heart, and she had remained in love with him all these years. Her lover had even seen her through one of her depressions. "He loved me as much as anyone ever has." Recently, she revealed, he had sent her a birthday card; indeed, it seemed he still sent her a card every birthday.

"Sometimes," she mused, "you can't have some mysterious person, and you think it would have been wonderful." No one else had mattered much. After forty years as a psychiatrist I have learned to wonder about people who claim to have lost their unavailable "only" love. Something usually seems to have gone wrong with their ability to take people in.

Just as she did not turn the lights on in her house, just so Maus's mind did not let in sunny thoughts. The dead seemed to her so much more real than the living. I asked Zelda Maus, as I did everyone, what was the most annoying aspect of growing older. She replied, "Going downhill, losing the strength you used to have. . . . A person realizes that they are coming to the end of the line, and that's the worst part." Although Maus feared living to be 90, she also feared death in a way that most of the Study members did not.

Major depressive disorder is a terrible disease, but it has nothing to do with old age. Epidemiological studies show that despite their many losses and poor physical health, the old are actually less depressed than the rest of us.[22] Maus's crankiness came from feeling "sick," not from old age.

Despite her gloom Zelda Maus squeezed my hand when I left, silently letting me know that she had enjoyed my concern. Most Terman women were respectable old ladies whom I wouldn't have dreamed of hugging. But Maus was like a homeless panda, with just enough charm and neediness that I wanted to pick her up and rescue her. I could not, so I squeezed her hand too. I left her house wishing that adult development had only happy endings.

* * *

So do our personalities change over time or do they not? Our genes matter, and genes do not change from birth. But it is also our genes that are programmed to permit us to grow and to change. If the road is rough and we are without shoes, it is our genes that develop calluses upon our soles. Similarly, if our childhood environment is rough, our genes, like those of Anthony Pirelli, help us to reshape our memories and to find surrogate parents. And even when our inborn temperament does not help, our environment can and often does change. Sir Michael Rutter is almost certainly correct when he writes, "The notion that adverse experiences lead to lasting damage to personality 'structure' has very little empirical support."[23] The exceptions, of course, are extreme traumas like childhood sexual abuse and wartime atrocities that can lead to lifelong post-traumatic stress disorder.

Recovery from the slings and arrows of outrageous fortune can create an illusion of personality change in the same way that we are often nicer to know after we have had a cup of coffee in the morning or when we no longer have the flu. But underneath we are the same person. After the fact, it is easy to prove almost any theory. For example, the success of Anthony Pirelli, the Inner City tycoon from chapter 1, had to spring from somewhere. As a psychoanalyst I can argue that it was his ability to internalize love from his sister, Anna, from his brother, Vince, and from his wife that allowed life to change. A geneticist could respond by pointing to Pirelli's first-class temperament and note that Vince, his older brother who had helped Pirelli through accounting school, later became a bank president. The geneticist could also point out that long ago in Italy a maternal great-grandfather had also been a bank president. These observations are all true.

And indeed, it was only by blind luck that Pirelli got the family genes for financial wizardry rather than his mother's genes for manic depression and his father's genes that facilitated alcohol dependence. My point is that in advance no one could have predicted that Pirelli would become assertive and a model of positive aging or that Pirelli's son would receive a Ph.D. in mathematics. In advance no one would have predicted that Bill Loman and Zelda Maus would have been miserable in old age.

So how does this book teach us to predict the future? I would suggest, rather than count up the risk factors in a person's life — the ones that resilience researchers believe condemn disadvantaged children to a substandard future — count up the positive and the protective factors. Pirelli enjoyed all seven of the protective factors outlined in chapter 7. He did not smoke or abuse alcohol; he loved his wife; he used mature defenses; he obtained fourteen years of education; he watched his waistline; and, like the Harvard men, he exercised regularly.

Even these protective factors, however, might have been for naught had it not been for four personal qualities that are harder to quantify — qualities visible in the lives of Jim Hart, Susan Wellcome, and Anthony Pirelli and qualities that applied equally to all of the Study's diverse cohorts. The first quality is future orientation, the ability to anticipate, to plan and to hope. The second quality is a capacity for gratitude and forgiveness, the capacity to see the glass of life as half-full, not half-empty. Put differently, Thanksgiving is not "just another day" and paranoia and injustice collecting can destroy old age. The third quality is being able to imagine the world as it seems to the other person, the capacity to love and to hold the other empathically — but loosely. The fourth quality, related to the third, is the desire to do things *with* people, not to do things *to* people or ruminate that they do things to us. As we grow older, we all need to recall Susan Wellcome's example and leave the screen door unlatched.

CHAPTER TWELVE

POSITIVE AGING: A REPRISE

> Grant unto me the seeing eye, that I may see the beauty in common things . . . and that I may know that each age from first to last is good in itself and may be lived, not only well, but happily.
>
> Edmund Sanford, "Mental Growth and Decay"

The old AA watchwords become helpful in old age and in gardening. For with old age and with gardens we must remain brave enough to change the things we can; serene enough to accept the things we can't; and wise enough to know the difference.

• *Let go and let God:* God grows the garden; you do not have to. The seasons change, and you accept them. There is no way that you can hurry a garden up. The tomatoes will not ripen until they are good and ready. Accepting that fact bestows serenity.

• *First things first:* Watering young plants, especially if they have been recently transplanted — like grandchildren — takes precedence over everything. In old age, however, you no longer have to keep up with the neighbors.

• *Keep it simple:* The task of successful aging is to follow the advice in Voltaire's *Candide* and cultivate our garden. The rat race is over; the pagers and beepers have been returned; and no shrill small voices call out at 4 A.M. with earaches. Yes, it takes sweat and kneeling to weed; but the garden looks better for it. In *De Senectute,* Cicero reminds us that elderly Romans cared not for literature and philosophy, but rather for viniculture, improving barren soil, orchards, bees, and gardens.

• *Carpe diem:* Seize the day, but only one day at a time. The past and the future can be for the moment ignored. In gardens you can live in today; besides, in old age what is not done today can be put off until tomorrow. And easy does it. In old age your back is precious.

• *Finally, use the telephone:* Don't nurse resentments or the poor-me's, but ask for help. Henry Emerson and Richard Lucky were complainers whom people loved to help. Alfred Paine never complained. Instead, he tugged and tugged on his own bootstraps and nothing ever happened. Successful aging, like sobriety and feeling tickled, can best be achieved in relationship.

Change is not always easy for the old. Thus, a wonderful quality shared by trees, azalea bushes, and perennials is that, unlike bifocals, they will stay where you put them. Pussycats and car keys are not like that. When old, one needs to be able to leave things behind and have them take care of themselves. This is so that you can leave suddenly to go to a grandchild's birthday across the state or leave lightheartedly to go to a movie or leave unexpectedly to go to the hospital. Gardens can look after themselves; dogs, potted plants, and children — even to a surprisingly advanced age — are not like that.

Gardens take work, it is true — but not work that requires a sprint, rather, work that can be done slowly. Gardens provide wonder and joy — so do children — but to raise a child you have to be able to run, and you can't go south for the winter. Gardens never need to be chased, and they are tolerant about being left alone under snow.

Golf is a little like gardening. Each hole is the first day of the rest of your life. With golf you don't have to run, and golf stays with you when you go south. But gardens supply more wonder and joy than golf — and less self-recrimination. Gardens allow you to take the stroke over again, and gardening can provide solace even if your partner dies.

Gardens, like Sophocles, understand the metaphor of the Resurrection just as they also understand that the seeds of love must be eternally resown. When we die, gardens live on after us. There is a kind of immortality about gardens, at least until next spring — and the spring after that.

In a nursing home, it is a joy to be brought flowers from one's garden. Even a photograph of one's garden a decade out of date is heartwarming. But an old putter in the corner or the golf ball you sank five years ago for a senior's tournament-winning birdie means very little. True, the memory of a hole-in-one or of dew still on the April fairway or the memory of dogwoods blooming beside the second tee can still bring joy — but, you see, my mind's eye has again wandered from golf to gardens. Indeed, the best thing about golf may be that it is played on an eighteen-hole garden.

Again, gardens remind the old that although happiness is harder to come by in old age, joy remains. The old man gets up in the morning. He is not happy with the nagging ache in his knee, nor with the sagging pot around his middle, nor with the persistent wagging tremor in his hand. But then, suddenly, outside the window there is his garden — God's work as much as his own — and he feels joy.

Peter Raven, director of the Missouri Botanical Garden, put it beautifully when he told Roger Rosenblatt in a *Time* interview:

"We have relatively short lives and yet by preserving the world in a condition that is worthy of us, we win a kind of immortality. We become stewards of what the world is.

"'Gardeners?' I ask him.

"'Gardeners,' he confirms."[1]

And so in old age gardening becomes both a model and a metaphor for our waning lives. Good gardeners are by definition generative. With age they, like Keepers of the Meaning, become repositories of gardening lore. And in November they understand Integrity. They do not mourn the roses and tomatoes that are past. With satisfaction and good cheer they cover their dormant perennials with leaves, confidant that in the future they will rise again.

E. B. White described his wife, Katharine, in her final years: "The small, hunched-over figure, her studied absorption in the implausible notion that there would be yet another spring . . . sitting there with her detailed [garden] chart . . . in the dying October calmly planning the resurrection."[2]

Thus, perhaps, successful aging is most akin to successful fall gardening, completing the harvest and tenderly putting the garden to bed for the winter. True, we should steel ourselves to the fact that the final 1 or 2 percent of our life may not be much fun; but, always, always, successful living means understanding that death is part of the journey. Besides, as I mentioned earlier, centenarians on average do pretty well until they pass their 97th birthdays.[3]

Positive Aging — A Third Pass

In chapter 1 I offered Anthony Pirelli as a model of how to grow old, and suggested that aging well has something to do with forgiveness, gratitude, and joy. In chapter 7 I spoke of healthy aging, as if the principal task was to live a long time without disability. In this chapter I shall try to synthesize the preceding eleven chapters with yet a third model: how to grow old with grace. In this book I have repeatedly highlighted 75- to 80-year-old Study members with the following characteristics:

First, she cares about others, is open to new ideas, and within the limits of physical health maintains social utility and helps others. Unlike King Lear, who demanded that his daughters take care of him, she remembers that biology flows downhill.

Second, he shows cheerful tolerance of the indignities of old age. He acknowledges and gracefully accepts his dependency needs. When ill, he is a patient for whom a doctor enjoys caring and remembers to be grateful. Whenever possible he turns life's lemons into lemonade.

Third, she maintains hope in life, insists on sensible autonomy (to do for oneself what one is able), and cherishes initiative. She remembers that all life is a journey and that development goes on for all of our lives.

Fourth, he retains a sense of humor and a capacity for play. He willingly sacrifices surface happiness for basic joy. As Voltaire suggested, he cultivates his garden.

Fifth, she is able to spend time in the past and to take sustenance from past accomplishments. Yet she remains curious and continues to learn from the next generation.

Sixth, he tries to maintain contact and intimacy with old friends while heeding Anne Morrow Lindbergh's injunction that "the seeds of love must be eternally resown." (Appendix K describes my transformation of these six points into a 15-point scoring system for "graceful aging.")

The life of Bradford Babbit tells a sad story of someone who missed achieving these characteristics. He was blessed with a Harvard diploma, a graduate degree, and a retirement income of $125,000 a year. When I interviewed him in 1998 he had no mortgage, no medical bills, and no grandchildren to educate. His house was set on a lovely green spacious yard in a comfortable, expensive Philadelphia suburb. But the inside of the house in which he had lived for twenty years looked more like a barren cheap motel than the home of a man who had discovered how to embroider life. There was no color anywhere; everything seemed empty and brown. There was no sign of life's mementos or hobbies. It was as if Babbit's social radius had never expanded beyond himself.

On his study wall there were just four pictures — enlargements of recent snapshots from a trip to Mexico. There were no pictures of people. There were no belongings, no books, no treasures, no past. He was the only serviceman I have ever met who spent two years in Japan and did not bring something back to decorate his life. Babbit simply did not take life in.

Brad Babbit was obese. He looked to me like an old, sick man, but he got a point for not being a complainer. I asked Babbit how his health had been since retirement, and he said, "Good." Sometimes his knees hurt him, but it was not a big problem. For him the most annoying aspect of growing older was "not being able to bend over." He told me joylessly about some grass seed that he realized he would have to plant. But Babbit was no gardener.

I asked Babbit, "What is it like being home for lunch?" He explained that his wife still worked during the day as a bank teller. Babbit himself volunteered his time to work evenings at the checkout desk of the local library. Not only did they not have lunch together; they usually did not have dinner together. Babbit ate alone at his desk in the library. But he liked having a thirty-hour-a-week job where he could chat with the library patrons. I asked Babbit how he and his wife collaborated. "My wife watches her TV in the next room. We go our own way during the day. . . . We lead pretty independent lives. We are very compatible."

Babbit's unmarried daughter was a profound disappointment to him, and he was without grandchildren. I asked Babbit what he had learned from his daughter, and he laughed bitterly. He began with, "Jen has been a big disappointment . . . after all we have done for her." Like King Lear, Babbit blamed his troubles on others. He then returned to my question. "Have I learned anything? It is not what we dreamed of, but I have to stand behind her." If he had no great love for his daughter, he maintained loyalty.

Babbit had learned to read when he was 4, but there were no books in sight. Instead, in retirement, Babbit reported spending twenty hours a week watching television. Indeed, there is nothing wrong with watching television if it brings pleasure. But Babbit regarded the present as the unhappiest time of his life because it was "hard to retire." In his job as a certified public accountant, he spent much time enforcing procedures and inspecting how people did their jobs. Babbit had liked the structure, the organization, the rules and regulations. A widening social radius — or a garden — was the last thing he had ever wanted. When I asked Babbit who was his oldest friend, he curtly retorted, "No, let's give that one up." Yet, in an earlier questionnaire Babbit acknowledged, "I keep people at a distance more than I really want to." He was not happy in his choices.

Poverty, mental illness, lack of education, or brain disease would be the usual explanation for such barrenness. But none of these obtained. Babbit had never seen a psychiatrist nor taken a tranquilizer. He was not, nor had he ever been, clinically depressed; there was simply no joy or decoration in his life. His genetic heritage seemed positively salubrious. Indeed, among the men in the Study, Babbit was almost unique in that there was no admitted mental illness among seventy-four known relatives. In college he had been called an "A" by the Study staff for "psychological soundness." He was basically a nice man. He called me "George" often, and he was quite attentive to my coffee cup.

As Babbit told me of his life, I looked out the windows at his beautiful lawn. It was spring. The sky was bright blue. The out-of-doors was filled with color and light. But somehow none of the color penetrated the windows into his house. The more he told me of his life, the more my mind conjured up an image of Sahara sand sifting into the floor of his den. In reviewing my notes, I noted that every time he laughed I had jotted down a qualifying adverb conveying pain. I could not recall Babbit ever laughing with pleasure. But perhaps if I was daydreaming about the Sahara, I was not paying attention.

The physically healthy Babbit had received only 3 points on the scale for graceful aging (see Appendix K), while the deceased Henry Emerson from chapter 6 had received 13 out of a possible 15 points. So did Dr. Eric Carey, who also died young. Babbit did well on only one item: Trust, Autonomy, and Initiative, for he had not had an unhappy childhood. But there was little in his life to convey the other five facets that the Study deemed important for graceful aging: social utility, sustenance from the past, capacity for joy and humor, self-care, and maintenance of relationships.

But nothing is that black and white. As e. e. cummings reminds us, "only sons-of-bitches measure spring with a thermometer." Successful aging is nothing if not complex. Is it not important that Emerson had spent one hundred days in the hospital and is now dead and that Babbit never spent time in the hospital and is still alive? Perhaps, but when Emerson died, his vineyard lived on, and I do not know if Babbit ever got around to planting his grass seed. For his sake, I hope so.

·   ·   ·

In contrast, Iris Joy was one of the most successful "gardeners" that I met while working on the Study. Iris Joy was a "gardener" in the sense of being a great cultivator of her own life and the lives of many others. She began, lived, and closed her life with an income below the poverty line. But of all of the 824 lifetimes in the Study of Adult Development, she provided perhaps the best model of positive aging — a perfect 15 out of 15. I do not ask the reader to agree. I simply calls them as I sees them.

From her own experience Iris Joy could have written this book. Besides keeping life simple, retaining a sense of humor, re-sowing the seeds of love, and, in Hercule Poirot's words, "exercising the little gray cells," she had remembered to choose her parents with care. Although below the poverty line, Joy's childhood environment had also been scored as high as any in the Study. Her parents had helped her through Erik Erikson's first four stages of life — achieving basic trust, autonomy, initiative, and industry, which is about as much parental education as a body needs to take in.

Genetically, her parents did not leave her at increased risk for alcoholism or depression, and they did leave her with the gift of succeeding at school. Iris Joy had been blessed in all these ways. In school Iris Joy had always finished her math homework "by the time the teacher finished taking the roll." She neither smoked nor abused alcohol. In her long and loving life, she had been frequently and profoundly grief-stricken but never clinically depressed. Her own IQ and that of her only child were 158. Iris Joy's emotional intelligence, in my opinion, was off the charts.

Iris Joy's garden was her house. In 1936 she and her husband had bought their San Francisco carriage house — built with square nails, heavy wood beams, and a white picket fence out front — for $1,500. The Joys had kept the window that the horse had chewed on just as it was, but they had hired a good carpenter to level the floor. They had replaced the carriage loft doors with windows that they gleaned from a torn-down building, and they had shellacked the warm redwood paneling that covered every wall. Joy explained that the brick walk of the cottage was made of bricks that she and her husband had harvested around the neighborhood.

Joy's small living room/dining room looked like the inside of a tasteful gift shop. It was very bright, very warm, very cozy. On the mid-December day that my wife and I went to see her, we found her writing Christmas cards. There was a gas fire going in her converted Franklin stove. Every corner of the room had something in it — a set of antique spoons on the wall, a warm rag rug on the floor. The Christmas tree was decorated. Joy's desk was open — and frightfully tidy — but each pigeonhole was brimming over with well-sorted letters.

One wall was filled with books — simple books as well as classics. There were the complete works of Zane Gray, bestsellers from the '40s and '50s, and a well-thumbed Funk & Wagnall's encyclopedia. It was the library of a bright woman who had never gone to college, whose father had been a pipefitter, and whose husband had never read a book in his life until she taught him how.

Greens and candles ran down the middle of the table, and a nutcracker soldier stood guard. Nothing in the room looked as if it had cost very much, but there was nothing in the room that looked cheap. The oil paintings on the wall were original; they were done by members of her family. The inexpensive chairs had wooden arms, but they boasted cozy and clean slipcovers, and bright homemade pillows adorned the sofas. Walking into Joy's house was a little like walking into an enchanted cottage, but probably Iris Joy's infectious warmth distorted my vision. In psychiatry such a phenomenon is called positive countertransference.

When Joy was young, her answers on the questionnaire had seemed too good to be true. Getting to know her first through pencil and paper, I wondered if she was just a Pollyanna or Dickens's Mr. McCawber or Voltaire's Dr. Pangloss. But after spending two hours in her presence I did not think so. It was clear that Joy papered over what seemed socially undesirable. But if for seventy-seven years you can always look on the bright side, maybe it starts to become true.

Iris Joy's father was a plumber and a mailman. When she was growing up, her father kept a last in the house so as to repair his children's shoes, and her mother sewed all their dresses. Although there were only twenty books in the house, there was a great big garden out behind their house to play in. The Joys may not have had very much money, but "there was always a little extra money for treats." "We had a great family life," she insisted. "I was brought up in the most fortunate way that I could be." One day when the four Joy children were fully grown and out of the house, they were discussing their roles in the family. All were amazed to discover that each of them had always believed that he or she was their parents' favorite.

Her parents "never fought, and each was wonderful in different ways." They saw to it that all their children graduated from high school. Later Joy's brother, also in the Terman Study, graduated from night law school and eventually became a prosperous lawyer.

When I met her, Joy was short and dumpy. Her hair was dyed black, and she had a large mole on her cheek. With very few wrinkles, she looked 60, not 77. She wore a bright red blouse with red slacks, house slippers, and simple stud earrings. Without being dramatic or resorting to charm she had a remarkable capacity to warm her audience. She did not smile very much; but when she laughed, unlike Babbit, she made my wife and me laugh too. She displayed a breathless enthusiasm and frequently used jokes to make her point. Part of the stage effect was the brightly lit Christmas tree and her skillful use of decorations. But part of the effect was the contentment and serenity of Iris Joy. During the interview I scribbled on the margin of my notes, "There is a constant light in her face. Her eyes glow."

Joy's grammar, accent, and use of language did not at first convey intelligence. Then I began to appreciate that her remarkable ability to use simple words to convey exactly what she wanted was more reminiscent of Churchill and Hemingway than of the average American who never attended college. She would talk frankly about people and affective issues; then, suddenly, she would switch gears and give a detailed financial accounting. She explained that she received about $300 a month from Social Security, and about $300 from a pension. She also had a small income from investments, but she had let the interest compound. She then added with good humor, "I think I have lived below the poverty line all of my life. Ignorance is bliss."

Then, suddenly, Joy interrupted her narrative, "Oh, can I brag?" With virtually no training she had managed the payroll for a Woolworth's store, and had done it very well. "I was proud of that." She hastened to assure us that it was the people under her who had really done the work and had made her look good. But just the same, "I felt good." She was at peace with her past.

Perhaps what was most outstanding about Joy was her capacity to keep life simple. She had married the town minister's son — an unemployed plumber who was almost illiterate. At the end of World War II her husband had bought a farm in Alberta, in a town with a population of 100. In summer they lived in a tiny prairie home that they built themselves, scratching out a living from the unyielding prairie soil and the stern Alberta climate. In 1950 Joy wrote to Lewis Terman, "We are happier here these last four years, working together on a farm, than we ever were living in town on separate jobs . . . we farm as partners." They lived largely on a barter economy. They spent their winters in San

Francisco, which allowed Joy the opportunity to have her half-time job at Woolworth's doing accounting for hard money, and gave their son the opportunity to attend a good urban public school.

After her husband's death Joy continued to live six months of the year in Canada, since her Canadian citizenship meant that she could obtain free medical care. She had always been deft at living on bargains and barter arrangements. In Alberta, in their little Swedish hamlet, Iris Joy, who in high school had wanted to become a doctor or a novelist, had become the village wise woman. "I am consulted on all matters: first aid, all diseases, mathematics, good manners . . . part of the time I know the answers. I have helped neighbors in sickness, in threshing, and in other emergencies. I am beginning to feel that real contentment lies in being needed." Her friends would come over to her farmhouse for coffee and then leave their babies and grandmothers behind to be cared for. She had felt a sense of "peace within myself" from converting to the Catholic Church at age 34. At 50 she helped older people regain the use of their limbs after strokes, as well as "changing bandages, lancing boils, and taking splinters out." She taught the Chinese shopkeeper's children English. In order to be wise, you do not need to attend college.

Someone once told Joy that an old person should have daily contact with 20 people of different ages. Thus, she encouraged people to continue coming to her with their problems. Two of her Canadian friends had told her that they always felt glad when Joy returned each spring, because they felt that "I have control of things." In her faith tradition, she explained, "We are not supposed to feel pride, but it's only human to feel proud when you have helped someone." Self-esteem is such a boon to successful aging!

Joy's marriage had lasted for forty-five years "because my husband was such a fun guy." Her husband had known that "I was smarter and better educated, but he was better at sizing up people. He loved children, could imitate accents — better yet, he could be very funny." When she married him, he had never read a book right through, so she got him interested in reading Jack London and the *National Geographic*. He was good-looking, and "he liked what I did . . . every morning he would bring me a cup of coffee in bed, and then I'd spoil him the rest of the day." With diffident enthusiasm she added, "And we had a wonderful sex life . . . when he died, I thought to myself, not many people get to live with a person like him." Iris Joy could always see the bright side of everything. But, remember, when she was a child her family life had also received the highest possible score. Good pasts matter.

I asked Joy whether in forty-five years of marriage she had ever come close to divorce; she instantly quipped back, "Divorce never, murder, yes!" Then, she hastened to assure us that she and her husband never hit each other. "But we had arguments, and I was as responsible as he was!" She revealed that when she fussed at him, her husband would send her two miles down the dirt road to visit a neighbor, Mandy. It seemed that Mandy had eight children; and so after spending two hours with Mandy and her unruly brood, Joy would return home feeling grateful for how lucky she was. When her husband would get mad, he, too, would leave the house and go to town. Eventually, he would return with a pineapple or some chocolate. He was Norwegian, she explained; thus, he would never say anything. Besides, she added, "There's nothing so good to settle an argument as a good old double bed."

The last fifteen years of Joy's life had not been easy. In 1973 her only sister died. She said her sister and she were so close that "I still can't have her picture out." She was a little bit choked up as she told us. In May of 1974 her mother had died, and two days after her mother's funeral "I had a heart attack." In 1980 her husband died. She immediately reminded us that she was lucky because her youngest brother was "a rock of Gibraltar." He now came over for dinner every night except Wednesday.

Since 1974 she had had "a long spell of heart condition." Each year she had to have an exam in order to get a driving license.

Every two years or so she had had to go to the hospital with angina. The last time she'd been in the hospital was the previous August. Her other medical problems included a hiatal hernia, sinus troubles, and arthritis. She admitted that many years before, while going through menopause, "I did think, 'If this is getting old, I don't like it.'" But that was perhaps the only time that she had felt "sick."

Her recent medical troubles did not faze her. One time she had had severe heart pains. She prayed, and the heart pain immediately stopped. She laughed, and told us, "I thought to myself, it happened this fast?!" Over rough spots she explained, "I count my blessings, and I take one thing at a time. . . . And humor is free." She associated to the time when she had fretted to her rich brother that she wasn't sure there would be enough money to bury her when she died. Her brother replied, "Don't worry, Iris, they won't leave you on top of the ground very long." She then associated to a 91-year-old woman who had told her daughter that she was surprised that the Lord hadn't taken her. Her 60-year-old daughter piously explained, "Well, Mother, that's because He still has work for you to do." The nonagenarian retorted, "Well, I can tell you here and now, if the Lord comes and tells me to do one more thing, I ain't a-goin' to do it!"

That anecdote notwithstanding, Joy kept plenty busy herself. Recently, she had been asked to join a women's club. She explained that it was not a do-good organization, but that it was "for cultural and social purposes . . . the table is set pretty, and they have a receiving line and the officers pour tea." She said this was a good thing, because after her husband had died, she had let her clothes go. The women's club inspired her to dress up. She also belonged to a bridge club. She said the members were mostly ten years older than she was, and that was a good thing too. "Their memories aren't so good. So now I get to win a lot." Joy also belonged to a historical society; then for the third time she asked us to excuse her if she boasted. "I'll show you something." She came back carrying some oyster shells in a pie plate filled with water. They had been dug up from an old Indian shell mound nearby. She was fascinated by the idea of their being three hundred years old. She had not forgotten how to say, "Wow!"

Her answers to five of our standard interview questions were illuminating. First, asked if her intelligence was a blessing or a burden, Joy exclaimed, "Oh, a blessing! I read Shakespeare, Plato, and Freud for pleasure instead of to impress others." Every place she had ever worked had wanted to keep her as a steady employee. "It makes your life so much easier. . . . I was valuable because I could do everything without any help." Then she gave credit where it was due. She reminded us that intelligence was a gift, not a virtue. "The Lord was good to me." Of course, her responses might have been bogus and intended to impress, except that Joy seemed a very independent woman who was not trying to impress anyone, least of all herself. Asked how the Terman Study had affected her, she blurted out, "This may be the wrong answer, but I always felt it was nagging me."

Second, asked what were the characteristics of someone who aged well, Joy replied that it was important to keep an open mind. When she was younger everything seemed black and white, but now she was able to keep both sides of an issue in mind. "I am into the gray period." She exercised her vocabulary by playing Scrabble in the evening with her brother and checking the dubious words in the fat dictionary that she kept next to her. She told us about a paper that she had written on gradual retirement, recommending that as they got older, people should work fewer and fewer hours with each passing year. That way they could ease into learning how to spend their spare time, while making way for younger people. The paper had not been published, because, she explained, she was ahead of her time. She told us this humorously, and without any effort to take herself seriously, but at the same time enjoying her intelligence. Laughing, she then announced that she had invented the Peace Corps before President Kennedy. In an article that she did publish in the 1950s, she had suggested that it would help American college kids if, before graduating, they went to an underdeveloped country, and practiced their skills for a couple of years. Then, armed with practical experience, they would come back to graduate. She still continued to write, but she explained that it was more important for her to maintain constructive contact with people. I thought to myself that it must be easy to age well if you are smart enough to figure it all out in advance, as Iris Joy seemed to have done.

Third, asked what she enjoyed most about retirement, Iris Joy, without any pause, exclaimed, "Being with children!" Being with children had been a hobby all of her life; children had been her husband's hobby also. When Joy was 14, she had already begun working at Woolworth's. Her job was decorating Easter eggs for children. She explained that her biggest retirement responsibility now "comes with the children." Her brother's children had come to her Alberta farm for seven summers, and her granddaughter had come for fourteen summers. Some summers they'd had as many as five children at a time. The children enjoyed feeding the pigs and had also loved the experience of living with oil lamps. They were very sorry when she and her husband finally brought electricity to the farm. For a while she'd also invited a girls' club to her house once a week, when about eight girls would come for cooking lessons and slumber parties. Her greatest legacy, she felt, was going to be "the children . . . you don't have as much effect as you think, but if you can leave happy memories in the children. . . ." That would be enough for any life. Asked if she still "collected kids," she said she did; but at 77 she no longer had them stay overnight.

She told us of a neighbor child, Rachel, across the street, who as a very young girl had been in a full-body cast. Joy had baby-sat for her while the girl's mother went to school. "And now Rachel comes over and helps me." She was delighted that Rachel copied the way she kept house. In return, Joy helped Rachel with her reading. "She got straight A's last year." She spoke with excited speech, but then tempered her boast. She acknowledged that Rachel's A's had been mainly due to the girl's being bright, rather than to her own excellent tutoring. Joy made her caveat funny, not just a disclaimer. She closed on a more somber note. "I only had one child, but we can't always choose that."

Fourth, we asked Joy, "What have you learned from children?" Instead of pausing like so many in the Study, she responded immediately, "The freshness of their outlook." She explained that children saw things differently. "It just renews your youth to see things through their eyes as they talk to you. . . . We're each made up of all the people we've come into contact with." Although adults did not notice it, she explained, "We are made up of the impressions that our children make on us, just as much as children are made up of impressions from their parents."

Needless to say, she and her son had a loving relationship, and they saw each other frequently. One activity she particularly enjoyed with him was being taken to plays in San Francisco. Her peak experience had been *My Fair Lady*. . . . "You can't do better than that!" The enthusiasm with which she spoke about the musical was that of a teenager. She described how exciting it was to see Rex Harrison. Growing old does not mean that you have to grow stuffy.

Fifth, asked to describe her closest friend, Joy replied, "There are two right up there [in Alberta]." Sharon was young; she was in her 40s and ran the post office. Mary was young too. She was the one who each year when Joy came back to Alberta felt that everything was going to be all right. In San Francisco, Joy said, she had three close friends in her bridge club. They saw each other every two weeks and sometimes in between. They had all raised their children; they had all raised their grandchildren; and "now we're working on our great-grandkids." Her oldest friend, she reflected, "must be Rosie." Rosie was in Joy's women's club. They had known each other since 1919. "Oh, that was a wonderful time to be," she reminisced, describing how she and her family had gone out to the Golden Gate before the bridge was built and had watched the last convoy of sailing ships glide into San Francisco Bay. As she talked, she made life magic.

Iris Joy's religious faith was simple and practical. She explained it to a young nephew. If he got lost on their 150 acres of wooded farm, he was to sit down on a log and pray to God for help. After praying, he should get up and walk until he came to a fence. Then, if he followed the fence, he would certainly find a house and help. Clearly, Joy's God helped those who helped themselves; but she never stopped believing in a benevolent God. One overriding emotion, joy, filled the interview; another word for it would be gratitude.

To conclude, I believe that the life of Iris Joy illustrates most of the lessons for successful aging. She chose loving parents, and she did not smoke or abuse alcohol. She understood how to savor joy and how to turn lemons into lemonade. She spent a life cultivating her "garden" both in California and in Canada. She was able to learn from her children, but she never forgot that biology flows downhill. She remembered that all life is a journey and that the seeds of love must be eternally resown. Finally, she heeded psychologist Edmund Sanford's century-old advice: "The real secret of a happy old age [is] once more in service for others carried on to the end of life — a service which, on the one hand, gives perennial interest to life by making the old man [or woman] a participant in the life of all those about him, and on the other, surrounds him with love in return."[4] So how should the reader of this book live out her or his final years?

* * *

I can do no better than to quote from a valedictory address (June 3, 1987) given by a wise schoolteacher at the Noble and Greenough School in Dedham, Massachusetts, Timothy Coggeshall. (E. B. White deserves a little of the credit, too.) The address echoes Sophocles but with a lighter touch. In addition, the address permits us all to identify; for it uses as a model a very human modern mouse, not an ancient blinded king. Coggeshall's valediction ends:

The child feels in touch with primitive things — a summer shower and a rainbow; the murmur of the wind in the deep green wood; the sparkling ocean air; dune land burning with the smell of sand and golden sun. Throughout your life, tune in to the marvelous mysteries that were fresh and new and amazing when you were young. . . .

I hope you will keep other companions from your childhood alive in your hearts . . . Pooh clutching his balloons and riding high in the sky, Alice floating down the rabbit hole and stepping through the looking glass. Jody frolicking with his fawn, Flag, and then learning from his father that "life is fine, powerful fine, but 'taint easy. When life knocks you down, you take it for your share and go on." . . .

Besides my sister, my favorite teacher is a two-inch-tall mouse named Stuart Little. Stuart told the children to remember three important rules:

"Be a true friend.

"Do the right thing.

"Enjoy the glory of everything."

We can imagine him outside now in the sunshine, paddling past us in his tiny birch bark canoe, *Summer Memories,* heading north, upstream on his quest, traveling light and . . . reminding us that a person who is looking for something doesn't travel very fast, and waving farewell to his childhood and boyhood, that secure and sun-warmed past that is over and done with and gone for all time.

"Yet Stuart knew this:

"If a flower blooms once, it goes on blooming somewhere forever.

"What is changed is never gone unless we let it go.

"You will remember —

"And you will be remembered."

APPENDICES

APPENDIX A: The Three Cohorts

The Harvard Sample

The "Grant Study" of Adult Development was begun at the Harvard University Health Services (then called the Department of Hygiene) thanks to a generous gift to Dr. Arlie Bock from his grateful patient, William T. Grant, the founder of the W. T. Grant dime stores. It was the very first grant of the now well known Grant Foundation. In making the gift, Grant hoped to discover the qualities of a good store manager.

Arlie Bock, in a press release dated September 30, 1938, described their mutual aims: "Large endowments have been given and schemes put into effect for the study of the ill, the mentally and physically handicapped. . . . Very few have thought it pertinent to make a systematic inquiry into the kinds of people who are well and do well."

The Harvard deans who made the final selection chose sophomores who, in the words of Arlie Bock, were "able to paddle their own canoe" or, in a freshman dean's words, were "boys we would be glad that we admitted to Harvard." About 80 of the 100 students selected each year agreed to participate in the Study — a demanding commitment of more than twenty hours of multifaceted scrutiny along with an implicit consent to be studied for the rest of their lives.

The men came from families that were relatively stable. By the age of 19 only 14 percent had lost a parent by death and only 7 percent had lost a parent through divorce. These figures, however, did not differ appreciably from the American middle class of that era.

Sixty-one percent of the Study subjects were graduated with honors in contrast to only 26 percent of their classmates. Indeed, perhaps too many men in the sample lived up to the definition of normality offered by a staff member: "A healthy person is someone who would never create problems for himself or anyone else." As one of the most successful men in the Study said, what he enjoyed most in life was "being beholden to no one and helping others."

In college the Study investigators did try to classify the subjects according to their "psychological soundness:" "A" (most sound), "B" (sound) and "C" (future in some question). But as the Study director mused during a case conference, "Are we putting in B and C the fellows who are really doing something in life? And are we putting in A categories the boys who are willing to take it and will get through somehow?" Indeed, the staff actually predicted that the "B's" and "C's" would make the headlines and the history and that the "A's" would merely become the "backbone of society." Their predictions did not quite turn out that way, for health turns out to be anything but dull.

By modern standards the study was old-fashioned. The men's blood was classified in four groups, I-IV; the ABO convention was not yet in universal use. A single-channel electroencephalograph — at the time a brand-new technological wonder — was administered. In order to intuit each Grant Study lad's personality, the electroencephalograph squiggles were read like tea leaves. A physical anthropologist studied each boy and recorded not only his somatotype (i.e., ectomorph, mesomorph, or endomorph) but also whether his physical measurements were in proportion or, heaven forbid, were "disproportionate." It took thirty years for the Study staff to conclude that physical anthropology was irrelevant to personality. But the Study of Adult Development is almost unique in having both the data and the follow-up to draw such a conclusion.

In 1940 the Study left many questions relevant to the vicissitudes of middle life and old age unasked and unanswered. In Berkeley, Erik Erikson was only just beginning the research that was to make adult development a popular and comprehensible intellectual concept. The disciples of Harry Stack Sullivan and Melanie Klein were only just beginning to convince psychoanalytic psychiatry that interpersonal relationships were of greater importance than fantasy. Thus, the Harvard men were queried about masturbation and their dreams but not about friendships and sweethearts. A great pity.

The historical accident of World War II permitted the Harvard men to be compared with their fellow citizens on grounds other than academic excellence. The Study men performed well on the battlefield. Instead of an expected 36, only 3 were rejected for psychiatric reasons. If just 10 percent of the Study men went into the army with commissions, 71 percent were officers at discharge. During combat they reported fewer symptoms of nausea, incontinence, and palpitation than have been reported by other studies of men under battle conditions; but on the battlefield the Study men won more than their share of medals for heroism.

The Study illustrated the instability of social class in America. Through their Harvard degree the men, whatever their social origins, were given a ticket of entry to the upper middle class. But not all of them came to Harvard with a silver spoon in their mouth; and even when they did, their parents often had humble beginnings. For example, there was one prep school graduate among the Harvard men whom I had always thought the scion of privilege. He had possessed a trust fund from birth; his father had been head of a New York Stock Exchange; his grandfather was a successful merchant banker. What I only just discovered, however, was that his rich grandfather had made his first thousand dollars as an itinerant pioneer picking up buffalo horns on the Great Plains at night and shipping them back to New England for resale.

The father of another Study member, Brian Farmer, worked as a painter and paperhanger. Soon after Brian's birth, however, work grew scarce and his father found it necessary to move his family to South Dakota, to a farm that his wife hoped to inherit from her mother. In order to make ends meet, Mr. and Mrs. Farmer and their six children went into the sugar beet fields as common laborers. For their combined efforts the family received only eleven dollars for every acre they cleared. They had scarcely enough to eat. A kindly neighbor told them that they could have all the beans and potatoes they could gather from his fields. Together, they gathered enough beans (which they canned) and potatoes to last them a winter, with a surplus stock which they traded in for staples such as sugar, salt, etc., and some groceries. Mr. Farmer picked up odd jobs here and there; but their neighbors were so poor that they, too, were unable to pay in cash. During these years the Farmers did not know what it was to taste fresh vegetables and fruits. When Brian Farmer entered Harvard, his father was still earning only five dollars a day. At age 75 another Study member confessed, "Having been known, according to friends, as a very happy guy, I must admit the Life Satisfaction Chart gave me a hard time. . . . My early life was clouded by the fact my mother was an alcoholic. She had this problem until she was in her early sixties. I had a terrible time in my second, fourth and sixth grades. I got trial promotions probably because the teachers wanted to get rid of me. Throughout this period, also, there was hardly any income in the family. My folks had lost the variety store and gas station. During the winter, warmth at night consisted of getting under a pile of blankets. The winter days of my early years were spent curled up on a bench behind a big potbelly stove in a variety store listening to men talk. I would stay there because it was warmer than it was in the house."

The Inner City Cohort

Born between 1925 and 1932, most of the Inner City men, children of the Great Depression, have early memories of discrimination and deprivation. But by the 1950s they had become beneficiaries of the GI bill and of America's postwar economic recovery. In addition, as children of once devalued Irish and Italian immigrants, they had been able to pass their minority status on to urban African Americans. They became the voting majority and the political masters of Boston. While only one in ten of their fathers belonged to the middle class, half of the Inner City men at age 47 met such criteria.

Besides the obvious biases in ethnicity and school performance resulting from matching the controls with delinquents remanded to reform school, the Inner City selection criteria imposed several other sources of bias. The Gluecks' original sample included no African Americans and no women. In addition, the Gluecks excluded the 10 percent of the men's classmates who by age 14 had manifested any serious delinquency. Thus, just as the Harvard sample probably excluded many passive, underachieving, but otherwise perfectly healthy college students, the Inner City sample probably excluded some adventurous, energetic students who manifested early delinquency but who enjoyed subsequent good outcomes.

A final and important source of bias was that at age 68 (1999) the Inner City men's health had deteriorated to the same degree as had the health of Harvard and Terman samples ten years later at age 78. In other words, although ten years younger than the two highly educated samples, the Inner City sample had suffered similar disability and mortality.

It may seem remarkable to some, but for thirty years there had been no contact between the Harvard Grant Study and the Harvard Glueck Study. Once I integrated the two studies, the Glueck Study (Inner City) men uncontacted for fifteen years had to be relocated. Thanks to the thoroughness with which Eleanor Glueck had recorded the addresses of relatives and thanks to the ingenuity and perseverance of my Study colleagues, *all* surviving Inner City men were contacted after age 40. It took twenty years and the invention of the Internet, however, to locate the 456th man! We currently know whether all but two of the 456 Inner City men are alive or dead at age 60 (and whether all 268 of the Harvard men are alive or dead at age 75). Time and again we would give up on finding a man only to be rewarded five years later with success.

Trying to reinterview some of the men, however, was not easy. For example, we had expected Inner City Study member Bill O'Neill at age 48 to be discharged from the Cambridge Detoxification Center on Wednesday, February 3. Accordingly, in hopes that he would be there, our interviewer visited O'Neill's home on February 4. No one was home, so the interviewer returned three hours later. A short man came out of Mr. O'Neill's apartment carrying a large bag of trash into the hallway. He was a disheveled man in his late 40s with a head of curly gray hair, and he appeared to be cleaning out the apartment. Unshaven, he moved slowly. Asked if he was William O'Neill, the man replied that "Bill" was due to be discharged from the Detoxification Center the next day at around 3 P.M. On February 5 our interviewer returned; there was no one home.

On February 6 our interviewer again visited O'Neill's home. This time a tall, dark-haired man answered the door; a few other men were visible inside watching TV. Asked if he was William O'Neill, the tall man said he was not. After determining that the interviewer was not a bill collector, he summoned Bill O'Neill to the door. The short, curly-haired man who came to the door was the same man who, two visits previously, had explained that Bill was not yet home from the hospital. The only difference was that now O'Neill had had a haircut and a shave. Without reference to the prior meeting, he acknowledged that he was indeed the long lost William O'Neill. He explained he had just come home from the hospital and did not feel well. Claiming he did not want to risk answering the Study investigator's questions incorrectly, he suggested that perhaps the interviewer would like to come back in a couple of weeks. The interviewer allowed that sooner might be better. Reluctantly, O'Neill agreed to the interview; then, recalling that his friends were present, he decided that he was too weak after all. He proposed meeting two days later — Monday, February 8, at 2:00 P.M.

To the interviewer's surprise, O'Neill himself answered the door. He was dressed in a clean if threadbare pair of trousers and an old T-shirt. He took a final moment to reconsider. "How long will this take?" The interviewer promised to expedite things. O'Neill led the interviewer into the kitchen, made coffee, and gave a cooperative interview for two hours. During the interview the tall, dark-haired man sat silently next door in the living room watching TV. Sounds of cowboys, Indians, and cartoons provided background music for the interview. For the next seventeen years O'Neill remained an illusive quarry. Finally, at age 65, he once more consented to a brief interview. Again he was gracious to the interviewer. O'Neill revealed that in his 50s he had joined Alcoholics Anonymous and for the last ten years had enjoyed stable sobriety. This was confirmed from independent sources. He died at age 66 from cancer.

However hard the interviewers may have had to work to relocate the Inner City men, the latter deserve still greater credit for making a reciprocal effort to cooperate. Their collective loyalty to the Study over its sixty years of existence has been extraordinary.

The Terman Women Sample

In the 1920s California was still a young state. The population of Los Angeles was 500,000 and the population of Oakland 20,000. The schools had grassy playgrounds, and the worlds of the Terman women were closer to the childhoods of East Coast American children in the nineteenth century than to the modern urban "blackboard jungle." Long before the bridge was built, a Study member could recall watching the last sailing ships glide through the Golden Gate. The Terman women themselves were the descendants of pioneers. One woman's grandmother had saved her own life by killing an intruder with a tomahawk. As a high school teacher in Leadville, Colorado, the father of a Terman woman routinely used to disarm his students before class. The father of still a third Terman woman won a stagecoach line to Arizona in a poker game. The Terman women did not grow up as Valley Girls.

Twenty percent of the Terman women's fathers were in blue-collar occupations and 30 percent, a proportion ten times that of their public school classmates, were in "the professions" — a broad definition that included high school teaching. Only one Terman woman's father was an "unskilled laborer"; he worked as a janitor at the University of California at Berkeley so that his five bright children could all go to college for free!

As children the Terman women had been precocious. They had walked one month earlier than their schoolmates, and they had talked three months earlier. Twenty percent of the women learned to read before age 5, and 60 percent had graduated from high school at 16 or younger. The high intelligence of the Terman women — mean IQ of 151 — did not handicap them psychologically. Rather, their mental health was demonstrably better than that of their classmates. In personality traits, the Terman women showed significantly more humor, common sense, perseverance, leadership, and even popularity. They were as likely as their classmates to marry, but their physical health was better. Compared to their classmates, they had better nutrition, better mental stability, fewer headaches, and fewer middle ear infections. Their siblings suffered only half the childhood mortality experienced by the siblings of their classmates. Finally, at age 80, like the Harvard sample the mortality of the Terman women has been only half what would be expected for white American women in their birth cohort. Like the Harvard sample, more than half of the Terman women survived past 80.

There was evidence that the Terman women's high tested intelligence was based on biology as well as on environmental privilege. For example, their children were clearly more gifted, as defined by standardized IQ tests, than the children of the educationally and economically more advantaged Harvard men. While negative environmental factors can profoundly lower tested IQ scores, positive environmental factors can elevate tested IQ by only ten or fifteen points.

The career opportunities for these highly intelligent women were filled with paradox. On the one hand, the Terman women's mothers did not have the right to vote until their daughters were 10 years old. On the other hand, California college tuition was cheap (twenty-five to fifty dollars per term for both Stanford and Berkeley) and a college degree was a realistic expectation for bright California women. On the one hand, the Depression, which began when they were 20, and World War II, which began when they were 30, put pressures on these women to enter the workforce. On the other hand, the jobs provided for the Terman women were limited in scope, compensation, and opportunity. When asked what occupational opportunities World War II had opened for her, one Berkeley-educated woman replied, "I finally learned to type. The phenomenon of 'Rosie, the riveter' provided an economic boon to the high school dropout but became an economic millstone for the gifted Terman women."

In short, it was the college-educated middle class Terman women, most of whose relatives had been in the United States for generations, who in this study most dramatically illustrated the negative effect of social bigotry upon adult development. At least 253 of the Terman women had full-time jobs for most of their lives. Most had gone to college and many to graduate school. Nevertheless, their mean maximum annual income ($30,000 in 1989 dollars) was identical to that of the Inner City men with an average of ten to eleven years of education and a mean IQ of 95. In contrast, World War II and the GI bill that paid for graduate school allowed the men of the Terman Study the chance to create the Los Alamos and Livermore laboratories and, ultimately, Silicon Valley. They added their brilliance to the Los Angeles entertainment industry. Lewis Terman's children, a boy and girl, were both included in his study of gifted children. Both graduated from Stanford and worked for the university for much of their lives. The son served as provost for Stanford University and as mentor to many of the founders of Silicon Valley. Terman's daughter served in a clerical position in one of the dormitories.

In 1987, Caroline Vaillant and I interviewed these women at an average age of 77 to 78. Our interviewing style was for me to review the longitudinally gathered record of the woman's entire life. Then my wife, blind to their past and more sensitive to women's lives than I, interviewed the women while I took notes. This allowed the interview not to be biased by halo effects from the past. After the interview we integrated our findings.

Since most of the 50 women whom we did not interview had been followed for half a century, they could be included in many of the data analyses. (Indeed, one of the extraordinary advantages of multidecade prospective study is that even dropouts have been followed long enough to be well characterized.) Except for vastly inferior physical health, and possibly greater alcohol and cigarette abuse, the 50 uninterviewed women did not differ significantly from the 40 women whom we did interview.

APPENDIX B: An Illustrated Glossary of Defenses

Definitions of Mature and Immature Defenses

To illustrate defenses I shall use an imaginary woman. She married at age 30 and after one miscarriage tried unsuccessfully for the next seven years to have a living child. She had always felt inadequate to her younger sister, who already had four children and had been the one in the family who won praise as "being good with kids." The woman's husband desperately wanted children. At age 38, following a cervical biopsy that showed early cancer, she underwent a total hysterectomy. (Note that her conflict involves instinctual wishes, parental expectations, reality, and the needs of those she loved.) Below are a number of vignettes (similar to those used to identify defenses in Study members) illustrating her possible responses to her surgery. The first six vignettes illustrate immature defenses; the last five illustrate mature defenses.

Immature Defenses

Following a slight postoperative wound infection, she wrote long, angry letters to the papers blaming the hospital for unsanitary conditions. Blaming her doctor for not doing a Pap smear earlier, she contemplated instituting malpractice proceedings against him. (Projection)

Emerging from anesthesia she felt no regret but instead enjoyed what she felt was a religious experience. Postoperatively, she told all her friends that her pain gave her a sense of joyous communion with sufferers everywhere. She felt an intense inward sense of good fortune that she had been favored by God to have her cancer discovered so soon and to have come through surgery so well. (Dissociation)

She asked the nurse not to permit visitors because they made her "sad." She threw out all her flowers and instead lost herself in photographs of babies. She would go down the corridor to the newborn nursery daydreaming about what she would call each child if it were hers. Once a floor nurse had to ask her not to whistle Brahms' "Lullaby" quite so loudly. (Fantasy)

She became worried that the cancer might have spread to her lymph nodes and belabored her visitors with accounts of tiny lumps in her groin and neck. When her sister came to visit, the patient threw the flowers she brought into the wastebasket and angrily accused her of caring so much for her own children that she did not care if her own sister died of cancer. (Hypochondriasis)

When the intern, while inserting an intravenous line, missed her vein, she smiled at him and told him not to worry; "When you're just a medical student, it must be hard to get things right." Unable to sleep, she watched her IV run dry. Only then, at 4 A.M., did she call the night nurse to wake the intern to restart the IV. She cheerfully told him that she had not rung for the nurse earlier because she knew how busy everyone in the hospital was and she was sure he would remember to check. (Passive aggression)

Shortly after leaving the hospital she was unfaithful to her husband with four different men in a month, twice picking up men in cocktail lounges and once seducing an 18-year-old delivery boy. Prior to that time she had had no sexual interest in any man but her husband. (Acting out)

Mature Defenses
A month after surgery, she organized a group of other women who had had breast and uterine surgery to counsel and visit patients undergoing gynecological surgery. From their experience they tried to provide information, advice, and comfort to surgical patients. (Altruism)

She read Marcus Aurelius and Ecclesiastes in the hospital. She took great care to hide her tear-stained tissues from her husband and made no complaint (even though the process was painful) while her sutures were removed. Knowing that baby pictures upset her, she deliberately gave away an unread copy of her favorite magazine, which featured an article on childcare. (Suppression)

She got great pleasure from the get well cards from her sister's children; she agreed to teach a Sunday school class of preschoolers; she had a poem published in her hometown weekly on the bittersweet joys of the childless aunt. (Sublimation)

She laughed so hard tears came to her eyes and her ribs ached when she read the *Playboy* definition of a hysterectomy: "throwing out the baby carriage but keeping the playpen." She explained her private mirth to a startled and curious nurse with "The whole thing is just so damned ironic." (Humor)

Her doctor was surprised to find out how relaxed and practical she was about her postoperative course and the calm frankness with which she could express her regret at being cheated of children. His surprise was due to the fact that she had spent her preoperative visit anxiously worrying about possible surgical complications and weeping over the fact that she would never be able to bear children. (Anticipation)

APPENDIX C:
Methodology for Assessing Maturity of Adaptive Mental Mechanisms (a.k.a. Defenses)

The methodology is spelled out in much greater detail in G. E. Vaillant, *Ego Mechanisms of Defense: A Guide for Clinicians and Researchers*, Washington, D.C., American Psychological Association, 1994. Since defense mechanisms like "creativity" and "perseverance" are abstractions, distinction between mature defenses (good denial) and immature defenses (bad denial) becomes important. For each of the three cohorts the fifteen individual defenses used frequently enough to count were clustered into three groups: mature (sublimation, suppression, anticipation, altruism, and humor); intermediate, or neurotic (displacement, repression, isolation, and reaction formation); and immature (projection, schizoid fantasy, passive aggression, acting out, hypochondriasis, and dissociation).

In order to control for marked variation in the frequency of identified defensive vignettes across Study members, ratios of defenses at different levels of maturity, rather than absolute numbers of defenses, were employed. By this I mean that suppression as a style of defense received the same weight if it were noted three times in someone for whom 10 vignettes were counted and nine times in someone for whom a total of 30 vignettes were counted.

The relative proportion — the ratio — of defense vignettes in each of the three general categories (mature, intermediate, immature) was determined. In order to obtain a nine-point scale of defense maturity, the ratio between immature and mature defenses was used to distribute a total of eight points. Of the eight points, one to five points could be assigned to each of the three levels of maturity, but the total had to be eight, and every level had to be assigned at least one point. For example, someone who manifested ten examples reflecting mature defenses, four examples reflecting neurotic defenses, and *no* examples of immature defenses would be scored as follows: mature defenses = 5, neurotic defenses = 2, and immature defenses = 1. Someone who exhibited six examples reflecting mature defenses, eight examples reflecting neurotic defenses and nine examples reflecting immature defenses would be scored: mature = 2, intermediate = 3, immature = 3. Then the (1–5) rating for mature defenses was subtracted from the (1–5) rating for immature defenses, providing a total score of +4 to −4 (i.e., a nine-point scale). For purposes of computation, the score for overall maturity of defensive style for each person was transformed into a 1–9 scale by adding five points to the total. Thus, a score of 1 reflected the most mature style and a score of 9 reflected the least mature adaptive style (i.e., immature = 5, mature = 1). This procedure produced a normal (bell curve) distribution of scores and a rater reliability (Pearson correlation coefficient) of .84 for the Inner City men and .87 for the Terman women.

APPENDIX D: Assessment of Childhood Scales

1. Child Temperament Scale

Childhood emotional problems (age 0-10)

1 = very shy, tics, phobias, bedwetting beyond age 8, dissocial, severe feeding problems, other noted problems

3 = average (no problems, but not quite 2)

5 = good natured, normally social, an "easy child"

2. Childhood Environmental Strengths Scale

(The score on this scale equals the sum of the points given for the following items. Range 5-25.)

a. Global Impression

1 = rater's overall hunch — a negative, nonnurturing environment

3 = neither negative nor positive feeling about subject's childhood

5 = a positive, intact childhood; good relationships with parents, siblings, and others, environment seems conducive to developing self-esteem; a childhood that rater would have wanted

b. Relationship with Siblings

1 = severe rivalry, destructive relationship, sibling undermines child's self-esteem or no siblings

3 = no good information, not mentioned as good though not particularly bad

5 = close to at least one sibling

c. Home Atmosphere

1 = any noncongenial home, lack of family cohesiveness, parents not together, early maternal separation, known to many social agencies, many moves, financial hardship that impinged greatly on family life

3 = average home: doesn't stand out as good or bad; or lack of information

5 = warm, cohesive atmosphere, parents together, doing things as a family, sharing atmosphere, maternal and paternal presence, few moves, financial stability or special harmony in spite of difficulties

d. Mother/Child Relationship

1 = distant, hostile, blaming others (such as father, teachers) for wrong methods of upbringing, overly punitive, overprotective, expecting too much, mother absent, seductive, not encouraging feeling of self-worth in child

3 = mostly for lack of information or lack of distinct impression about mother

5 = nurturing, encouraging of autonomy, helping child develop self-esteem, warmth

e. Father/Child Relationship

1 = distant, hostile, overly punitive, expectations unrealistic or not what child wants for self, paternal absence, negative or destructive relationship

3 = lack of information, no distinct impression about father

5 = warmth, encouraging of autonomy in child, helping to develop self-esteem, does things with child, discusses problems, interested in child

APPENDIX E:
Basic Trust at Age 50 Associated with Childhood Environment and Future Successful Aging

True/False statements answered at about age 50

	Aging Age 75		Childhood Age 10-20	
	Happy-Well N = 43	Sad-Sick N = 25	Warm N = 29	Bleak N = 28
A. View Emotions as Absent				
Others have felt that I have been afraid of sex	12%	30%	0%	32%
Marriage without sex would suit me	0%	16%**	0%	7%
I have had a difficult sexual adjustment	5%	33%**	0%	18%*
Sometimes I feel numb when I should be feeling a strong emotion	19%	48%	17%	39%
B. View Emotions as Overwhelming				
I have sometimes thought that the depth of my feelings might become destructive	2%	32%***	14%	32%*
I sometimes fear that I will wear people out	19%	48%**	10%	42%**
People usually let you down	0%	24%***	3%	11%
Sometimes I feel I am a considerable strain on people	26%	60%**	24%	39%
Answered "True" to two or more of the above 8 statements	21%	81%***	25%	63%***

* p < .05 ** p < .01 *** p < .001

APPENDIX F: Scale for Subjective Physical Health (Instrumental Activities of Daily Living)

Study questions are asked in bold. The answers of a 79-year-old Study member are presented in regular type. The scoring system is provided in parentheses. The Study member received 17 out of a total of 23 points. For the purpose of the Happy-Well/Sad-Sick classification a score of 19 points or higher was considered "not disabled."

1. **Because of health are you unable to do some things that you could do at age 60?**
   No cutbacks (2), some cutbacks (1). For example:
   I do not cut as much firewood, but I don't need much with the advent of natural gas heat. (1)

2. **In the past year, have you:**
   a) **Participated in hard physical activities?** Yes (3), Yes, but slowly (2), No (1).
   Gave up downhill skiing last year (age 77). Loved it but cannot subject my families (all distant) to care if some young ski boarder hits me from behind. Got my first skiis at age 5. Damn. (1)
   b) **Climbed two flights of stairs without resting?** Yes (3), Yes, but slowly (2), No (1).
   No. (1)
   c) **Have you walked more than two miles or more than 20 city blocks without resting?**
   Yes (3), Yes, but slowly (2), No (1).
   Yes, did 25 fast blocks in downtown Chicago last month. (3)

3. **Do you still move light furniture, carry a light suitcase through airports, etc.?**
   Yes (2), No (1).
   Exercise is endless living in the country. (2)

4. **Has your health led you to reduce a major activity (e.g., reduced yard work)?**
   Yes (1), No (2). Describe:
   Having trouble with night vision but am not restricted just yet. No more long trips. (1)

5. **Has your health led you to stop a major activity (e.g., fishing, looking after yard)?**
Yes (1), No (2). Describe:
No. Really enjoy keeping up with several much younger lady friends. Took three of them to Paris last April, Santa Fe in January, Florence and Venice come October. (2)

6. **Does your health prevent you from driving a car or using some forms of public transportation?**
Yes (1), No (2).
No. (2)

7. **When you go downtown, do you need help (e.g., wheelchair, cane, someone to carry packages?**
Yes (1), No (2).
No. (2)

8. **Because of your health, do you need some help to complete daily activities (e.g., bathing, dressing, shopping for necessities)?**
Yes (1), No (2).
No. I am called an ambulatory ragbag by some who have never seen a Brooks Brothers suit. (2)

APPENDIX G: Scale for Objective Mental Health (Age 50–65)

1. Career prior to age 65	1 = working full-time
	2 = significant reduction of workload
	3 = retired before age 65
2. Career success	1 = current (or preretirement responsibilities/success as great or greater than at age 45
	2 = demotions or reduced effectiveness (prior to retirement)
3. Career or retirement enjoyment	1 = meaningful, enjoyable
	2 = ambiguous
	3 = working only because he must or feels retirement demeaning/boring
4. Vacations	1 = 3+ weeks and fun
	2 = less than 3 weeks if working or unplayful retirement
5. Psychiatrist use	1 = no visits
	2 = 1–10 visits
	3 = psych hospitalization or 10+ visits
6. Tranquilizer use (maximum use in any one year)	1 = none
	2 = for 1 to 30 days
	3 = for more than one month
7. Days sick leave (exclude irreversible illness)	1 = less than 5 days/year
	2 = 5+ days
8. Marriage from age 50 to 65	1 = clearly happy
	2 = so-so
	3 = clearly unhappy or divorced
9. Games with others	1 = regular social activities/sports
	2 = little or none
Total (Low score is good: a score greater than 14 excluded a person from the Happy-Well)	9–14 = score compatible with being classified Happy-Well
	15–23 = bottom quartile; excludes individual from the Happy-Well

APPENDIX H: Scale for Objective Social Supports (Age 50–70, Harvard Cohort Only)

1. Assessment of marriage (using multiple questionnaires from both husband and wife and interview)
   - 0 = marriage rocky or divorce
   - 2 = marriage = so-so
   - 4 = marriage excellent and of long duration

2. Play and activities with others
   - 0 = no games with others
   - 1 = true for one period
   - 2 = games with others at age 47 and 65

3. Relationship with siblings
   - 0 = no siblings or poor relations
   - 1 = so-so
   - 2 = good relations with at least 1 sibling

4. Religious involvement
   - 0 = no involvement
   - 1 = a little
   - 2 = attend church/temple regularly and religion plays a very important role in life

5. Closeness to children from interview data and children's questionnaires)
   - 0 = no children or distant from them all
   - 1 = likes them but does not see them often
   - 2 = intimate relationship to at least one child that he sees often

6. Confiding relationship 1967–1991
   - 0 = no confidante
   - 1 = only wife or physician
   - 2 = at least one active confidante besides wife

7. Social network
   - 0 = no social network
   - 1 = so-so
   - 2 = clearly involved in social activities, club memberships, rich pattern of friends

Total: Sum of items 1–7 (social support over the last 20 years). A score less than 6 excluded a man from the Happy-Well.

APPENDIX I: Scale for Subjective Life Satisfaction

Please show us what your satisfaction has been with each of the following areas of life OVER THE LAST 20 YEARS by checking the column which best describes your experience:*

Life Area	(2) Highly Satisfying	(1.5) Generally Satisfying	(1) Somewhat Satisfying	(0.5) Not Very Satisfying	(0) Not at all Satisfying
Income-producing work	X (2)				
Hobbies		X			
Your marriage	X (2)				
Your children	X (2)				
Friendships		X (1.5)			
Community service			X		
Recreation/sports	X (2)				
Religion					X
Other (specify)					

Total score calculated by adding the scores for the four underlined areas (job, marriage, children, friendships) and the single most satisfying of the other five life areas (hobbies, community service, sports, religion, other). An illustrative example is given; the subject's answers are marked with an X. His assigned total score is 9.5 (A score less than 7 excluded men from the Happy-Well.)

*(Asked of Harvard men in 1995 and 1997 and Inner City men in 1998 and 2000)

APPENDIX J: Table Contrasting the Happy-Well with the Sad-Sick and the Prematurely Dead

	Odds Ratios (95% Confidence Intervals)[a]	
	Harvard n = 162[b]	Inner City n = 217[c]

Controllable Protective Factors (range)

Smoking < 30 Pack-Years (yes/no)	4.81 (0.84, 27.7)[d]	4.56 (2.29, 9.11)***
No alcohol abuse (yes/no)	see footnote[e]	1.11 (.527, 2.35)[f]
Mature defenses (yes/no)	2.65 (1.22, 6.80)*	2.98 (1.40, 6.10)**
Stable marriage (yes/no)	1.94 (0.70, 5.35)	2.75 (1.24, 6.81)*
BMI > 21 and < 29 (yes/no)	3.05 (0.99, 9.40)[h]	1.71 (0.85, 3.43)
Some regular exercise (yes/no)	3.09 (1.30, 9.75)*	n.a.
Education (in years)	n.a.	.855 (0.77, 0.96)*[g]

Uncontrollable Protective Factors

Without depressive diagnosis (yes/no)	10.4 (4.75, 23.2)*	3.51 (1.20, 9.99)*
High parental social class (I–V)	1.46 (0.91, 2.36)	1.12 (0.63, 1.96
Stable childhood temperament (1–5)	.919 (0.68, 1.24)	1.10 (0.85, 1.42)
Warm childhood (5–25)	.980 (0.89, 1.12)	.985 (0.92, 1.11)
Ancestral longevity (in years)	1.00 (0.97, 1.04)	.998 (0.97, 1.00)

a. Controlling for the other ten variables (education n.a. for Harvard and exercise n.a. for Inner City cohorts)

b. 75 Harvard men classified as Intermediate Aging [Successful Aging = 2] excluded

c. 114 Inner City men classified as Intermediate Aging [Successful Aging = 2] excluded and 1 man excluded due to missing data

d. p = .079

e. Since no Harvard men who abused alcohol were among the Happy-Well, the odds ratio could not be calculated, but alcohol abuse was left in the model.

f. Alcohol abuse appeared to make no independent contribution due to its colinearity with smoking.

g. For each additional year of education, the likelihood of being Sad-Sick or Prematurely Dead at 65 was reduced by .85.

h. p = .051   *p < .05   **p < .01   ***p < .001

APPENDIX K: Graceful Aging Scale

1. Maintains social utility, open to new ideas, cares about others (within the limits of physical health) 0–3
2. Eriksonian Integrity, accepts the past and can take sustenance from past accomplishments 0–2
3. Maintains other Eriksonian skills: Basic Trust (hope in life), sensible Autonomy, and Initiative. (In old age Industry, Generativity, and Intimacy are not always possible) 0–3
4. Enjoys life, retains sense of humor, capacity for joy and play. (Since "old age is not for sissies," happiness may not be possible) 0–3
5. Cheerful acceptance of "indignities of old age," graceful about dependency issues, takes care of self, and when ill becomes a patient that a doctor would want to care for 0–2
6. Cultivates relationships with surviving old friends and is successful in making new ones 0–2

TOTAL

Summary Scale

13–15 = Unusually vigorous aging. Meets almost all of the criteria for successful aging and is beloved by physician and grandchildren.

10–12 = An old age adjustment that the rater would be content to have at 75.

7–9 = Real strengths, but some serious limitations.

4–6 = So-so adjustment — fits the young person's stereotype of old age. More rigid and discontented than otherwise. Fails many of the above criteria.

0–3 = Moderate depression, complaining, dependency, rigidity, withdrawal, timidity, self-centered, unable to accept old age. The kind of elderly person doctors don't like and that young relatives withdraw from.

NOTES

Chapter 1 The Study of Adult Development

1. H. Amiel, *Journal Intimé* (London: Macmillan, 1985).
2. J. W. Rowe and R. L. Kahn, *Successful Aging* (New York: Dell, 1999).
3. P. B. Baltes and K. V. Mayer, eds., *The Berlin Aging Study* (Cambridge, England: Cambridge University Press, 1999).
4. M. Rutter, B. Yule, D. Quinton, W. Yule, and M. Berger, "Attainment and Adjustment in Two Geographical Areas, III: Some Factors Accounting for Area Differences," *British Journal of Psychiatry* (1974), vol. 125, pp. 520–533.
5. E. E. Werner and R. S. Smith, *Vulnerable but Invincible* (New York: McGraw-Hill, 1982).
6. W. Garmezy, "Stressors of Childhood" in *Stress, Coping and Development in Children,* N. Garmezy and M. Rutter, eds. (New York: McGraw-Hill, 1983).
7. M. Cowley, *The View from Eighty* (New York: Viking Press, 1980).
8. C. W. Heath, *What People Are* (Cambridge, Mass.: Harvard University Press, 1945).
9. S. Glueck and E. Glueck, *Unraveling Juvenile Delinquency* (New York: Commonwealth Fund, 1950).
10. S. Glueck and E. Glueck, *Delinquents and Nondelinquents in Perspective* (Cambridge, Mass.: Harvard University Press, 1968).
11. Glueck and Glueck, *Unraveling Juvenile Delinquency.*
12. R. Sampson and J. Laub, *Crime in the Making* (Cambridge, Mass.: Harvard University Press, 1993).
13. Glueck and Glueck, *Delinquents and Nondelinquents in Perspective.*
14. G. E. Vaillant, *The Natural History of Alcoholism Revisited* (Cambridge, Mass.: Harvard University Press, 1995).
15. L. M. Terman, *Mental and Physical Traits of a Thousand Gifted Children, vol. 1. Genetic Studies of Genius* (Stanford, Calif.: Stanford University Press, 1925).
16. G. E. Vaillant and C. O. Vaillant, "Determinants and Consequences of

Creativity in a Cohort of Gifted Women," *Psychology of Women Quarterly* (1990), vol. 14, pp. 607–616.

17. R. R. Sears, "The Terman Gifted Children Study" in *Handbook of Longitudinal Research,* S. A. Mednik, M. Harway, and K. M. Finello, eds. (New York: Praeger, 1984), pp. 398–414.

18. M. H. Oden, "The Fulfillment of Promise: 40-Year Follow-up of the Terman Gifted Group," *Genetic Psychological Monographs* (1968), vol. 77, pp. 3–93.

19. C. K. Halloran and R. R. Sears, *The Gifted Group in Maturity* (Stanford, Calif.: Stanford University Press, 1995).

20. A. J. Garfein and A. R. Herzog, "Robust Aging Among the Young-Old, Old-Old, and Oldest-Old," *Journal of Gerontology: Social Sciences* (1995), vol. 50B, pp. 577–587.

21. G. E. Vaillant and K. Mukamal, "Positive Aging," *American Journal of Psychiatry* (2001), vol. 158, pp. 839–847.

22. A. B. Hollinghead and F. C. Redlich, *Social Class and Mental Illness* (New York: Wiley and Sons, 1958).

23. D. Goleman, *Emotional Intelligence* (New York: Bantam Books, 1995).

24. G. E. Vaillant and J. T. Davis, "Social/Emotional Intelligence and Midlife Resilience in Schoolboys with Low Tested Intelligence," *American Journal of Orthopsychiatry* (2000), vol. 70, pp. 215–222.

25. G. E. Vaillant, *Adaptation to Life* (Boston: Little, Brown, 1977).

26. G. E. Vaillant, *The Natural History of Alcoholism Revisited.*

27. O. Hagnell, E. Essen-Moller, J. Lanke, L. Ojesjo, and B. Rorsman, *The Incidence of Mental Illnesses over a Quarter of a Century* (Stockholm: Almquist and Wiksell International, 1990).

28. From S. de Beauvoir, *The Coming of Age* (New York: G. P. Putnam's Sons, 1972).

29. From D. J. Levinson, *The Seasons of a Man's Life* (New York: Knopf, 1978), p. 34.

30. From B. Friedan, *The Fountain of Age* (New York: Simon & Schuster, 1993), p. 87.

Chapter 2 Ripeness Is All: Social and Emotional Maturation

1. W. James, *The Principles of Psychology* (New York: Henry Holt, 1890), vol. 1, p. 121.

2. S. Freud, "Femininity" (1933), in J. Strachey, ed., *The Standard Edition of the Complete Psychological Works of Sigmund Freud* (London: Hogarth Press, 1965), vol. 22, pp. 134–135.

3. H. C. Covey, "Old Age Portrayed by the Ages-of-Life Models from the

Middle Ages to the 16th Century," *The Gerontologist* (1989), vol. 29, pp. 692–698.

4. A. Quetelet, *A Treatise on Man and the Development of His Faculties* (Edinburgh: William and Robert Chambers, 1842).

5. I. L. Nascher, *The Diseases of Old Age and Their Treatment* (Philadelphia: Blakiston, 1914).

6. G. S. Hall, *Senescence* (New York: D. Appleton, 1922), p. 100.

7. C. Bühler, "The Curve of Life: Life as Studied in Biographies," *Journal of Applied Psychology* (1935), vol. 19, pp. 405–409.

8. Rheinischen Museumsamtes, *Die Lebenstreppe* (Cologne: Rheinland-Verlag, 1983).

9. E. Frenkel-Brunswik, "Studies in Biographical Psychology," in *Character and Personality* (1936), vol. 5, pp. 1–34 (pp. 4–6).

10. W. Shakespeare, *As You Like It,* Act II, Scene 7.

11. E. Frenkel-Brunswik, *Studies in Biographical Psychology,* p. 8.

12. E. Erikson, "The Life Cycle," in *The International Encyclopedia of the Social Sciences* (1976), vol. 9, pp. 286–292.

13. E. H. Erikson, "Identity and the Life Cycle," *Psychological Issues* (1959), vol. 1, p. 59.

14. E. H. Erikson, J. M. Erikson, and H. Q. Kivnick, *Vital Involvement in Old Age* (New York: W. W. Norton, 1986), p. 60.

15. E. Erikson, *Childhood and Society* (New York: W. W. Norton, 1950).

16. N. Haan, R. Millsap, E. Hartka, "As Time Goes By: Change and Stability in Personality over Fifty Years," *Psychology and Aging* (1986), vol. 1, pp. 220–232.

17. Carol Gilligan, the author of *In a Different Voice* (Cambridge, Mass.: Harvard University Press, 1980), deserves credit for suggesting this model as an alternative to Erikson's upwardly leading staircase.

18. R. Havinghurst, *Developmental Tasks and Education* (New York: David McKay, 1972).

19. C. E. Franz, "Does Thought Content Change as Individuals Age? A Longitudinal Study of Midlife Adults," in T. F. Heatherton and J. L. Weinberger, eds., *Can Personality Change?* (Washington, D.C.: American Psychological Association, 1994).

20. E. Erikson, *Childhood and Society,* p. 232.

21. E. H. Erikson et al., *Vital Involvement in Old Age.*

22. G. E. Vaillant, *The Wisdom of the Ego* (Cambridge, Mass.: Harvard University Press, 1993).

23. G. E. Vaillant and E. M. Milofsky, "The Natural History of Male Psychological Health, IX: Empirical Evidence for Erikson's Model of the

Life Cycle," *American Journal of Psychiatry* (1980), vol. 137, pp. 1348–1359.

24. A. J. Stewart, J. M. Osborne, and R. Helson, "Middle Aging in Women: Patterns of Personality Change from the 30s to the 50s," *Journal of Adult Development* (2001), vol. 8, pp. 23–37.

25. Ibid., p. 25.

26. G. E. Vaillant and E. M. Milofsky, "The Natural History of Male Psychological Health, 1: The Adult Life Cycle from 18-50," *Seminars in Psychiatry* (1972), vol. 4, pp. 415-427.

27. Ssu Shu, *The Four Books: Confucian Anelects* (c. 470 B.C.), trans. J. Legge (Shanghai: Chinese Book Company, no date), pp. 13–14.

28. W. R. Miller, A. L. Leckman, H. D. Delaney, and M. Tinkcom, "Long-Term Follow-up of Behavioral Self-Control Training," *Journal of Studies on Alcohol* (1992), vol. 53, pp. 249-261.

29. Project MATCH Research Group (T. F. Babor, W. R. Miller, C. DiClemente, R. Longabaugh, eds., "Comments on Project MATCH: Matching Alcohol Treatments to Client Heterogeneity," *Addiction* (1999), vol. 94, pp. 31–69.

30. F. M. Benes, "Human Brain Growth Spans Decades," *American Journal of Psychiatry* (1998), vol. 155, p. 1489.

31. F. M. Benes, M. Turtle, Y. Khan, and P. Farol, "Myelinization of a Key Relay in the Hippocompal Formation Occurs in the Human Brain During Childhood, Adolescence and Adulthood," *Archives of General Psychiatry* (1994), vol. 51, pp. 477–484.

32. S. Freud, "The Neuro-Psychoses of Defense" (1894), in *Standard Edition,* vol. 3, pp. 45–61.

33. G. E. Vaillant, *Ego Mechanisms of Defense: A Guide for Clinicians and Researchers* (Washington, D.C.: American Psychiatric Press, 1992).

34. G. E. Vaillant, "Adaptive Mental Mechanisms: Their Role in a Positive Psychology," *American Psychologist* (2000), vol. 55, pp. 89–95.

35. G. E. Vaillant, "Natural History of Male Psychological Health, V: The Relation of Choice of Ego Mechanisms of Defense to Adult Adjustment," *Archives of General Psychiatry* (1976), vol. 33, pp. 535–545.

36. E. Semrad, "The Organization of Ego Defenses and Object Loss," in D. M. Moriarty, ed., *The Loss of Loved Ones* (Springfield, Ill: Charles C. Thomas, 1967).

37. G. E. Vaillant, "Theoretical Hierarchy of Adaptive Ego Mechanisms," *Archives of General Psychiatry* (1970), vol. 24, pp. 107–118.

38. N. Haan, *Coping and Defending* (San Diego, Calif.: Academic Press, 1977).

39. G. E. Vaillant, "Adaptive Mental Mechanisms."

40. N. Haan, *Coping and Defending.*

41. H. Steiner, K. B. Araujo, and C. Koopman, "The Response Evaluation Measure (REM-71): A New Questionnaire for the Measurement of Defenses in Adults and Adolescents," *American Journal of Psychiatry* (2001), vol. 158, pp. 467–473.

42. S. Folkman, R. S. Lazarus, S. Pimley, J. Novacek, "Age Differences in Stress and Coping Processes," *Psychology and Aging* (1987), vol. 2, pp. 171–184.

43. P. T. Costa and R. R. McCrae, "Personality Continuity and the Changes of Adult Life," in M. Storandt and G. R. Vanden Bos, eds., in *The Adult Years: Continuity and Change* (Washington, D.C.: American Psychological Association, 1989), pp. 45–77, p. 58.

44. C. J. Jones and W. Meredith, "Developmental Paths of Psychological Health from Early Adolescence to Later Adulthood," *Psychology and Aging* (2000), vol. 15, pp. 351–360.

Chapter 3 The Past and How Much It Matters

1. G. E. Vaillant, "Natural History of Male Psychological Health, II: Some Antecedents of Healthy Adult Adjustment," *Archives of General Psychiatry* (1974), vol. 31, pp. 15–22.

2. M. Rutter, *Material Deprivation Reassessed, 2nd ed.* (Hammondsworth: Penguin Books, 1987).

3. G. E. Vaillant, *The Natural History of Alcoholism Revisited.*

4. G. E. Vaillant and C. O. Vaillant, "Natural History of Male Psychological Health, X: Work as a Predictor of Positive Mental Health," *American Journal of Psychiatry* (1981), vol. 138, pp. 1433–1440.

5. G. E. Vaillant, "Natural History of Male Psychological Health: Effects of Mental Health on Physical Health," *New England Journal of Medicine* (1979), vol. 301, pp. 1249–1254.

6. A. Lazare, G. L. Klerman, D. J. Armor, "Oral, Obsessive and Hysterical Personality Patterns," *Archives of General Psychiatry* (1966), vol. 14, pp. 624–630.

7. G. E. Vaillant and E. M. Milofsky, "Empirical Evidence for Erikson's Model of the Life Cycle."

8. M. Rutter, *Maternal Deprivation Reassessed.*

9. A. B. Zonderman, P. T. Costa, R. R. McCrae, "Depression as a Risk for Cancer Morbidity and Mortality in a Nationally Representative Sample," *Journal of the American Medical Association* (1989), vol. 262, pp. 1191–1195.

10. L. Tolstoy, *Childhood, Boyhood, Youth* (New York: Scribners, 1852, 1904), p. 109.

Chapter 4 Generativity: A Key to Successful Aging

1. Ninety-three percent of the 14 generative women and 56 percent of the nongenerative women at forty reported attaining orgasm "usually" or "always" (chi square 37.3, d.f. 12, p < .001).
2. G. E. Vaillant, L. N. Shapiro, P. P. Schmitt, "Psychological Motives for Medical Hospitalization," *Journal of the American Medical Association* (1970), vol. 214, pp. 1661–1665.
3. J. Kotre, *Outliving the Self* (Baltimore: Johns Hopkins University Press, 1984), p. 10.
4. E. Erikson, *Childhood and Society*, p. 141.
5. A. Lindbergh, *The Unicorn* (New York: Pantheon, 1954), p. 32.

Chapter 5 Keeper of the Meaning

1. C. D. Ryff, "Successful Aging: A Developmental Approach," *Gerontologist* (1987), vol. 22, pp. 209–214 (p. 210).
2. W. James, *The Principles of Psychology*, vol. 2, p. 110.
3. F. W. Purifoy, L. H. Koopmans, and R. W. Tatum, "Steroid Hormone and Aging: Free testosterone, Testosterone and Androstenedione in Normal Females Aged 20–87 Years," *Human Biology* (1980), vol. 52, pp. 181–191.
4. E. Hemingway, *The Green Hills of Africa* (New York: Scribners, 1935).
5. R. Helson and P. Wink, "Personality Change in Women from the Early 40's to the Early 50's," *Psychology and Aging* (1992), vol. 7, pp. 46–55.
6. P. Wink and R. Helson, "Personality Change in Women and Their Partners," *Journal of Personality and Social Psychology* (1993), vol. 65, pp. 597–605.
7. D. L. Gutmann, *Reclaimed Powers* (New York: Basic Books, 1987).
8. C. Jung, *Modern Man in Search of a Soul* (New York: Harcourt, Brace and World, 1933), p. 109.
9. S. de Beauvoir, *The Coming of Age*, p. 77.
10. E. H. Erikson et al., *Vital Involvement in Old Age*, p. 60.
11. F. L. Wells and W. L. Woods, "Outstanding Traits: In a Selected College Group with Some Reference to Career Interests and War Records." *Genetic Psychological Monographs* (1946), vol. 33, pp. 127–249.

Chapter 6 Integrity: Death Be Not Proud

1. M. Barrett, *Second Chance* (New York: Parabola Books, 1999), p. 95.
2. M. Cowley, *The View from Eighty*, pp. 3, 4, 41.
3. Quoted in M. Cowley, *The View from Eighty*, pp. 45–46
4. This life task was pointed out to me by the perennially wise and now retired Harvard University Health Service psychiatrist Elizabeth Reid.

5. Quoted in S. de Beauvoir, *The Coming of Age,* p. 206.

6. Ibid., p. 201.

7. H. Zinsser, *As I Remember Him* (Boston: Little Brown, 1940).

8. Sophocles, *Oedipus at Colonus,* trans. G. Garrett, in D. R. Slavitt and P. Bovie, eds., *Sophocles* (Philadelphia: University of Pennsylvania Press, 1999), ll. 6–8.

9. *Oedipus at Colonus,* ll. 1328–1331.

10. *Oedipus at Colonus,* ll. 1213–1214.

11. *Oedipus at Colonus,* ll. 686–688.

12. *Oedipus at Colonus,* ll. 1679–1684.

13. C. H. Whitman, *Sophocles* (Cambridge, Mass.: Harvard University Press, 1951), p. 251.

Chapter 7 Healthy Aging: A Second Pass

1. L. Breslow, "A Quantitative Approach to the World Health Organization Definition of Health: Physical, Mental and Social Well Being," *International Journal of Epidemiology* (1972), vol. 1, pp. 347–355 (p. 348).

2. T. T. Perls and M. H. Silver, *Living to 100: Lessons in Living to your Maximum Potential at Any Age* (New York: Basic Books, 2000), p. 74.

3. P. B. Baltes and M. M. Baltes, *Successful Aging* (Cambridge: Cambridge University Press, 1990), pp. 1–34 (p. 18). My choice of these six dimensions has been influenced by the work of Paul and Margret Baltes, who for many years have studied successful aging at the Max Planck Institute in Berlin and the Free University of Berlin.

4. P. B. Baltes, and M. M. Baltes, *Successful Aging.*

5. N. Shock, *Normal Human Aging* (Washington, D.C.: U.S. Government Printing Office, 1984).

6. H. Thomae, "Conceptualizations of Responses to Stress," *European Journal of Personality* (1987), vol. 1, pp. 171–191.

7. K. W. Schaie, "The Seattle Longitudinal Study: A 21-Year Exploration of Psychometric Intelligence in Adulthood," in K. W. Shaie, ed., *Longitudinal Studies of Adult Psychological Development* (New York: Guilford Press, 1983), pp. 64–135.

8. R. Bosse, C. M. Aldwin, M. R. Levenson, and K. Workman-Daniels, "How Stressful Is Retirement? Findings from the Normative Aging Study," *Journal of Gerontology: Psychological Sciences* (1991), vol. 46, pp. 9–14.

9. E. W. Busse and G. L. Maddox, *The Duke Longitudinal Studies of Normal Aging: 1955–1980* (New York: Springer, 1988).

10. H. M. Krumholz et al., "Lack of Association Between Cholesterol and Coronary Heart Disease Mortality and Morbidity and All-Cause

Mortality in Persons Older than 70 Years," *Journal of the American Medical Association* (1994), vol. 272, p. 1335.

11. Heath, *What People Are.*

12. Wells and Woods, "Outstanding Traits."

13. P. P. Schnurr, C. O. Vaillant, and G. E. Vaillant, "Predicting Exercise in Late Midlife from Young Adult Personality Characteristics, *International Journal of Aging and Human Development* (1990), vol. 30, pp. 153–161.

14. T. R. Dawber, *The Framingham Study* (Cambridge, Mass.: Harvard University Press, 1980).

15. L. F. Berkman, L. Breslow, *Health and Ways of Living: The Alameda County Study* (New York: Oxford University Press, 1983).

16. X. J. Cui and G. E. Vaillant, "Antecedents and Consequences of Negative Life Events in Adulthood: A Longitudinal Study." *American Journal of Psychiatry* (1996), vol. 152, pp. 21–26.

17. G. E. Vaillant, *The Natural History of Alcoholism Revisited.*

18. G. E. Vaillant, P. P. Schnurr, J. A. Baron, and P. D. Gerber, "A Prospective Study of the Effects of Cigarette Smoking and Alcohol Abuse on Mortality," *Journal of General Internal Medicine* (1991), vol. 6, pp. 299–304.

19. G. E. Vaillant and K. Mukamal, "Positive Aging in Two Male Cohorts," *American Journal of Psychiatry* (2001), vol. 158, pp. 839–847.

20. S. de Beauvoir, *The Coming of Age,* p. 571.

21. H. Heimpel, "Schlusswort," in *Hermann Heimpel zum 80 Geburtstag,* Max Planck, ed., Institut für Geschict (Göttingen: Hubert, 1981), pp. 41–47.

22. C. Erhardt, J. E. Berlin, *Mortality and Morbidity in the United States* (Cambridge, Mass.: Harvard University Press, 1974).

23. K. S. Kendler, C. A. Prescott, M. C. Neale, and N. L. Pedersen, "Temperance Board Registration for Alcohol Abuse on a National Sample of Swedish Male Twins, Born 1902 to 1949," *Archives of General Psychiatry* (1997), vol. 54, pp. 178–184.

24. G. E. Vaillant, *The Natural History of Alcoholism Revisited.*

Chapter 8 Retirement, Play, and Creativity

1. Bosse et al., "How Stressful Is Retirement?"

2. L. T. Midanik, K. Soghikian, L. J. Ransom, I. S. Tekawa, "The Effect of Retirement on Mental Health and Health Behaviors: The Kaiser Permanente Retirement Study," *Journal of Gerontology: Social Sciences* (1995), vol. 50B, pp. S59–S61.

3. D. J. Ekerdt, L. Baden, R. Bossé, E. Dibbs, "The Effect of Retirement on Physical Health," *American Journal of Public Health* (1983), vol. 73, pp. 779–783.

4. G. F. Streib and C. J. Schneider, *Retirement in American Society: Impact and Process* (Ithaca, N.Y.: Cornell University Press, 1971).

5. Ekerdt et al., "The Effects of Retirement on Physical Health."

6. S. R. Sherman, "Reported Reasons Retired Workers Left Their Last Job: Findings from the New Beneficiary Survey," *Social Security Bulletin* (1985), vol. 48, pp. 22–30.

7. Quoted in de Beauvoir, *The Coming of Age.*

8. R. C. Atchley, "The Process of Retirement: Comparing Men and Women," in M. Szinovacz, ed., *Women's Retirement* (Beverly Hills, Calif.: Sage Publications, 1982).

9. J. T. Bethel, "John Harvard's Journal," *Harvard Magazine* (2000), Sept.– Oct., p. 61.

10. S. Freud, "Creative Writing and Day-dreaming" (1908), in *Standard Edition,* vol. 8, p. 145.

11. M. Konner, *The Tangled Wing* (New York: Holt, Rinehart and Winston, 1982), p. 246.

12. M. Csikszentmihalyi, *Creativity: Flow and the Psychology of Discovery and Invention* (New York: HarperCollins, 1996).

13. J. Huizinga, *Homo Ludens* (London: Temple Smith, 1971).

14. B. H. Price and E. P. Richardson, "The Neurological Illness of Eugene O'Neill — A Clinico-Pathological Report," *New England Journal of Medicine* (2000), vol. 342, pp. 1126–1133.

15. H. C. Lehman, *Age and Achievement* (Princeton, N.J.: Princeton University Press, 1953).

16. D. K. Simonton, "Does Creativity Decline in Later Years? Definition and Theory," in Marion Permutter, ed., *Late Life Potential* (Washington, D.C.: Gerontological Society of America, 1990), pp. 83–112 (p. 103).

17. M. Csikszentmihalyi, *Creativity,* p. 229.

18. G. E. Vaillant and C. O. Vaillant, "Determinants and Consequences of Creativity in a Cohort of Gifted Women."

19. C. V. Mobbs, "Neuroendocrinology of Aging," in E. L. Schneider and J. W. Rowe, eds., *Handbook of the Biology of Aging* 4th ed. (San Diego, Calif.: Academic Press, 1996), pp. 234–282.

Chapter 9 Does Wisdom Increase with Age?

1. P. B. Baltes and J. Smith, "Toward a Psychology of Wisdom and Its Ontogenesis," in R. J. Sternberg, ed., *Wisdom: Its Nature, Origins, and Development* (New York: Cambridge University Press, 1990), pp. 87–120.

2. Sternberg, *Wisdom: Its Nature, Origins, and Development.*

3. I *Kings* 3:7.

4. I *Kings* 3:11.

5. K. S. Kitchener and H. G. Brenner, "Wisdom and Reflective Judgment: Knowing in the Face of Uncertainty," in Sternberg, *Wisdom: Its Nature, Origins, and Development*.

6. S. Streufert, R. Pogash, M. Piasecki, and G. M. Post, "Age and Management Team Performance," *Psychology and Aging* (1990), vol. 5, pp. 551–559.

7. J. Smith, U. M. Staudinger, and P. B. Baltes, "Occupational Settings Facilitating Wisdom-Related Knowledge: The Sample Case of Clinical Psychologists," *Journal of Consulting and Clinical Psychology* (1994), vol. 66, pp. 989–999.

8. L. Orwell and M. Perlmutter, "The Study of Wise Persons: Integrating a Personality Perspective," in Sternberg, *Wisdom: Its Nature, Origins, and Development*, pp. 160–177.

9. Baltes and Baltes, *Successful Aging*.

10. Orwell and Perlmutter, "The Study of Wise Persons: Integrating a Personality Perspective."

11. J. Loevinger, *Ego Development* (San Francisco: Jossey-Bass, 1976).

12. P. Wink and R. Helson, "Practical and Transcendent Wisdom: Their Nature and Some Longitudinal Findings," *Journal of Adult Development* (1997), vol. 4, pp. 1–15.

13. R. Nozick, *The Examined Life* (New York: Simon and Schuster, 1989), p. 268.

Chapter 10 Spirituality, Religion, and Old Age

1. E. Erikson, *Childhood and Society* (New York: W. W. Norton, 1950), p. 228.

2. J. Piaget, *The Moral Judgement of the Child* (London: Kegan Paul, 1932).

3. J. Fowler, *Stages of Faith* (New York: Harper and Row, 1981).

4. J. Loevinger, *Ego Development*.

5. G. E. Vaillant, S. E. Meyer, K. Mukamal, and S. Soldz, "Are Social Supports in Late Midlife a Cause or a Result of Successful Physical Aging?" *Psychological Medicine* (1998), vol. 28, pp. 1159–1168.

6. E. B. Palmore, "Predictors of the Longevity Difference: A 25-Year Follow-up," *Gerontology* (1982), vol. 22, pp. 513–518.

7. P. R. Williams, D. B. Larson, R. E. Buckler, R. C. Heckman, and C. M. Pyle, "Religion and Psychological Distress in a Community Sample," *Social Science and Medicine* (1991), vol. 32, pp. 1257–1262.

8. K. S. Kendler, C. O. Gardner, and C. A. Prescott, "Religion, Psychopathology and Substance Use and Abuse: A Multi-Measure, Genetic-Epidemiological Study," *American Journal of Psychiatry* (1997), vol. 154, pp. 327–336.

9. H. G. Koenig, H. J. Cohen, D. G. Blazer, C. Pieper, K. G. Meador, F. Shelp, V. Goli, B. DiPasquale, "Religious Coping and Depression Among Elderly Hospitalized Medically Ill Men," *American Journal of Psychiatry* (1992), vol. 149, pp. 1693–1700.

10. H. G. Keonig, L. K. George, B. L. Peterson, "Religiosity and Remission of Depression in Medically Ill Older Patients," *American Journal of Psychiatry* (1998), vol. 155, pp. 536–542.

11. S. Radhakrishnan, *Indian Philosophy* (London: Unisin Hyman, 1989).

12. L. Tornstam, "Gero-Transcendence: A Theoretical and Empirical Exploration" in L. E. Thomas and S. A. Eisenhandler, eds., *Aging and the Religious Dimension* (Westport, Conn.: Auburn House, 1994).

Chapter 11 Do People Really Change Over Time?

1. C. G. Jung, "The Stages of Life," in J. Campbell, ed., *The Portable Jung* (New York: Viking, 1971), p. 12.

2. R. R. McCrae and P. T. Costa, *Emerging Lives, Enduring Dispositions* (Boston: Little, Brown, 1984).

3. J. Block, *Lives Through Time* (Berkeley, Calif.: Bancroft Books, 1971).

4. G. Elder, *Children of the Great Depression* (Chicago: University of Chicago Press, 1974).

5. N. Haan, *Coping and Defending* (New York: Academic Press, 1977).

6. G. Sheehy, *Passages* (New York: E. P. Dutton, 1976).

7. D. Levinson, *The Seasons of a Man's Life* (New York: Alfred A. Knopf, 1978).

8. Z. Rubin, "Does Personality Really Change After Twenty?" *Psychology Today* (May 1981), pp. 18–27.

9. J. J. Conley, "Longitudinal Consistency of Adult Personality: Self-Reported Psychological Characteristics across Forty-Five Years," *Journal of Personality and Social Psychology* (1984), vol. 47, pp. 1325–1333.

10. M. P. Farrell and S. D. Rosenberg, *Men at Midlife* (Boston: Auburn House, 1981).

11. P. T. Costa and R. R. McCrae, "Objective Personality Assessment," in M. Storandt, I. C. Siegler, and M. F. Elias, eds., *The Clinical Psychology of Aging* (New York: Plenum Press, 1978), pp. 119–143.

12. J. Block, "Some Enduring and Consequential Structures of Personality," in A. I. Rabin et al., eds., *Further Exploration in Personality* (New York: John Wiley and Sons, 1981), p. 27.

13. J. R. Harris, N. L. Pederson, G. E. McLearn, R. Plomin, J. R. Nesselroade, "Age Differences in Genetic Influences for Health from the Swedish Adaptation Twin Study of Aging," *Journal of Gerontology: Psychological Sciences* (1992), vol. 47, pp. 213–220.

14. E. R. Kandel, "A New Intellectual Framework for Psychiatry," *American Journal of Psychiatry* (1998), vol. 155, pp. 457–469.

15. C. J. Jones and W. Meredith, "Developmental Paths of Psychological Health from Early Adolescence to Later Adulthood," *Psychology and Aging* (2000), vol. 15, pp. 351–360.

16. P. Mussen, D. H. Eichorn, M. P. Honzik, S. L. Bieber, W. M. Meredith, "Continuity and Change in Women's Characteristics over Four Decades," *International Journal of Behavioral Development* (1980), vol. 3, pp. 333–347.

17. E. E. Werner and R. S. Smith, *Vulnerable but Invincible.*

18. G. E. Vaillant, and C. O. Vaillant, "Natural History of Male Psychological Health, X: Work as a Predictor of Positive Mental Health," *American Journal of Psychiatry* (1981), vol. 138, pp. 1433–1440.

19. A. Hollingshead and F. C. Redlich, *Social Class and Mental Illness* (New York: Wiley, 1958).

20. G. E. Vaillant, "Poverty and Paternalism: A Psychiatric Viewpoint," in L. Meade, ed., *The New Paternalism: Supervisory Approaches to Poverty* (Washington, D.C.: Brookings Institution, 1988), pp. 279–304.

21. E. E. Werner and R. S. Smith, *Overcoming the Odds* (Ithaca, N.Y.: Cornell University Press, 1992).

22. Baltes and Mayer, *The Berlin Aging Study.*

23. M. Rutter, "Resilience in the Face of Adversities," *British Journal of Psychiatry* (1985), vol. 147, pp. 598–611.

Chapter 12 Positive Aging: A Reprise

1. Roger Rosenblatt in P. Raven interview, *Time,* April 26, 1999, p. 51.

2. Quoted in M. Cowley, *The View from Eighty,* p. 69.

3. Perls and Silver, *Living to 100,* p. 74.

4. E. C. Sanford, "Mental Growth and Decay," *American Journal of Psychology* (1902), vol. 13, pp. 426–449.

ACKNOWLEDGMENTS

The Terman Study was begun sixteen years before I was born. The Grant (Harvard) Study of Adult Development was begun in 1937 when I was three years old, and the Glueck (Inner City) Study was begun when I was six. I did not join the Grant Study staff until 1967. In writing this book, then, I have harvested a crop that for decades many others have planted and devotedly tended. I hope that the many people who have helped in the creation of these studies whose names do not appear below will understand that the limiting factor is space and not gratitude.

First, I am deeply indebted to the foresight of Lewis Terman, of Eleanor and Sheldon Glueck, and of Arlie V. Bock for having planned the three studies on which this book is based. I am equally indebted to Clark W. Heath and Charles C. McArthur, who guided the Grant Study for the first thirty-five years of its existence before I became director. I am equally grateful to the many associates who for the past thirty years have helped me gather data from the Inner City men and the Harvard men. I am particularly grateful to Ruthanne Cowan, Lewise Gregory, Sara Koury, Robert Richards, Tara Mitchell, Eleanor Walker, and Robin Western for providing the personal warmth that cemented living men and women to the abstraction of a study of adult development.

Over the years I have enjoyed many teachers whose guidance has indirectly helped to shape this book. Among the most .important was Elvin Semrad, who first conceived the hierarchy of defenses described in chapter 2. Additional intellectual guidance came from two important sources, the Center for Advanced Study in the Behavioral Sciences (CASBS) and the Henry A. Murray Center for the Study of Lives at the Radcliffe Institute for Advanced Studies. In 1978–1979 at the CASBS I was blessed to have as colleagues Paul Baltes, James Birren, James Fries, Matilda Riley, and Martin Seligman. For twenty years as a contributor to the Murray Center, I have benefited from the generative leadership of its former director, Anne Colby. For the past twenty years, the friendship and wisdom of these colleagues have shaped my intellectual development.

Over the thirty-five years that I have worked on the Grant Study there have been several men who have provided the intellectual climate and institutional support needed to conceive, research, and write this book. My patient department chairmen, Paul Myerson, then John Mack, then Miles Shore, then Gary Tucker, now Jonathan Borus; my host at the Terman Study, Albert Hastorf; and the Harvard University Health Service director Dana Farnsworth, followed by Warren Wacker, and now David Rosenthal, have seen to it that I have had time and space in which to be curious. (In more material terms, the Grant Foundation, the Positive Psychology Network, and grants MH-00364, MH-10361, MH-38798 from the National Institutes of Mental Health (NIMH), and grant MH-42248 from NIMH and the National Institute of Aging, and grant AA-01372 from the National Institute of Alcohol Abuse and Alcoholism have all provided generous financial support.)

There are many individuals who are coauthors of this book even more directly. Some have helped as research associates, some as independent raters, and some as both. They include Xing-jia Cui, J. Timothy Davis, Charles Ducey, Paul Gerber, Stephanie Meyers, Phyllis Remolador, Liv Bjornard Hyatt, Ana-Maria Rizzuto, Diane Roston, Henry Vaillant, Caroline Vaillant, Stephen Soldz, Eva Milofsky, Kenneth Mukamal, Jonathan Wolf, and many others.

Joanna Vaillant, Michael Buehler, Anne Vaillant, and Jonathan Wolf critically read individual chapters. Beth Rashbaum, Maren Batalden, Joanna Settle, and Caroline Vaillant were all patient enough to critique the entire book. They have helped immensely.

Finally, Robin Western deserves quadruple credit for serving as an interviewer, as shepherd to lost and reluctant Study members, as independent rater, and for typing uncomplainingly the myriad drafts that this book has undergone. Of equal importance, William Phillips, in the great tradition of Maxwell Perkins and the alchemists of old, has served as a magical editor who transformed dross into intelligible prose.

Only the loyalties and generous spirits of the Study men and women themselves have made a more critical contribution to the birth of this book.

George E. Vaillant, M.D.

INDEX